Fiber Optics
in Architectural Lighting

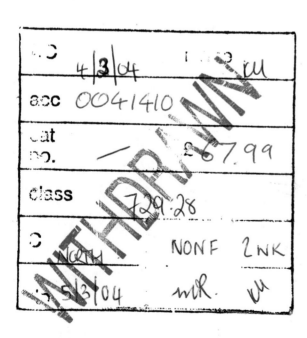

Fiber Optics
in Architectural Lighting

Methods, Design, and Applications

Gersil N. Kay

Boston, Massachusetts   Burr Ridge, Illinois
Dubuque, Iowa   Madison, Wisconsin   New York, New York
San Francisco, California   St. Louis, Missouri

To Del Bennett of Flair Lighting, who did so much to simplify the physical rules of fiber-optic lighting; and my husband, Bill Duffy, whose task it was to point out those confusing phrases in the manuscript needing further explanation.

Contents

Appendices **265**

Foreword

Fiber optics, one of the forms of remote source lighting, has already much to offer the lighting designer, not least of which features are safety, low maintenance, and miniaturization of fittings. The paraphernalia of light generation can be now relegated to easily accessible remote locations, with light accurately distributed to where it is required, leaving the visual scene and displays virtually unencumbered by intrusive fixtures and avoiding the dangers from heat, ultraviolet radiation, and electrical connections.

There is no shortage around us of exceptionally poor lighting installations. Design and installation requires both good engineering expertise and artistic sensitivity to achieve success. In this publication, the author demonstrates that she abounds in an enviable balance of both these qualities. As a result of her work in the United States and around the world, she has developed an eye for detail and a love of good architecture that provides such a sound basis for the guidance she gives in this leading book.

Peter Lawson-Smith, OBE, Dip. Tech (Eng), C.Eng., FIEE, FCIBSE, Mcons.E, ACT (Birm), FIIExE. Mr. Lawson-Smith is the distinguished founder of a leading British Building Services Consulting Engineering firm. His commissions include work on royal residences, National Trust properties, and important museums. He has been an early advocate of fiber-optic lighting.

The chapters are stepping stones that will encourage manufacturers, designers, and users toward the most exciting prospects that fiber optics and similar technologies have to offer in connection with lighting. I hope they will fire the imagination of readers to explore and develop applications limited only by their own ingenuity.

Preface

Light is ephemeral. It can neither be held in the hand nor controlled without a physical barrier. For this reason, the art of illumination is not a cut-and-dried science, but must be handled with a combination of technical skill, practical experience, common sense, and imagination. Since the discovery of fire, there has been an ongoing search for better lighting. One such innovation, employing fiber optics, is the subject of this book. It offers a different approach to the lighting process. Readers should keep in mind that ALL LIGHT, whether natural or artificial, is injurious to fugitive organic materials if allowed to play on them long enough. Some types of light, however, like fiber optics, are much safer than others.

Rather than bewilder those who are neophytes in basic lighting techniques with a highly technical discussion on the laws of physics pertaining to optics, this book gives the most important features of creating good illumination with any medium, as well as principles specifically pertaining to fiber optics. A brief glossary of useful general lighting terms will be found in Glossary A, along with definitions of words used exclusively in this field.

It should be noted that fiber-optic technology is not meant to be the only choice; it is simply another practical tool for the design professional. There will be times when a combination of conventional and fiber-optic techniques is the most appropriate method. Every effort has been made to offer an objective presentation of the facts to enable the reader to arrive at his or her own conclusions. To avoid looking like a goods catalog or a promotion for professionals, credits for case histories appear in the Notes at the end of the book.

While many suppliers and designers worldwide were asked to submit examples, not everyone responded. Therefore, mention here does not constitute a preference or an endorsement, nor is it to be taken as a comprehensive list of all participants in the field. Firms are coming into and out of this emerging business at such a rapid pace that it would be meaningless to list them. Rather, naming contributors to this publication is merely to acknowledge all those gracious and generous enough to join in this exercise.

Acknowledgments

The list of those around the world who have generously and patiently introduced me to fiber optics and light pipe is long. The roster below will indicate how many people are already involved in this technology. Each added another dimension to the ongoing search for knowledge in this field. My sincere gratitude to all for "enlightening" me, especially:

Miles J. H. Pinniger
Charles Marsden-
  Smedley
William Alexander
  Allen
Paul Ruffles
Abe Feder
Paul Marantz
Dennis Keough
Bill Scheinfisch
W. Philip Cotton, Jr.
Alfred Borden IV
Louis Gauci
Robert G. Neiley

Stephen Cannon-
  Brookes
Christopher Tuttle
Nick Ferzacca
Russell Leslie
Luke Tigue
Ann Kale
Jules Fisher
Matt Cunniff
Robert Hughes
Richard Forster
Helen Diemer
Dan Rahimi
Hugh Hardy

Cathy Luo
Peter Lawson-Smith
Helmut Guenschel
Nicholas Boileau
Charles Stone
Daina Yurkus
LeMar Terry
Joseph Brassell
William Leaman
LaVerne Roston
Malcolm Dunkeld
Paul Mathiesen
John Belle
Helen Bennett

Donald F. Nardy
Robert Skaler
Francesca Bettridge
Charles D. Linn
Lorne Whitehead
Reuven Azoury
Rich Einhorn
Anne E. Scott
Stephen J. Kelley
Wanda Jankowski
Alvin Holm
Stuart Lewis
John Longenderfer
Peter Langhorn
June Swann
Teri Jefferson
Christina Norsig
Mickey Nathanson
Paul Tear
Ian Grant
David Palmer
Heather Seniow
Bert Laugenslager
Winthrop Aldrich
Voith & Mactavish
Zack Zenolli
Michael Harrington
William Taylor
C. C. Sullivan
Craig DiLouie
Jill Brookman
Maurice Brill
Patrick Ward
Timothy C. Dwyer

Walter Spiegel
Ken Billington
Claude Engels
Lindsay Audin
Bill Havens
Deborah Gottesman
Wade Zimmerman
Kathryn Respond
Richard Foster
Lois I. Burgner
Donald Insall
David Roccosalva
Dextra Frankel
Alan Parnell
Duncan Campbell
James Holder
Cynthia Hinson
Rodney Melville
Dana Knapp
Rosie Winston
Monica Dance
Mark Faithfull
Brian Ellis
Margot Gayle
Cheryl O. Meyne
Russ DeVeau
Betty Lou Pacey
Alan Ritchie
Elaine Gray
R. J. Thornberg
Lloyd W. Jary
Javier Ten
Mathew Gilbert

Henry Moy
Mark Hughey
Christina Trauthwein
Paul Yunnie
Ronald A. Rueb
Lyn Kessler
Jack Murray
Joseph Salimando
Sir Bernard Feilden
Sir William Whitfield
John Fidler
Enjua Meain
Kurt Barnhart
Julian Harrap
Bryan S. Rogers
Lewis Sternberg
Eric Anton
Peter Inskip
Lee Waldron
Terence Dodge
Walter Palmer III
William Seale
John Waite
Laurie Stansfield
Enrique Carrera
Mark Newman
William Maiman
Ray Grenald
Carl Gardiner
Chambers, Murphy &
   Burge
John Boncher
Jeff MacKay

Introduction

Anyone looking through this book will have the usual who, what, when, where, why, and how questions. Here are some answers:

Who? Quite simply, this book is for everyone involved in buildings, grounds, monuments, and sites, such as building owners and managers; architects; engineers; interior and lighting designers; exhibit builders; maintenance staff; governmental and/or regulatory agencies; general and subcontractors; preservationists; electricians and other craftsmen; homeowners; curators; conservators; administrators; exhibit and/or display staff; historical societies; industrial plants; house museums; museums; landscape architects and designers; builders of ships, trains, automobiles, and planes; kitchen and pool designers; attorneys; accountants; city planners; financial institutions; and funding agencies. It can also serve as a textbook for educational institutions and apprentice-training schools.

What? The purpose of this book is to explain a completely different tool for the lighting process. It is intended as a practical help for all those requiring and providing artificial lighting. The revolutionary technology explained here contains many of the desired properties of illumination sought ever since fire was discovered, namely, safety, longevity, cost-effectiveness, and clarity. Although illustrated, it is not a "coffee table" book. This is a distillation of 40 years of field experience and 20 years of teaching those already in the building business who are interested in this system. The queries discussed in it are recurring ones brought up in lectures and courses given around the world. It begins at the beginning, indicates where and how to get started, and shows practical methods to do the job.

When? The time is now to employ "something completely different" in technology that can solve many problems in energy efficiency, maintenance, safety, and creating good lighting.

Where? Applications can be for commercial, institutional, industrial, residential, hazardous, historic, landscape, or purely decorative purposes, or a combination thereof.

Why? Just as people climb mountains "because they are there," this book was written because there simply wasn't any comprehensive publication answering questions about a technology that has tremendous potential for use worldwide. Although fiber-optic lighting has been employed for over 30 years in Europe and the Middle and Far East, very little has been taught or written about it. Consequently, the topic is generally unfamiliar or confusing to many in the industry. A wide-ranging primer for every level, from the student to the practicing professional, seemed to be in order.

How? This book brings together in one convenient spot useful material from many sources: architectural history as it pertains to illumination, fundamental lighting techniques, sound construction methods, and practical engineering rules. Written in easily understandable terms, it purposely keeps masses of statistical data and jargon to a minimum. It explains the basic technical workings of this system vis-à-vis conventional ones. It presents a holistic approach to lighting in its relation to all other disciplines composing a building. It even discusses fundamentals of computer-generated lighting design.

The reader can also expect to learn something about the energy- and cost-saving details of this system. Checklists based on empirical knowledge gained from actual on-the-job experience offer helpful shortcuts and caveats for owners, design professionals, and contractors.

Special attention is given to venues over 50 years old. There are over 1,200,000 commercial, institutional, and industrial properties erected before 1940 in the United States, plus at least 20 times more residential units. Multiply these numbers for countries older than the United States, where tourism, the largest business in the world, is a major economic force. Each of these sites could benefit from retrofitting with this energy-efficient lighting system.

Often, nonprofit owners of older buildings think they cannot afford the services of design professionals. If they do the work themselves without sufficient technical data, they may create illumination that may be not only unsafe for the property, its contents, and occupants, but also costly in energy and maintenance. This book will indicate what is a "do-it-yourself" project, and when specialists should be consulted. The object is to obtain the best lighting at the lowest initial and ongoing costs.

The figures just quoted do not take into account all the newly constructed buildings and those postwar structures that are not considered historic but are also in need of having their lighting upgraded to satisfy energy legislation.

Here is the first book to provide a straightforward explanation of fiber optics with an unbiased view of all the systems currently available. The author has spent the past 12 years investigating many versions around the world. Few readers would have the opportunity or inclination to interview all the clients, design professionals, and contractors who have been contacted and visited. With correct facts at hand, the user will be able to make intelligent decisions on how to proceed.

In some parts of the world, fiber-optic equipment has been considered just another tool for lighting, like fluorescent channels or track lights. However, its standards, procedures, definitions, and specific criteria have never been formally set. These are given as follows:

Chapter 1. Offers a brief history of lighting and the definitions and components of light pipe, glass fiber optics, and plastic fiber optics. It lists types of projects where each system can most suitably be used.

Chapter 2. Gives suggestions on how to get started on a project, from determining the scope of work to selecting design professionals and suppliers.

Chapter 3. Deals with designing illumination with fiber optics.

Chapter 4. Covers installation of the equipment.

Chapter 5. Touches on economic considerations.

Chapter 6. Contains a great variety of representative case histories. Some examples proceed from initial concept through planning, supply, and installation. All are aimed at getting the reader to think about alternative ways to do the task. Applications are roughly divided into commercial and institutional classes, although they are not mutually exclusive.

The reader is urged to read Chapters 1 to 4 carefully before jumping to the applications in Chapter 6. Usually, the first question is about cost, which is mentioned earlier. Because a successful installation is based on many details, there will be a number of lists of what to do or not to do. These items could have been presented in narrative form, but the busy person, in a hurry to get a quick answer, may find this plan faster for reference.

Hundreds of people have commented that fiber-optic lighting opens a door leading away from boring, repetitive illumination that does not use their innate talents to best advantage. As mentioned in the text, fiber optics is addictive. It will color your life forevermore, as the concept of time-and-motion studies has altered many a person's way of doing things. And, it is fun!

History and Technology of Fiber Optics and Light Pipe

Brief History

Fiber optics and light pipe are two forms of an idea that is not new. They were devised to create illumination with properties allowing better control of the environment. Often, throughout the centuries, it was neither practical nor possible to use whatever lighting system was currently available, because of inaccessibility of installation, difficulty in maintenance, cost, or the desire to avoid unwanted by-products of the light. *The innovation was to put the light source away from where the illumination was required, but in a location always convenient for its renewal.* The actual light rays can be conducted to where needed along a series of light guides (flexible or inflexible) emerging from the distant light source. The specific workings will be explained further on.

Some of the drawbacks of using fire for earliest lighting were the obvious inherent danger, heat, odor, inconvenience of procuring fuels, and choking smoke that blackened surrounding surfaces and contaminated foodstuffs. Maintaining rushes, wicks, and other paraphernalia was a burdensome chore, especially when a sudden gust of wind or rain could extinguish the fire after a lot of work had gone into building it. So, efforts continued to eliminate or minimize the existing shortcomings of available methods for illumination.

When candles arrived, they still generated heat and smoke; were expensive (only the rich could afford masses of flaming candles, and then only for special occasions); did not provide unmoving light, since the flame flickered; and they got shorter as they burned, needing frequent replacement. A chance breeze could blow out the flame unexpectedly, even indoors. (See Fig. 1-1.)

Oil-based light sources, usually encased in sheltering glass, were an improvement, yet remained very smelly and discolored the surrounding area. At the end of the nineteenth century, the introduction of a workable incandescent electric lamp, developed independently by Swan in England and Edison in the United States, removed the stench, dirt, and possibility of being blown out accidentally. They lasted a very long time, although the light levels produced were not high. They were part of the revolutionary changes seen in almost every walk of life, which have occurred during the

(a)   (b)

Fig. 1-1 (a) Candle in 15th-century building. (b) Street lamplighter, 18th century.

past 100 years. However, until alternating current was perfected, direct current–powered electric lights still flickered.

By 1897,[1] electric lighting was an established science, and there were numerous lamp types available.

> The Edison and Swan lamp patents had expired by 1893 so newcomers like Robertson started making filament lamps, first carbon, then tungsten. The early development of public electricity supply was driven by the demand for electric lighting. Artificial lighting at that time ranked third in importance among the necessities of civilization, preceded only by clothing and shelter!
>
> Early in this century, for high intensity lighting, there were various arc lamps suitable for street lighting and shop windows. Low pressure gas discharge lamps, amazingly up to 200 feet long and called Moores tubes, were constructed on site by "glass plumbers" and were the forerunners of cold cathode lighting. The predecessor of the fluorescent tube was also in existence. It was known as the Cooper Hewitt lamp which used a U tube of 1″ diameter and 50″ of light-giving length. There were even compact quartz mercury vapor lamps for industry and shops.
>
> The early 1900s was a great period of experiment. Carbon filaments were replaced by the Nerst lamp from AEG (Germany). Then the squirted Osium lamp, metalized carbon and tantalum, all preceded ductile tungsten drawn wire filaments in 1907. The gas-filled lamps developed by Langmuir in 1913 were called ½-watt lamps because the power per candle was reduced from about 1 watt to ½ watt—a commercial claim only ever achieved for the higher power lamps!

In the 1920s, most offices were lit by filament lamps with "coolie hat" shades. Gas street lighting was still around, even when the first mercury and sodium discharge lamps appeared. But for many people, lighting had advanced very little since the days of Charles Dickens. The average illuminance figures for the 1930s were considered generous at 10 footcandles (100 lux). Values that were little higher than bright moonlight served for manual tasks and circulation areas.

When fluorescent tubes appeared in the 1930s, the heat normally produced by light was lessened and overall ambient light was more readily obtainable. These lamps became so ubiquitous that a solitary fluorescent tube can be found everywhere, even in ancient temples in third-world countries. However, the lamp colors were not always flattering to the human skin, and the directional quality of the incandescent bulb, which facilitated doing close work, was lost. So, the search for a "better mousetrap" carried on.

The two decades immediately following the Second World War saw amazing progress in improvements in light output, color, and variety. Applications in every commercial and industrial activity were made. Cornice lighting or other built-in systems using fluorescents were in vogue, leading to overall luminous ceilings.

In the 1960s, the introduction of high-intensity discharge lamps (HID), like low- or high-pressure sodium, quartz, and early metal halide, still did not provide all the lighting improvements desired. The following gives a comparison[2] of earlier lamps:

LAMP	CURRENT LUMINOUS EFFICACY	YEAR LAMP FIRST MARKETED	EFFICACY WHEN INTRODUCED LUMENS/WATT
Incandescent Lamps:			
Carbon filament	up to 4	1880	3–4
Tungsten filament	up to 18	1906	8
Tungsten halogen	up to 30	1958	18
Gas-Discharge Lamps:			
Mercury	up to 60	1932	32
Linear fluorescent	up to 104	1934	25
Metal halide	up to 100	1961	65
High-pressure sodium	up to 140	1965	90
Compact fluorescent	up to 80	1981	50

*This table was taken from a British source.

Throughout the hunt for improved lighting, glass was always recognized as an excellent conductor and enhancer of light. This transmittance property makes low-iron glass very energy efficient. (The more iron content, the more resistance to transmission of light, requiring more power to be seen.) A 1966 exhibition, "Lighting Unplugged," at the Museum of Art, Rhode Island School of Design, showed that as early as the thirteenth century, lantern makers used ovals of rock crystals, and later glass roundels, to direct the light in a beam, much like the modern-day flashlight (torch). Makers of Renaissance candleholders added glass to these implements to increase their radiance. Beginning in the sixteenth century, *water lenses* (candlelight shining through a glass flask of water) magnified both the light and the objects being illuminated, enabling artisans to do intricate tasks like embroidery and calligraphy. (See Fig. 1-2.)

Facets of cut-glass chandeliers holding candles added further sparkle to an eighteenth-century room. By the nineteenth century, wood engravers replaced the candle light source for the water lens with an oil lamp.

What were the properties of artificial light which were considered so beneficial? Illumination has been sought which would:

- Avoid the danger of accidentally catching fire or being blown out
- Provide illumination that would last a very long time, even under hostile conditions
- Be cool

(a)   (b)

Fig. 1-2 (a) A 16th-century "water lens." (b) A 17th-century Étainière (a "tin-knocker" for lighting fixtures).

- Not accelerate deterioration of organic materials by fading (by ultraviolet rays) or drying out (by infrared rays)
- Require minimal maintenance
- Be very energy efficient
- Be directional, but discreet, so that it would not impact on any décor or landscape, historic or contemporary
- Be glare proof, silent, and able to be made vandal resistant
- Have the flexibility to reach high and inaccessible places
- Be able to be retrofit into existing lighting fixtures
- Be safe in hazardous and wet locations
- Offer a wide variety of components to accomplish every lighting purpose
- Be able to be focused while lit, so that technicians can see what they are doing
- Provide the highest levels of light at desired distances, with unexcelled clarity and color rendition

This is actually a description of the properties of glass fiber-optic lighting, a concept certainly cleaner (as opposed to smoky, smelly fuels), brighter, and more efficient than anything yet devised.

However, it took a long time for the commercial development of the two practical systems, one now called *fiber optics*—very flexible octopus-like "tails" providing multiple points of *directional light* powered by a source placed a distance away; and the other, *light pipe*—a long run of rigid hollow tubes of *ambient* light served either by one lamp, or by two located at each end of the conduit.

Serious inventing began in the last century. In 1870, a man named John Tyndall spoke about "total internal reflection," which early glass blowers had probably observed. This is the phenomenon of light bouncing back and forth within the walls of a closed container. (A more complete explanation follows.) According to a 1996 telephone interview with Canadian professor Lorne A. Whitehead, a modern pioneer in this discipline, "In 1882, in the United States, William Wheeler patented a lighting method based on a relatively inefficient metallic reflection light guide. He used a system of mirrors to guide the light along a network of hollow pipes. These mirrors had a relatively high rate of light absorption, making this concept inventive, but not practical." Thus, "doing it with mirrors" may not work well with light, because after hitting a few corners, the light rays are considerably dissipated. This requires starting out with much larger components to end up with the actual light level needed.

Mr. Wheeler was aware of electric carbon lamps but thought that Edison's incandescent bulb would not succeed. Therefore, he advocated a mechanism to pipe light through hollow conduits to multiple locations from a central light source. One problem impeding commercial success of this invention was the effect of *attenuation* (the inevitable light loss as it travels along its path). Research is being done in many countries to reduce this natural physical impediment, just as comparable strides are being made in superconductivity.

At the same time as Mr. Wheeler's activity in the United States, several inventors in Russia were carrying out similar work. Then, for years, nothing further developed until, beginning in the 1960s, these efforts were renewed. Throughout the former Soviet Union, scientists designed, patented, and installed a variety of lighting systems based on metallic reflection light guides. These were the first to be manufactured in substantial quantity. Simultaneously in Europe, bundled flexible *glass* fibers were beginning to be used in scientific instruments for their preciseness, and in highway signs.

In the 1950s, a cladding to keep light from leaking out of optical fiber was developed.[3] In the late 1970s, small-diameter acrylic fiber optics was introduced.[4] The patent was later sold,[5] becoming the plastic version of fiber optics. Eventually, light pipe and fiber optics, of either glass or plastic, emerged as three different products for three different usages. Each will be discussed in chronological order of appearance.

The modern concept of "integrated engineering"—where all systems in a building work together to achieve the best indoor environment and energy efficiency—is a pragmatic approach to design and construction advocated by many. The lighting technology described in this book fits in very well with this philosophy, because it reduces energy costs, as well as maintenance and ventilating/air conditioning requirements, while extending the life of the landscape or building and its contents, by removing the harmful aspects of all light (desiccation from infrared and fading from ultraviolet rays). Besides, more and more design professionals and building contractors are being drawn to this field because they find "it is fun." Run-of-the-mill new construction is unchallenging for those who enjoy exercising their innate skills.

Because of the ubiquitous use of fiber optics for communications, when the words *fiber optics* are heard, they are often interpreted as meaning the material for this use and not for illumination. Even if lighting is mentioned, no differentiation between glass and plastic is made. In Europe, glass is usually understood as the material. In the United States, it is just the opposite, because of the relative unfamiliarity with glass.

Light Pipe Technology

Although Europeans were already working with glass fiber optics for several decades, Canada and the United States generally became aware of light pipe first, before fiber optics. In 1979, Lorne Whitehead, a graduate student of physics at the University of British Columbia in Canada, looked for a better way to light his lab. Starting with Wheeler's premise, he developed a material with a precise prismatic boundary surface that sent internally reflected light efficiently along its length. This "total internal reflection" occurs when relatively parallel rays of light are introduced into a hollow prism light guide (PLG) within a long square or round enclosure. Rays that approach the prisms within the critical angle (approximately 30°) are refracted back into and along the guide. Other rays escape in a controlled manner, allowing an even distribution of light (within 14 percent of the average illumination, according to the manufacturer) along a relatively long length (up to 80 ft [25 m]. By 1983, Dr. Whitehead had established his own company.[6] In 1985, a technology called *microreplication* appeared. This produced optical lighting film (OLF),[7] which made practical the large-scale manufacturing of prism light guides (PLG).

The guiding principle of light pipe is identical to that of fiber optics. Unlike the latter, however, "piped" light is not encouraged to escape from the far end of the light guide. In most cases, the surface is reflective, causing the striking rays to return along the length of the guide, to be released eventually. The object of the light pipe system is usually to provide *even* illumination over a significant length from a single source, often in otherwise difficult installation areas. And unlike the tiny (usually much less than ½ in [12.5 mm] in diameter) bundled hair-thin glass fiber-optic flexible strands, a standard inflexible light pipe ranges from 3 to 8 in in diameter (75–200 mm).

The resultant apparatus is a large-scale (more than 20-ft [600-cm]-long) luminaire with an efficiency of approximately 52 percent, that can provide significant illumination along its length, all from one or two light sources. Prism light guide material uses microprisms etched into a thin polymer sheet, to create the same effect as the 4-mm (0.16-in) rigid walls of the light pipe with a 20-mil (0.02-in) flexible sheet. By integrating a reflective material into a corner unit, a light pipe can be made to turn corners.

According to Dr. Whitehead's 1996 statement, "As far as we know, there is no limit to the lifetime of prism light guides, providing that the materials are not subject to excessive temperature, ultraviolet, or highly concentrated solvents, conditions which are easily met. The oldest one is now 13 years old, and working fine." In a manufacturer's words:[8]

There was a need: The imagination of the lighting designer has been inhibited by the practical need to provide access to all points of a lighting system for the purpose of lamp replacement and luminaire maintenance. To free the designer from the limitation imposed by conventional linear lighting systems (fluorescent, neon, cold cathode), light pipe technology was developed.

The answer: Single point source luminaires beam light onto hollow linear light guides to produce, through the principle of total internal reflection, lines of brilliant white or colored light.

The applications: The results can be dramatic, as for building highlighting; creative, when used with light sculptures; or highly functional, as for canopy lighting. Shopping centers, commercial and institutional developments, and private and public monuments have all used back-lighting of design elements, such as glass block columns and translucent panels, made possible by accessible positioning of remote luminaires and color change units.

The system: It is designed for both indoor and outdoor use, and will tolerate adverse climatic conditions. It is robust, waterproof, and wind-tolerant. Performance is not affected by low temperatures. There are two types to choice from. The *end-feed* is ideal for uninterrupted runs of light up to 88 ft (a bit less than 30 metres), where luminaire access is available at both ends; and for runs of up to 44 ft where access is available at one end only. The *mid-feed* type is suited for uninterrupted runs of light in excess of 88 ft and where access to luminaires is desirable from the inside of a building.

Typical components: A light guide and an adjacent, but separate luminaire transmit light efficiently and uniformly. The light guide is a long, hollow assembly, with a 3 to 8″ outside diameter, lined with optical elements of continuous thin acrylic or polycarbonate film incorporating microscopic prisms with 90° geometry. The internal optical system is protected by a sealed acrylic outer housing. (See Fig. 1-3.)

The luminaire incorporates a universal-burning 250 watt metal halide lamp with a life of 10,000 hours, in a specially designed reflector. This assembly is coupled to, and aligned with the light guide, providing a collimated (narrowed) beam of light through its input window.

Each system is shipped complete with mounting brackets, light guide and fittings, lamps and remote ballasts. Although most components are common to both the end-feed and mid-feed systems, designing complete runs involves different constraints with respect to possible luminaire locations.

Light Sources

In addition to using the current metal halide lamps, much worldwide research continues to find even longer-lasting, more energy-efficient light sources. The *sulfur lamp*[9] is one such innovation, which should be commercially available soon. This operates like a microwave, and as of late 1996, had a life of between 45,000 and 60,000 hours, if the magnetron is changed every 15,000 hours. It contains a small amount of sulfur and inert argon gas. When the sulfur is bombarded by focused microwave energy, it forms a plasma that glows very brightly, producing light similar to sunlight. It produces light in what sounds like a rather indirect fashion: It first converts AC to DC, then DC to microwave power, much as an oven does. Originally at 135,000 system lumens, 6000 K, and a CRI of 79, once this 35-mm-diameter golf-ball-size lamp can be tamed and run on newly developed solid-state power supply, it could have great possibilities used with either light pipe or fiber optics for high-output ambient illumination. The first experimental installation was in the Smithsonian Institution's Air and Space Museum in Washington, DC. It features 3- to 100-foot-long prism light guides that run along the ceiling in the huge Rocket Hall. (See Fig. 1-4.)

Applications for Light Pipe

Because of the unbending nature of these light guides, uses for this type of illumination are necessarily fewer than for the flexible fiber optics. However, for expansive exterior decorative uses, or for providing ambient light in great interior areas, it is the current answer. Applications also include

Exploded View of End-Feed System

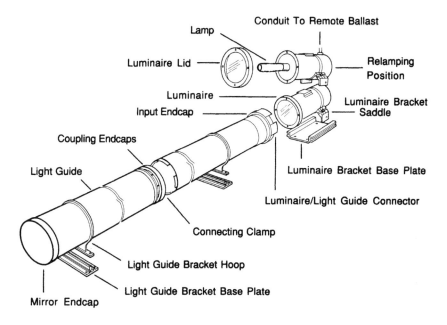

Exploded View of Mid-Feed System

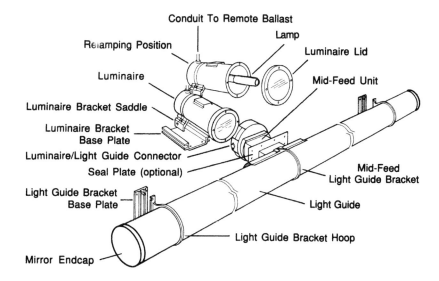

Fig. 1-3 Components of Light Pipe.™ Courtesy of TIR.

Fig. 1-4 Sulfur lamp provides ambient light. Auxiliary conventional lamps are needed for directional illumination. Photo courtesy of Fusion Lighting.

lighting where access is difficult, as in high-bays, delineation of long boundaries, space that must be isolated from radio frequency interference (RFI), and large hazardous locations.

There is always the debate whether to light the entire facade of a high-rise building, or just the top. If the structure is architecturally imaginative, there is a viewpoint for a perspective, and money to do it, why not include the whole thing? If space and funds are lacking, or the construction does not lend itself to having floodlights attached to it, just the building's pinnacle can be done. Stark, rectangular modern properties, devoid of decoration, cannot be done at all, because they are mostly glass, and there is really nothing to light.

Light Pipe™ Used on the Building Exterior

1. The design[10] for the exterior lighting of a skyscraper called for the outlining of a large pyramid at its crown. Although impressive, it presented obstacles in executing. Whatever conventional method explored could not provide the large-scale effect intended, and each had particularly difficult maintenance problems. Then, one day, someone suggested a product developed for hazardous locations, an outgrowth of

the glass fiber-optic revolution, which had swept the communications industry. Alternately called *prism light guides* (PLG) or *light pipe* by the manufacturer, this system had the potential to change certain aspects of the lighting industry. Mock-ups and tests were done, resulting in a glowing three-dimensional structure that has become a significant part of the nighttime skyline.

2. Light pipes were also used to create a dramatic special effect in an archway over the monorail tracks at a fair grounds.[11] Using a computer-controlled dichroic color filter changing system, instant color changes were produced along each 50-ft length of prism light guide. The triangular light pipes were contained within a metal strutwork. The color filter movements were controlled solenoids operated by a central computer that was programmed to deliver a varied array of visual patterns and sequences.

3. In 1987, light pipes were used to trace the outline of three inverted V-shaped gables on all four sides of a skyscraper in Philadelphia.[12] This modern-day version of the Chrysler Building in New York is mostly glass, so it could not be floodlit by traditional means. (The light would pass right through it.) Light pipe[13] was chosen over neon, cold cathode, or lasers because it could deliver a bolder image and required less maintenance. (See Fig. 1-5.)

Twenty-two-foot lengths of light pipe were each fed with a 400-watt metal halide source from the middle. Unlike the tower by the same architect[14] described in example 1, this lighting system is integrated into the curtain wall of the building, instead of being surface applied. Although lamps can be easily replaced from inside the structure, it did create some construction problems because the curtain wall manufacturer had never encountered anything like this before. However, once all contractual obligations were resolved, the system was installed. To retain the intentions of the designer, the light sources should be replaced regularly and not be allowed to die out, substantially altering the original effect.

Light Pipe™ Used in Building Interiors

There are two types of interior applications for light pipe. One is daylighting—capturing natural sunlight as a free light source, with light pipe as a conductor. The other employs only an artificial light source. (See Fig. 1-6.)

Fig. 1-5 Light Pipe™ at One Liberty Place, Philadelphia. Photo courtesy of Helen Diener, The Lighting Practice.

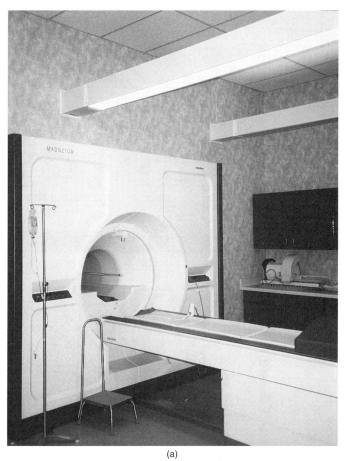

(a)

Fig. 1-6 (a) A magnetic resonance imaging (MRI) room uses standard Light Pipe™ with through-wall transition pieces and 400-W metal halide lamps. Locating the light sources and ballasts outside the shielded room eliminates magnetic interference. The Light Pipe™ is inserted through a wave guide tube, which is integrated with the wall shielding and is responsible for attenuating magnetic waves from the lamp and ballast of each Light Pipe™.

DAYLIGHTING

In 1987, Victoria Park Place, a Toronto office building,[15] used a series of eight sun-tracking heliostats to illuminate a 2000-square-foot floor of offices. Eight 25-ft-long light pipes, mounted in a conventional T-bar ceiling, distributed the concentrated sunlight. When adequate sunlight is not available, the same system disburses light from one or both 400-watt metal halide lamps located at each end of the run. The backup system is controlled by phototectors mounted in the roof. International research

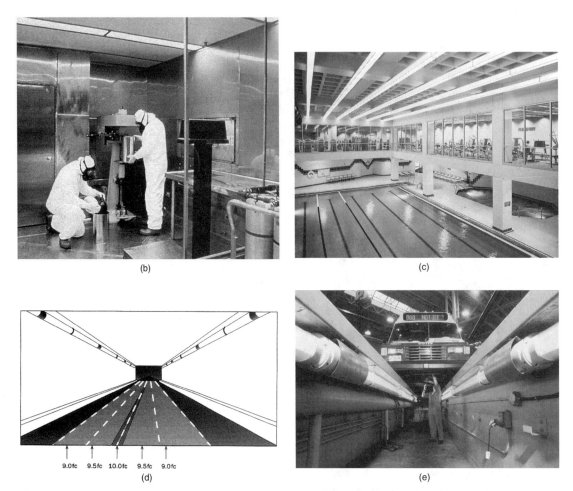

(b)

(c)

(d)

(e)

Fig. 1-6 (Continued) (b) Hazardous materials handling: Repeated, thorough clean-ups and decontamination in this facility require frequent, high-pressure, low-volume wash downs that will withstand danger of failure, spark of contamination. Glass fiber optics could also be used in a and b. (c) Swimming pool: 6–88-ft-long runs of Light Pipe™ provide uniform, high-quality illumination with 12- to 400-watt metal halide luminaires. The system is designed to give 80% downlight for direct illumination of the pool and 20% sidelight to highlight the coffered ceiling and enhance the architectural features. (d) Sketch of tunnel. Roadway uniformity at required maintained light levels can be up to 85%. The system is suitable for wall, ceiling, or a combination of configurations. (e) Garage. Courtesy of TIR.

continues to discover even more affordable combinations of light pipe or fiber optics for daylighting.

USING ONLY ARTIFICIAL LIGHT IN A CEILING

In a shopping center,[16] the main ceiling is 22 meters (66 ft), with a total area of 600 square meters. A 6-in-diameter light pipe system, powered by a 250-watt metal halide lamp for each pipe, runs 11 meters (33 ft) above

Fig. I-7 Rotshild Center, Rishon L'Zion, Israel. Glass panels never have to be removed. Relamping is easily performed from the car park floor level. The system mounts easily to any flat structural surface. Courtesy of the lighting designer.

the glass ceiling. For the smaller ceiling over the fast food section, 300 square meters of light pipe is used. (See Fig. 1-7.)

THE STILL-EXPERIMENTAL ANNULAR LENS GUIDE[17]

In mid-1997, a report of yet another related product appeared. Although it was not yet commercially sold, it was an example of the effort going on in all parts of the world in this field. The reader's patience in plowing through the technicalities of this imaginative system will be rewarded by getting ideas to use on future problematic cases. (See Fig. 1-8.)

> BC [British Columbia] Hydro's Edmonds Complex in Burnaby, Canada (an electric utility company) is representative of modern architecture and engineering. The focal point of the design is a central glass-walled atrium, which serves as a lobby, display hall and central meeting place. The 35 ft high, 1,500 square foot space features a large central planter.

Fig. 1-8 The annular lens. Courtesy of the University of British Columbia Physics Dept.

The space also had to contend with two problems. The first is Canadian West Coast weather—anything but cheerful on dark, rainy days, and there were no known means of mimicking sunshine entering a garden, as originally envisioned by the architect. The other difficulty stemmed from BC Hydro's energy-efficiency policies that precluded the addition of more energy-hungry lights.

While BC Hydro was searching for a solution, researchers at the University of British Columbia (UBC) were looking for an application for a lighting method they had just invented. Students in the Structured Surface Physics Laboratory at UBC were experimenting with a new way of guiding light, and a constantly improving new light source for powering it.

The laboratory called this "Annular Lens Guide," consisting of large prismatic lenses which were capable of directing light from one place to another *without resorting to a containment pipe* to hold in the light rays. They felt this concept could use the properties of large-scale "light piping" and, at the same time, avoid the "industrial plumbing" appearance of conventional light pipes. They envisioned a device for guiding light with periodic lens-like rings, which would have the added benefits of high efficiency, and unique visual impact.

The concept: Although light pipe solutions are practical to provide ambient light in large spaces, they could not solve the design challenge at the Edmonds Complex. First of all, their plumbing-like look would be architecturally incompatible with the character of the atrium. Secondly, light-emitting pipes have a high surface luminance. This, while acceptable on a ceiling, would not be appropriate for a structure suspended vertically in the center of the atrium and intended to direct light to the plants below.

BC Hydro's Power Smart Program's investigations into energy-related developments came across the annular lens guide concept. The UBC team agreed to collaborate with Power Smart on a design. It would combine an annular light guide and a sulfur lamp to provide the color and brightness of sunlight falling into the central garden, as well as create diffuse, shadow-free and, most importantly, *glare-free* illumination throughout the space.

With a sulfur lamp, a single unit of input power at 1.4 kilowatts produces 140,000 lumens, much more than conventional systems. Obviously, one floodlight of this size could not be used in the ceiling. In previous indoor lighting with this powerful lamp, its high intensity has necessitated spreading out the light in some kind of light guide. The only practical method has been the use of prism light guides (a previous development of UBC's laboratory, which resulted in a commercial company and a range of licensees around the world).

The resultant design consisted of a series of seven high-precision, lens-like rectangular rings mounted one above the other, to span the space from the ceiling to a location about 8 ft above the garden. Thin strong stainless steel cables, hanging from a hidden frame in the ceiling hold the lenses in this calculated configuration, with a strength satisfying the requirements for this seismic Zone 4 category.

The lenses themselves were designed according to the annular light guide theory. The light which shines into the central region of the top lens is guided downward until it is emitted from the central region of the bottom lens, forming a pool of light in the garden below. The designers also reasoned that a sulfur lamp could be positioned within the hanging ceiling system above the atrium. A reflector was used to ensure that all of its light would enter the lens guide, such that none of the light would cause glare by directly illuminating the space below. An important detail is that the prismatic material used to form the annular lens is, in one sense, imperfect. The laws of physics dictate that some light must reflect off the surfaces of such lenses as they carry out their primary goal containing light, by periodic redirection, within the guides.

Fortunately, this reflected light scatters in all directions, ideal to provide a diffuse glow of low brightness to illuminate the space and to highlight the sculptural aspects of the lenses themselves. Taking advantage of this effect, the system was planned so that half the light would bathe the garden in a bright pool of light, while the other half would provide soft, low-glare illumination in the rest of the space.

All the design constraints thus being met, there was a further detail of purely aesthetic impact. It was possible and desirable to have the shape of the lens change from top to bottom in order to create a visually more interesting element which matched the rectangular geometry of the garden itself.

In color and illumination level, the light falling on the planter resembles a beam of sunlight, and the surrounding glow achieves a bright cheery ambiance, even on the gloomiest of days. Furthermore, this system made it possible to turn off many of the less effective lamps used previously. The net result is a 60% reduction in power used for lighting this space. This resourceful discovery adds to the expanding arsenal of light guidance techniques. (SOURCE: Adapted from an article by Bernard Crocker and Dr. Lorne A. Whitehead in *Lighting Magazine*, Canada, April, 1997.)

Hint: It should be obvious that light pipe is definitely not a "do-it-yourself" job. The client is strongly urged to employ a competent lighting team.

While light pipe is excellent for such large, long spaces as previously illustrated, *directional* light, which relieves the flatness of *ambient* light and makes it possible to accomplish tasks, is best provided by fiber optics. To avoid confusion, the distinction should be made between plastic and glass versions.

Those who have seen the earliest examples of this technology are amazed to discover that the glass version is now capable of high light levels that can travel useful distances. Many may not be aware that the glass communications fiber which is so widely used today is substantially different, especially in attenuation and installation, from the material used for illumination.

End-Emitting Glass Fiber Optics

Although American manufacturers make millions of feet of glass fiber for communications, preferred because of its longevity of service, as of late 1997, they still were not producing glass fiber optics for lighting. This is a mystery in view of the tremendous potential market for retrofitting with this system to satisfy the universally decreed lowered energy usage for illumination. The highest-quality glass lighting product is found in Germany, Great Britain, and Japan.

The concept of glass fiber-optic functional architectural lighting is very simple. *The lamp assembly is located away from the area to be illuminated.* A single source, placed in a convenient spot, powers a quantity of points of light. The actual light rays are delivered out of the END of a number of very flexible glass guides sheathed in opaque material. Thus, because conventional breakable light sources themselves do not have to be installed in inaccessible places or over fragile objects where a broken lamp would be disastrous, the lighting designer is now free to create sophisticated illumination with concealed hardware, wherever needed. The bendable glass "tails" can be introduced wherever conventional copper wiring can go. For relamping, arranged display areas need not be entered, nor do heavily trafficked commercial areas have to be disrupted. This is because individual lamp and/or bulb changing at each point of light is eliminated completely.

The single-source idea also means many fewer lamps are needed to supply multiple points of high-level, directional lighting. The annoyance of individual burned-out lamps is gone, along with the negative impact of track lighting on important interior designs. Typical examples of both glass and plastic fiber-optic architectural lighting are listed in Chapter 6 on applications.

Over 30 years ago, glass fiber optics was used in scientific instruments where extreme accuracy and color rendition were required. Early medical devices to look down throats and into stomachs employed this material. It then progressed to outdoor highway signs because its components were impervious to weather, could be reused, and lasted decades with reasonable handling.

Later, everywhere else in the world except in the northern hemisphere, glass fiber began to be used for interior illumination, starting with just decorative applications. Then, actual architectural lighting evolved. Improvements in equipment were very rapid. Europe, the Middle and Far East were all enjoying this revolutionary system, while only a few North Americans were aware of its possibilities, even though they were embracing glass communications fiber wholeheartedly.

Now, glass fiber optics has grown up. It is no longer merely for "discos" and aquariums, but has become another useful lighting tool.

Terminology

There are glossaries included at the end of this book.

An excellent 1996 monthly series on communications fiber optics[18] stated, "Because the terminology is not yet codified, care must be taken to ensure that names and functions in different brands mean the same." There can be confusion both among professionals and between the practitioner and the general public. A "projector" could mean one thing to a lighting designer working with fiber optics, but something else to a lay person, who interprets it as a "movie projector." Light sources can alternately be called *illuminators, projectors,* or *light boxes.* Some terms deal with quantity of light, others with its color or application. They vary regionally and with personal preference.

As an example, in electrical contracting, the use of "TW," could mean a type of copper wire or a thin-wall metal conduit. The context will indicate which. Using the English language, semantics can get in the way because of localized terms and the gap between British English and American English. Between the United States, England, and Scotland, there are at least three names for exterior plasterwork—stucco, render, and harling. In fact, whoever writes a dictionary explaining all the different names in lighting and construction will be doing a good service to the industry, at least until the terms change again.

Again quoting the previously cited magazine article: "In most mature technologies, all materials are made to industry standards. This is not always so in developing ones, such as fiber-optics. Because of this, one make component may not work well with that of another." This statement is truer in the United States and Canada than it is elsewhere, where there is more compatibility and uniformity in components. It should be noted that, although air conditioning has been around since the 1920s, that business is only just now getting around to having open system protocols like BACnet, where components from different manufacturers may be employed interchangeably. There is also the threat of breach of warranty in combining incompatible products. For this reason, first-time users should seek guidance of those already experienced in the system, rather than trying to go it alone.

Components

In fiber optics, there are no lighting "fixtures" or "luminaires" as such. This system provides multiple points of light with nearly invisible hardware. It also makes it possible for the light guides to be retrofit unobtrusively into existing or reproduction chandeliers, wall sconces, table or floor lamps. Like Julius Caesar's "All Gaul," glass fiber-optic architectural lighting is divided into three parts: light source + light guides + fittings. (See Fig. 1-9.)

The Light Source—Called Projector/Illuminator/Light Box

The light source is simply a lamp housed in a metal container about the size of a large shoebox. However, not every lamp is suitable for this purpose. Glass fiber optics can only use those lamps, like a 6000-hour single-ended metal halide, or a shorter-life tungsten halogen lamp, whose light path will directly enter the harness most efficiently. Lamps whose light rays scatter in many directions, rather than go straight ahead, won't do. Also, a lamp with a long focus cannot direct the majority of light rays into the harness as well as the short-focused one can. (See Fig. 1-10.)

System Description

In general, a fiber optic lighting system consists of three **components**:

- ❏ Light source
- ❏ Fiber optic light guide
- ❏ Fittings

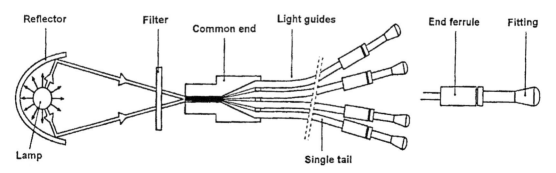

Fig. 1-9 Fiber optic lighting system. Drawing from Flair Lighting Ltd.

Fig. 1-10 A light source for glass fiber optics. The 6-in ruler indicates the size.

A word should be said about metal halide lamps, the present "workhorse" powering most fiber-optic architectural lighting. When first produced in the 1960s, there was indeed unexpected color shift. What should have been clear white light degenerated into pink, purple, and other startling colors. In fact, early metal halide was so unpredictable, interior designers blanched at the thought of using it. That was then. The new generation of lamps is much more color reliable, and they operate longer and much cooler than other sources.

Hint: Some manufacturers recommend that, if used in systems operating 24 hours a day, seven days a week, metal halide lamps should be turned off at least once a week for at least 15 minutes. Not to do so would affect the lamp performance. Others even suggest turning the lamps off once every 24 hours.

Large-size tungsten halogen lamps get hot enough when touched to burn off human flesh down to the bone. If the lamp is accidentally covered while operating, or if it falls onto flammable material, as witnessed by the ruinous fires at Windsor Castle in England, in an apartment building in Lincoln Center, New York, and in a mansion in Connecticut, it can be a dangerous fire hazard. For this reason, many universities are now banning their use in dormitories. Many a student has left socks to dry over a tungsten table or floor lamp, only to start a conflagration.

Naturally, before they approach the end of their lives, all lamps should be replaced promptly so that they don't start acting strangely. Multiple metal halide lamps in the same viewing area should all be relamped at the same time to keep the color and light level originally anticipated. Scheduled maintenance is essential for all types of lighting.

Since 1995, there has been a metal halide lamp[19] with a color temperature of 5600 K. It produces a more brilliant, whiter light, but has a shorter operating life (2000 hours). Early in 1997, a 100-watt metal halide lamp[20] was introduced exclusively for use with glass fiber optics (plastic fiber cannot withstand the heat and ultraviolet rays of the lamp). It is 20 percent brighter than the current 150-watt lamp, retains the 6000-hour life, and can be housed in a smaller container. And so, the race is on to produce lamps just for the burgeoning fiber-optics market.

Every manufacturer has a different configuration, size and shape of light source container, depending upon the type of lamp and accessories used. Illuminators which can operate in any available position (horizontal, vertical or angled) are obviously more useful than those which can only be run sitting on a horizontal plane. As improvements in the lamps are made, the size of the container decreases, making it even more convenient to conceal in tight interstitial spaces.

Certain features of the light source to be noted are:

- Box covers secured with loose screws (rather than the captive type) or hinges might present a problem if the screws could be easily dropped or lost (such as where the projector is mounted on a cat-walk). If the headroom where the projector is housed is limited, inhibiting ability to raise the cover to relamp, the cover might be fabricated on the side, instead of on top. The light source can even be put in a drawerlike base that slides out for service.

- As with all illumination, adequate space (a few inches) must be allowed around the light source to dissipate heat produced by the lamp. In most cases, one end of the glass fiber-optic illuminator contains a small silent fan. If the light source is installed vertically, sitting on the short side containing the fan, a louvered shelf must be provided for it so as not to impede the fan's operation.

- The location of the projector should be convenient and ALWAYS readily accessible for relamping.

The Harness—Also Called the Loom

The harness is a bundle of glass light guides (also called tails) that delivers the light where needed. There are two types of tails—end-emitting and side-emitting. The former is stocked in a large number of sizes, from size 1 to 380, because of its many applications. The latter comes in size 1 and 8, with as many as 60 strands (5 mm diameter). (See Fig. 1-11.)

- A glass tail is composed of multiples of 400 glass strands, each 50 microns, the size of a human hair.

- There is a very large variety of glass tail sizes, from size 1 (= 400 strands, making a tail with a diameter of 1.13 mm) all the way up to

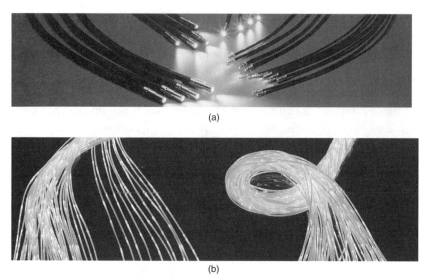

(a)

(b)

Fig. 1-11 (a) End-emitting glass. (b) Side-emitting glass.

size 380 (= 380 × 400 strands). The most-used sizes are under ½ in (12.5 mm) in diameter.

- The harness is a factory-assembled combination of various sizes and lengths of tails selected for a particular purpose. One end of each tail is gathered with all the others in the bundle and fixed permanently into the *common end* that is then inserted into the boss of the projector. The free octopuslike ends of the light guides can be manipulated immediately in any direction out of the light source, to where light is specified. *Note:* For certain applications, there are tail quantity and length limits.

- Only glass with a quality of 150 dB/km, or lower, should be used for illumination purposes. Anything inferior will perform poorly and be a complete waste of money.

- The metal halide projector can power a maximum of 160,000 glass strands in any combination of tail sizes. The tungsten source can only accommodate 135,000 strands. Once the upper limit of fiber is reached, another light source must be employed.

- Where exact color rendition is required, the rule of thumb is: The length of tails in any direction out of the light source should not exceed 8 to 10 m (24–30 ft). This figure can be doubled, with tails going in opposite paths out of a centrally placed illuminator. Beyond that length, it is a physical characteristic of light to begin breaking up gradually into colors of the spectrum, along with resultant lowered light levels.

- In actual practice, there are many installations with tails longer than 10 m, which still retain acceptable color. This is a function of the quality of the glass.

- The length of the end-emitting tail is figured from the distance where it emerges from the light source to the point where the rays emerge.

- If glass end-emitting fiber optics is used for emergency lighting at the baseboard (skirting) to lead building occupants to safety quickly, longer lengths of 12 to 15 m (up to 45 ft) are fine. Light, not color, is most important. Airlines have been using floor exit lighting for years. Hong Kong and the state of California have already adopted laws requiring emergency light at floor level, and Europe is not far behind. This is an improved method of lighting evacuation paths in smoke-filled areas, because exit signs placed above doorways cannot be seen. Moreover, the only breathable air will be down at the floor.

- Because the tails are factory cut to specification, this encourages the design team to plan ahead for best possible results. Often, those responsible for selecting the components comment that they start thinking about more innovative methods of lighting under the constraint of having to decide on tail lengths in advance.

- Larger glass tails, such as size 96 (= 96 × 400 strands), can throw a beam a distance of 100 ft.

- Using multiple tails focused on the same object or space can increase intensity. It can also be boosted by the use of collimating lenses, although the footprint of light is reduced.

- If uncontrolled by lenses, the *cone* of light emerges from all end-emitting tails at 68 to 70°, while the *footprint* of light increases with the size of the tail.

- End-emitting tails (light exits at the end) produce *directional* light. If used in a grid pattern, they can also provide ambient downlight. *Side-emitting* tails (light glows all the way around the tail, like neon) are for DECORATIVE purposes only. This type is just for delineating. It cannot provide even, overall illumination, or high light levels. For decorative or artistic works, there are two versions of side-emitting glass. One produces a continuous line of light. The other produces a sparkling effect. Groups of harnesses of 300 tails each can be employed as curtains or other textilelike objects. Color wheels are often used.

- The loss of light in transmission along the glass fiber (attenuation) is exponential. For example, a 1-meter-long tail of 150 dB/km glass, producing 2000 lux (200 footcandles), becomes 500 lux at 2 meters long (2000 divided by 2×2); it is 222 lux at 3 meters (2000 divided by 3×3); and so on. In addition, there is a slight loss at both the entrance of light into the glass fiber and at the exit point. This is why both the size and length of a tail must be considered when specifying. A larger size may have to be chosen for a very long length to compensate for attenuation.

- There is a selection of opaque sheathings for the end-emitting glass light guides, from ordinary PVC to Megolon™ (a proprietary product that does not emit poisonous fumes when burning), silicon (for extra flexibility), and metal (to protect tails where they may be subject to damage).

- In contrast to glass fiber optics for communication, glass fiber for illumination is much easier to install. It does not require expert cutting, polishing, or splicing as for telephone or computer applications. On arrival on job site, the common end of the factory-assembled harness needs only to be slipped into the opening boss of the light source.

- The glass tails are very flexible and can be fished through interstitial spaces just as copper electric wires can. Installation and lighting techniques are similar to conventional systems, as are the procedures for power and control wiring.

- An often-asked question is whether the individual glass tail can be shortened, lengthened, or otherwise altered in the field. As a practical matter, the answer is no, because of the need for special factory equipment and a clean environment to prepare the fibers and resecure the common end permanently. If done improperly, there would be a great loss of light in that tail, not to mention the possibility of getting the almost invisible glass fibers into human flesh, where they can't be seen, but certainly can be felt. Nevertheless, there is an ongoing search for an acceptable method of on-the-job replacement of a single tail in a harness.

- Unless accidentally broken, or in a catastrophe, glass fiber should last a very long time. There are operating examples over 30 years old. No one has ever asked about the "warranty" on the glass windows in a building.

- Light exits glass fiber at the same angle, regardless of the active diameter of the fiber bore. This angle is generally calculable at between 34 and 35° from the center line to either side.

- Glass fiber with reduced attenuation (below 150 dB/km) is being developed. This will extend the possible effective length and light levels even further.

FACTORS IN SELECTING HARNESSES FOR A DESIRED LIGHT LEVEL

Allow a knowledgeable supplier to assist in selecting the most effective sizes and lengths of light guides. In this way, ordering incorrect custom-made components can be avoided.

Appendix A contains a chart of approximate light levels produced by representatively sized tails. This can be the starting point for selection. Naturally, with added experience, the right tails will be picked almost intuitively. However, it takes more than simply choosing what appears to be the right-size tail from a list. The reader is cautioned not to depend solely on published figures, but to make actual on-site tests under existing conditions. Static numbers on a sheet of paper can be very deceiving. Besides published light levels, there are several more details to be addressed:

- One is attenuation, a factor of tail length.

- Another key element in the calculation, beside the size and length of the individual tail expected to produce a certain light level, is the number of fibers in each harness. You can focus the light source itself more tightly onto a smaller capacity harness than on a large one. In other words, don't load the harness to its maximum capacity if high light levels are needed.

- Most important is the effect of existing ambient light (including color of its lamps/bulbs and windows) and the nature (color, reflectivity, etc.) of the materials in the area, which further change the situation.

- To increase light level with the same-size tail, add a stronger collimating lens or use multiple tails aimed at the same area.

- To achieve even light, overlap the footprint of light from a series of tails arrayed horizontally or vertically.

Because of all these variables, over the past 15 years, successful European glass fiber-optic businesses have come to rely more on experimentation, past experience, and mock-ups in the field or research lab, than on data that exist only in a vacuum.

CORRELATED COLOR TEMPERATURE (CCT)

Unless the person is color-blind, mention of a primary or secondary color is readily understood. But after the basic red, yellow, blue, green, orange, and purple, names of hybrid "fashion" colors can be puzzling. What is called *shocking pink* one season could very well be called *strawberry* the next. For that reason, a standardized color reference[21] should always be used for a mock-up on-site before specifying.

Added to the shifting names of hues, the label "white" light can be thoroughly confusing. There are endless versions of the color white, from yellowish candlelight (1 footcandle) to the icy northern sky (10,000 footcandles). To identify it more precisely, its correlated color temperature (CCT) is quoted in Kelvin (K). A low CCT, such as 2700 K will be warm, while one of 6500 K will appear very blue and cold.

The 150-watt single-ended metal halide lamp has a color temperature, without adjustment from dichroic glass color filters, of 3000 K (yellowish warm) or 4000 K (cool white). If color filters are employed, most of which are based on a 3200 K light source, the warmer 3000° lamp should not be used, because it will drastically change the colors selected. Moreover, very dark color filters, and most reds and blues, will cut down the light considerably. Therefore, especially if the light has to pass through more than one medium (air, water, air, as in a fountain), only the lighter colors should be chosen.

In specifying fiber optics, the professional should also be aware of the color of other existing lighting in the same vicinity. The combination of yellowish incandescent bulbs, bright MR16 tungsten halogen, and white fiber optics, all in one space, could startle the viewer's eyes upon entering.

COLOR RENDERING INDEX (CRI)

In addition to the color appearance, there is color rendering ability—how accurately colors are seen in each type of light. The most common system considers the lamp's output in each of eight spectral bands and compares them with a theoretically perfect source. In a color rendering index (CRI), 100 is perfect, and anything above 80 is very good. Ordinary objects, when seen under an unfamiliar color of light (like green on red meat), actually take on a bizarre appearance. Not as drastic as this example would be a yellowish incandescent lamp on cool colors of green and blue, turning them into less-attractive muddy shades.

Miniaturized Fittings (Lenses and Holders)

If necessary, individual light points can be colored, controlled, or altered, by attaching lenses and holders to the threaded metal ferrules at the end of each light guide (See Fig. 1-12). (Changing the color of an entire harness may also be done by inserting a dichroic glass color filter within the light source.)

LENSES

Lenses should be made of high-quality polished glass. Remember that everything in fiber optics is greatly magnified, including defects. Light from imperfect tails or lenses will look like mountains on the moon when projected. There are times when lensing is not needed. Then, often only a

(a) (b)

Fig. 1-12 (a) Color wheels and bare glass fibers. (b) An assortment of lenses for glass fiber.

½-in opening in the ceiling, wall, or within a display case may be sufficient to provide glare-proof light.

- The fittings range in size from ½ (12.5 mm) to 2 in (50 mm) in length.
- These tiny lenses can be easily installed or removed by screwing them on or off the metal ferrule. Types include:

  Collimating—narrows the beam

  Diffusing—spreads the beam

  Downlight—light travels straight down from a ceiling or exhibit cabinet

  Wall-washer—covers an expanse of wall evenly

  Framing projector—restricts light to a specific shape (adjustable) so that it does not flow over a prescribed area. Example: light directed solely onto a painting, without spillover to the background

  Zoom lens—can be changed from a pinpoint to a larger spotlight

The lenses can be concave, convex, frosted, clear, or a combination thereof. They come in degrees, depending on the extent of collimating required. Refer to Appendix B for examples. Many fittings are adjustable to accommodate changes in use.

- Those lenses that are not completely recessed can be powder coated at the factory to match surroundings, making them as unobtrusive as possible.
- Proprietary realistic flickering candle- and gaslight are available from one supplier.[22]
- Vandal-proof coverings enable floor and/or pavement fittings to be walked on.
- Some suppliers can customize all components as needed.

METHODS OF SECURING TAILS AND LENSES

There are many methods of securing the tails and lenses from being accidentally moved off focus by vibration or carelessness. Depending on the construction methods and materials, they range from gravity to screwing or plastering in, using a template with holes cut for specific lenses, special holding fittings, adhesives, or any other innovative method best for the specific situation.

Additional Accessories

Accessories for dimming, color change, motion, or other special effects can be attached to the light source itself (such as 4- to 6-color wheels, dimming or flicker motors), or made to work multiple operations through an interface with sophisticated controls of a theatrical computer.[23] The light from an entire harness may be colored by inserting a dichroic glass color filter within the projector. In addition to separate color gels for each individual tail end, there are neutral density filters to dim selected tails. If certain light guides are temporarily not needed, they can be completely blanked out with a fitting. The tail can be split, as those used at a bank teller's window to indicate when free, so that it goes on and off.

> *Hint:* Please do not attempt to concoct homemade gadgets—they might damage the equipment beyond repair.

RETROFITTING EXISTING CONVENTIONAL LIGHTING UNITS WITH FIBER OPTICS

Where the client does not want to make extensive construction changes to existing illumination and décor, one manufacturer[24] offers an assembly that can substitute for low-voltage tungsten fixtures. Once the glass tails are fished in place of the copper wiring, this unit will fit most proprietary downlights and can be provided with an adjustable eyeball for additional flexibility of use. With this handy fitting, there is a minimum of breaking ceilings, repainting, etc., and business operation downtime.

Supplying Electric Power to the Fiber-Optic System

Light sources should be wired to keep the internal exhaust fan, if any, running at regular speed, no matter what light level is chosen through dimming. Otherwise, lacking the fan's normal dissipation of heat, for safety, the lamp will automatically turn itself off when the heat reaches a certain level. For this reason, where more than one projector is installed in the same location, the heat exhaust from one unit must be directed away from its neighbor. Some older, now obsolete, light sources did not have this thermal cutoff, causing problems with both plastic and glass illuminators, where older resins would "brown" if not corrected after several months.

If other motors attached to the projectors are running special effect wheels, wiring to control them must also stand alone from that powering the primary light source. Likewise, power for those portions of the system designated for emergency lighting must have auxiliary electricity supplied to keep them in operation when needed.

Properties of Glass Fiber Optics

The properties of this technology are eminently suited for functional illumination in commercial, residential, institutional, historical, and industrial applications. They provide directional light for task, display, illuminating interior and exterior architectural contours, and recreating historic effects. Fiber optics can also give an interesting mix of adequate ambient light, together with highlighting features. Some of the beneficial properties are:

1. Very cost effective

   Great longevity—it will outlast the wiring powering it.

   It is extremely energy efficient.

   It requires minimal maintenance.

   It does not produce heat from light, thus reducing air conditioning loads.

   Depending on the complexity, payback can be within a few years.

2. Provides discreet, sophisticated illumination

   It is COOL.

   It is glare proof and can give even light.

   It is silent.

   Pleasant environment increases personal comfort and productivity.

3. Provides safe illumination

   No electricity flows through the light guides, so it is safe, even in water.

   Nonmetallic, it is not affected by electromagnetic waves.

   Does not emit infrared and ultraviolet rays so destructive to organic materials; therefore, it delays the eventual fading and drying out caused by all light.

This feature is particularly useful for display in commercial, museum, and residential venues.

Can be used in high, inaccessible, hazardous, or confined space locations.

Plus:

- It can usually be installed more easily than conventional lighting systems. Light guides can be fished through interstitial spaces like copper wires.

- It can be made vandal proof, with components hidden.

- It can be retrofit into existing tungsten fixtures, reducing the need for constant relamping.

- There is a large variety of tail sizes and miniaturized fittings to suit every use.

- It is flexible for changing, as well as for permanent use.

- It can be used again in other locations—does not stiffen in place.

- It can be focused while lit.

- No color shift or disintegration of light guides over time.

- Not restricted to being run in straight lines.

- High light levels are possible.

- End-emitting tails provide EVEN light over an extended area (as opposed to just a single thin delineating line from decorative side-emitting light guides).

- It eliminates obtrusive track lighting.

- Color rendition is excellent.

- Historic light levels can be recreated.

- Impervious to weather or vibration.

- There are special effects, like proprietary flickering candle- or gaslight, color, motion, and dimming.

- Multiple effects can be automatically controlled through theatrical computers.

- No need to disturb displays or trafficked areas to relamp.

- No cutting, polishing, or splicing of light guides—harnesses come fully assembled.

- Glass fiber-optic applications are limited only by the imagination of the designer.

Applications for End-Emitting Glass Fiber Optics

Chapter 6 contains examples.

General:

- Retrofitting existing lighting fixtures
- Architectural contour lighting, interior and exterior
- Baseboard emergency lighting
- High, inaccessible locations
- Task and display

Commercial/industrial:

- Offices—task lighting, glare-proof computer installations
- Retail—display
- Supermarkets—fresh and frozen food displays
- Task lighting for manufacturing and inspection

Institutional:

- Historic Houses—re-create historic light levels

    To retrofit into existing or reproduction antique lighting fixtures

    To replicate safe flickering candle- or gaslight

- Government properties
- Libraries
- Museums—conservation display lighting in cases; on walls or floors; lighting for shops, restaurants, gardens, offices, labs and auditoriums

Houses of Worship

Hospitality—hotels and restaurants

Residential—task, display, architectural contours

Theatrical and places of assembly

Monuments, pools, and fountains

Gardens with plant materials sensitive to excessive heat from light

Marine—ships and off-shore oil rigs

Transportation—planes, trains, automobiles

Hazardous and confined space—hospital operating rooms, grain elevators, etc.

Seasonal—Christmas, Easter, Halloween, St. Patrick's Day, Thanksgiving, Fourth of July, etc.

Specialties:	Daylighting	Frozen food cases	Aquariums
	Doll houses	Architectural models	Saunas

Applications for Side-Emitting Glass Fibers

As mentioned previously, this neon-type product is decorative only.

- A continuous 5-mm-diameter band of light that can be used for decorative cove lighting.

- A "broken" tail that needs to be viewed directly. It sparkles.

Frequently Asked Questions About Glass Fiber-Optic Lighting

1. *Are the tails flexible?* Yes, much more so than copper wire or plastic. Glass tails can be taken in any direction out of the light source without stiff insulator protection from the lamp heat and UV (ultraviolet) rays.

2. *How far can they be bent?* A general rule is 10 times the diameter of the light guide. However, no glass should be bent beyond 90°. To do so might break some of the individual fibers, lessening the light intensity. Plastic is not as flexible.

3. *Can individual tails be shortened, lengthened, or removed from the harness in the field?* Currently no. This work must be done in a very clean environment with special equipment and materials.

4. *What is the maximum tail length for good color rendition?* From 8 to 10 meters (24–30 ft) in any direction out of the projector. If only emergency baseboard light to guide occupants out is required, tails can be up to 15 m in any direction out of the projector.

5. *How difficult is the installation?* Less so than for conventional or plastic systems. It is just another lighting job.

6. *How are the tail lengths determined?* Decide on a convenient location of the light sources, then investigate the clear path from the light source to where the light is needed.

7. *Can sufficient light levels at a distance be obtained?* Yes, with the large variety of glass tails.

8. *Can any lamp be used as a source?* No. Only a lamp whose path of light rays goes straight ahead (as opposed to going in 360°) will give efficient service. The narrow-beam 250-W, 24-volt tungsten halogen, or the single-ended 150-W metal halide are examples of suitable lamps.

9. *Can the metal halide lamp be dimmed?* Yes. With use of a motorized metal wheel, the lamp can be dimmed from 0 to 100 percent without color shift.

10. *Should a first-time user go it alone by selecting components from the catalogue?* No. Work with an experienced supplier.

11. *Can side-emitting glass be used for functional architectural lighting?* No—it is only a decorative substitute for neon, which only provides a band of light.

12. *Can glass fiber optics be used with conventional lighting?* Yes, as long as color temperatures and light levels are coordinated.

13. *Can special effects be obtained?* Yes. Dimming, color change, and motion can be created with motorized wheels. If more sophisticated results are required, a DMX512 input is used.

14. *Can the lighting design be done just using photometric data?* No. The best result is always with mock-ups, either on-site or in the research laboratory.

15. *Isn't it more convenient to cut the tails (plastic) on the site?* No. All lighting designs should be carefully planned before construction

starts for best results at lowest cost. The glass harness is delivered fully assembled, ready to be inserted in the projector, saving labor.

Plastic Fiber Optics

About 15 years ago, while glass fiber-optic architectural lighting was being steadily improved abroad, plastic fiber optics was introduced into the northern hemisphere. Much of this plastic was made in Japan, whereas the high-quality glass was manufactured in Germany and England, as well as in Japan. (When this manuscript was completed, there still was no American source for quality glass optical fiber for illumination.)

Again quoting from the previously cited magazine article,[25] it further says that "with the fiber industry developing so quickly, there will always be differing opinions on a variety of subjects. . . . [There may be as many thoughts on the topic as people asked.] You also do not want your job to be the guinea pig for some manufacturer's 'beta test-site' [first field test]." Today's glass fiber optics, being twice as old, has already gone through those experimental stages that plastic is now entering. The choice between plastic and glass fiber optics depends on the goals of the project. Note: Specifications vary with manufacturers.

Terminology[26]

- *Source isolation*—a term used to describe the light source when it is hidden or mounted away from the lighted path of the fiber optics, as behind a wall. The distant mounting of the light source can reduce noise pollution from the fan and/or stepper motor option.

  Note: Certain light sources for glass fiber optics are equipped with silent fans developed for European concert halls and run quietly.

- *Bend radius*—a 1-in (25-mm) bend will allow for even color intensity. A tighter radius may cause a bright spot. Multiple light bends may cause a dim linear run. There is no limitation on acceptable bends with glass fiber.

- *Fiber head capacity*—the fiber head holds the fibers in position at the light source. The maximum number of individual strands the fiber head of one brand can hold is 500. Some side-emitting fiber is available with 42, 84, or 126 strands, and in most cases, both ends of the fiber cable will need to terminate at the light source. If a smaller number of fibers is used, reducers inserted into the fiber head will hold them.

Components of End-Emitting Plastic

There are many similarities in the three categories of components (light source, harness, and fittings) in both glass and plastic fiber optics. Rather than belabor the point, the differences between the two materials will be indicated. Although at every lighting conference there is a greater proliferation of makers of plastic, only the specifications from three brands[27] were chosen as examples. This does not mean that other products are to be ignored. (See Fig. 1-13.)

Light Sources

These are mainly the same as for glass, except the newer lamps, which will damage plastic. Included are 75- and 250-W tungsten halogen; 150-W metal halide; and 400-W metal halide (1500 hours, 5600 K).

Harnesses

As with glass, there are end-emitting and side-emitting fibers.

END-EMITTING PLASTIC FIBER

There are two kinds. The small fiber is for multiple points of light for decorative purposes. The solid core has been employed for functional uses like display cases and exhibits.

- *Small plastic fiber:* This light guide is made with multiple fibers with a diameter typically between 0.005 and 0.08 inches. A bundle of small fibers is more flexible than of the large type. The bend radius is about 4 to 10 times the diameter of an individual fiber. Usually, there are three sizes available.
- *Large plastic fiber (PMMA):* This is also called *large core* or *solid core*. It is one-piece construction, rather than multifiber. It generally

comes in three to six or eight sizes between approximately ¼, ⅛, and ½ inch in diameter. Large-size plastic fiber is not likely to be broken accidentally, but it is not as flexible as small plastic fiber or glass, requiring larger bend radii than either of the former.

Connectors and cutter with Teflon-coated blades are sold specifically for this material. Because of its costs, some manufacturers offer to loan the cutter for short periods to facilitate reasonably sized installations. Some even say they will make quantity custom cuts and cap the fibers at the factory, approaching the fully assembled harnesses always done for glass. Otherwise, lengths are cut on-site as needed.

SIDE-EMITTING PLASTIC FIBER

Without opaque sheathing, the light emerges from all sides of the light guide. One brand[28] offers standard lengths of 120 ft. It can produce continuous runs of up to 250 ft (over 83 meters) or more with no splice. The operating temperature is 40°C. Its fiber is capable of withstanding heat up to 200°C. Another make[29] can be run up to 30 metres (98.36 ft), provided it is fed from both ends with two light sources. With a single projector, the maximum length is 40 ft. Any further distance would result in reduced light. "P" clips in either metal or clear plastic can be used to secure the tails in place. Solid-core side-emitting plastic is available in diffuse and low-flux (clear) versions. Mock-ups indicate that the diffuse is more visible at a distance. Another manufacturer[30] offers lengths per foot, or in spools of 500, 600, or 1000 ft.

The manufacturer cautions that, for the longest life of the fiber, the ultraviolet rays must be filtered out and the temperature that the fiber interface with the illuminator "sees" must be kept as cool as possible. One way to accomplish the heat isolation is with a glass coupler.

Fittings

A selection of typical fittings is shown in Fig. 1-13.

Applications

See Chapter 6 for case histories. Consensus is that, for short-term decorative or display uses where sophisticated lensing and high light levels are

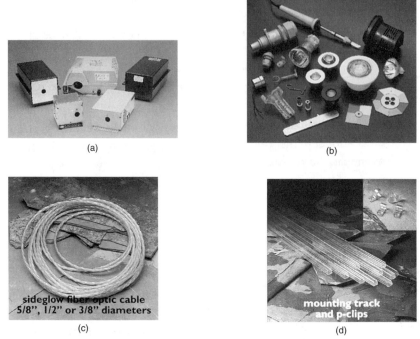

(a)

(b)

sideglow fiber optic cable
5/8", 1/2" or 3/8" diameters

(c)

mounting track
and p-clips

(d)

Fig. 1-13 Fittings for plastic fiber (a) Illuminators. (b) Accessories, tools. (c) Side-emitting plastic. (d) Mounting track and P-clips. Courtesy of SuperVision.

not critical, plastic is fine, especially in very long tail runs without too many sharp curves. Also, for those times where advance design is not possible, end-emitting plastic tails may have to be cut fast-track on the job. This does not guarantee the same results that adequate planning would achieve, but it does meet the deadline.

"Spectacular" signage displays employ single-strand unjacketed end-emitting fibers. (See Fig. 1-14.)

- Side-emitting light guides are very useful for signage and delineating structures decoratively with much less maintenance than for neon. They are not as bright as neon, but they are more energy efficient. They can withstand considerable abuse and will not break if hit. In external locations where there is a threat of vandalism, it would be better to use a transparent casing to support and protect the tails from slashes. Most versions of this material for outdoor

Fig. 1-14 A spectacular sign. Courtesy of SuperVision.

applications are UV protected and treated with algaecides and fungicides. (See Fig. 1-15.)

- Signage with side-emitting light guides can be single stroke, double stroke, or backlit; channel letters; pylon signs; and specialty. Other applications are glass block lighting, coves (sharp lines only); amusement park rides; or whatever other imaginative ideas occur.(See Fig. 1-16.)

- Typical configurations include:[31]

   Single run

   Looped

   Daisy chain

Properties of Side-Emitting Plastic Fiber

The features of side-emitting plastic fiber that neon cannot provide include:

- Color change

- Use-serviceable

- Less-expensive maintenance (just relamping required)

- Breakage-free handling

- Visible run (VR) sections around 90 ft (typical neon is 4 ft)

- Energy efficient: amps per VR for plastic = 1.8 versus typical neon = 7.6

(a)

(b)   (c)

Fig. 1-15 (a) Side-emitting plastic fiber as a substitute for neon outlining a building. (b) Side-emitting fiber to delineate steps. (c) Side-emitting fiber for cove lighting. Courtesy of Ultratec.

Fig. 1-16 Configurations of plastic fiber installations a to f. (a) Single stroke, exterior signage. (b) Double stroke, exterior signage. (c) Backlit, single-stroke backlighting. (d) Channel letters, exterior signage. (e) Pylon signs, exterior signage. (f) Specialty, guitar strings. Courtesy of SuperVision.

Installation

Please refer to Chapter 5 on installation, which is, for the most part, similar for both glass and plastic end-emitting and side-emitting fiber. Features specific to plastic are (See Fig. 1-17):

- The recommended maximum length of fiber tubing for side-emitting is 100 ft for most applications and 50 ft for signage.
- When a run of plastic cable requires more than one light source, space the units evenly to assure an evenly lit run.
- Dimensions are critical. Length cannot be added once cable is cut.
- Be sure to plan for approximately 3 ft of extra fiber tubing from each end at the illuminator for a service loop.

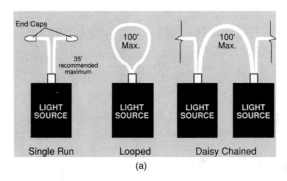

(a)

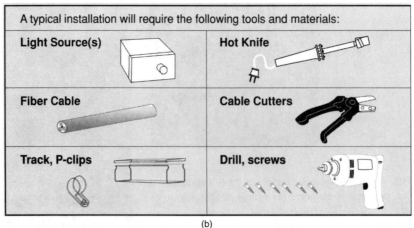

(b)

Fig. 1-17 Installation for plastic fiber (a & b).

- Light-colored surfaces are desirable for mounting the cable. However, dark backgrounds provide good contrast where there are high ambient light levels.

- If there are multiple light sources that require synchronization (so that they all work together), remember to provide access for control wiring between the light sources.

- The plastic fiber tubing may be masked, painted, plastered, cemented, or grouted over.

- Typically, under normal circumstances, 60 ft of side-emitting cable can be installed per hour.

- Typical tools and material required: light source(s); fiber cable (usually multistrand PMMA); track; P-clips; hot knife; cable cutters; electric drill; and suitable screws.

Hint: For glass block installation[32]

"Paint background white. Install track and fiber tubing 6–12″ behind glass blocks on white background at the midpoint of each course of glass block. Using adhesive and screws, install track as straight as possible.

Run a bead of adhesive inside the track to help keep the fiber tubing in place. Press the fiber tubing into the track, being careful not to kink or bend the fiber tubing more than a 2″ bend radius. Do not use cap. There is also the mortar joint method: Mount fiber tubing directly between glass blocks. Use glass block without edge coating on sides. If you do select a glass block that has edge coating, it must be removed to allow lighting transmission. Tack fiber tubing to the top of the row of glass block with hot glue to hold it in place and create a straight line along the top of the block. Run a heavy bead of silicone adhesive on both sides of fiber tubing. Apply mortar to joint and set the block.

On the ends of the glass block wall, a channel will have to be created to hide the fiber tubing where it passes from course to course. This channel must be a minimum of 2″ (50 mm) deep to avoid kinking the fiber tubing."

Differences Between Glass and Plastic Fiber-Optic Lighting

With parity in material price, the prospective user has to consider other factors to make a selection best suited to the lighting brief.

- *Longevity*

  Plastic can be attacked by the heat and ultraviolet rays of the lamp, even with the use of a buffer. Eventually, having the finite life of a man-made material, it will lose the ability to carry light and stiffen, discolor, or even melt under extreme conditions. Manufacturers sell hot knives to trim off the disintegrated tail end nearest the lamp when needed. This is why installers are advised to leave enough slack to take care of decreasing tail lengths. Failure of plastic before its estimated life could result in additional labor and material costs to remove and replace nonworking tails. Of course, as with any type of lighting, the lamp powering the system must be replaced before it begins to malfunction on reaching the end of its life.

- *Flexibility*

  Plastic is much stiffer and more difficult to maneuver through walls, ceilings, and floors than glass. It may require a long stiff barrier between it and the lamp, which means that the tails cannot be led immediately out of the projectors in the direction required. The glass tails can be manipulated as soon as they leave the illuminator. The minimum bend radius of plastic is 3 times the fiber diameter; the recommended bend radius is 10 times the fiber diameter. Please see Appendix C for bend radii for glass. No type of fiber should be bent past 90°.

- *Selection of components*

  There is a much greater variety of light guide sizes and miniaturized fittings for glass. This large "palette" enables the designer to create many more sophisticated effects.

- *Color rendition and light levels*

  Glass is one of the best conductors of light known. The clarity, color rendition, and light levels possible with glass are inherently superior.

- *Selection of light sources*

  The new, more efficient metal halide lamps developed specifically for fiber optics can only be used with glass because plastic can be damaged by the IR (infrared) and UV (ultraviolet) of the lamp.

- *Environmental impact*

  Components of glass fiber optics are "green" (environmentally safe). Plastic can emit poisonous fumes when burning.

- *Choice of sheathing*

  Glass has four different choices, depending on application.

- *Installation*

  Glass harnesses come complete, ready to be plugged into the light source. The tails are handled the same as electric wire. Coils of plastic require expert assembly. The purchaser of plastic is presented with a box of parts that have to be made up into harnesses on the job site, without the controlled factory environment. The cleanliness of the space and the expertise of the installer determine the results. For first-time users, there is a learning curve, which may eat up the labor budget. The relative ability of each worker may also make hourly costs quite variable. In both cases, there is the same power and control wiring to be done. Electrical contractors have found glass can be installed in less time.

- *Costs*

  Initial costs of plastic and glass equipment are comparable. As noted previously, labor costs to install glass are less.

- *Reusability*

  Glass remains supple. Plastic may "freeze" in the shape it is initially installed, and for this reason, cannot be reused elsewhere.

- *Maintenance requirements*

  Glass needs minimal maintenance (a slight dusting of the projector when relamping, unless conditions warrant more frequent cleaning). Between the adverse action of the lamp and the differing coefficients of elasticity inside and outside the light source, it may be necessary to trim the disintegrating plastic regularly. Plastic manuals advise to "leave a 3-ft service loop of fiber tubing at the illuminator." If the ends of the fibers appear damaged, the user is instructed to "re-install and re-cut fibers into the optical port."

- *Efficiency of glass and plastic fiber optics*

  Lumens delivered at the fibre ends can be easily measured using an integrating sphere, and represents one of the values for money factors in any comparison of fibre systems. The values do not allow easy comparison with conventional luminaires, due to the almost complete absence of scattered or unused lumens once the light is in the fibre. *The relatively low lumen efficiency from lamp to fibre end is compensated for by the delivery of lumens to the exact area where they are required. The* lumen values for a system depend critically on the size of the fibre bundles, how many are connected to one light source, and the type of light source. (SOURCE: Robert Hughes, Schott Fiber Optics, at a talk at Rensselaer Polytechnic.)

Other points relating to inefficiency are: At emergence from the projector, and then at the end of the light guide, some plastic can suffer up to double-digit light losses just from adsorption and then more from attenuation. For any fiber optics, if the wrong parabolic reflector or the wrong lamp is employed, which scatters light rays instead of concentrating them into the harness, the light source will be even more inefficient. Expecting side-emitting fiber to provide high light levels and even light over a distance is using the wrong tool, like trying to dig Suez with a teaspoon.

- *Attenuation and adsorption*

  Both the attenuation and adsorption of plastic fibers are higher than glass, typically 300/400 dB/km, compared to 130/150 dB/km for glass. The lower the number, the better the light transmission. According to one manufacturer's figures,[33] plastic of 300/400 dB/km has an attenuation of 6.7 percent per meter loss. This means that the color shift and light loss occur more quickly with plastic fiber than with glass (unless the glass is a very poor quality). Unlike glass, which has only a single-digit light loss exiting the projector and emerging at the end of the light guide (adsorption of glass of 130/150 dB/km translates to 2.9 percent per meter loss), with some types of plastic, this loss could be double digit.

Armed with basic technical data, the process of beginning to work with fiber optics begins.

Chapter 2

Getting Started with Fiber-Optic Lighting

Deciding on the Scope of Work

Although it is so visible, it seems that lighting is often the last element to be considered when developing the initial concept of any construction, and the first to be eliminated in a budget crunch. If you can smell fresh paint when called in to provide lighting, it is almost too late to do a proper job. It will cost more and be less effective, plus disrupt already completed space.

This is a pity, because, as the legendary American lighting designer, Abe Feder, said, "Lighting reveals the work of others"—others being everyone from architects, artists, manufacturers, and writers to Nature itself (landscapes). If it can't be seen, who will know it is there? Mr. Feder believed the emphasis should be on design for the specific purpose, rather than on generating sales of products.

Once the client decides that either new or upgraded lighting is needed, before any professionals are engaged, potential users themselves should think of all the features desired to accomplish the project and assign priorities to them. Not only immediate, but also near-future needs should be included for cost-effectiveness. This means that if light is wanted on one side of the room today but on the other side tomorrow, provisions for both points should be made at the same time. This example may seem like an oxymoron, but it actually happens often. Everyone but the owner benefits from these "extras."

A careful survey, area by area, of the building or landscape should be made to establish a logical plan for the right illumination to suit the people using it. Investigation into financing the new lighting should include benefits given by the Demand Side Management section of a local electrical utility company, the American Federal Green Lights Program, or other such energy-saving agencies in other countries. Some provide money up front for the installation of improved lighting. Others offer rebates on monthly service. If the structure is over 50 years old in the United States, the 20 percent Investment Tax Credit for Rehabilitation of income-producing properties might apply. The American National Park Service and the Internal Revenue Service administer this program. Nonprofit organizations have found that inviting prospective donors to see a small pilot fiber-optic project is a successful method to open the purse strings to fund further work. Once the fiber-optic lighting is seen in operation, it really sells itself.

If the use of fiber optics for its special properties is indicated, the next step would be to interview those already proven familiar with the technology and look at their last three commissions. A competent leader of the construction team should then be selected. Once comfortable with that person, other necessary disciplines should be called in at once, for further input and sharing of expertise. The introduction of any kind of lighting does not exist in a vacuum—there are always adjacent trades involved, which should be included in the discussions from the start.

Other Trades Involved in Lighting

Since "wireless" lighting has not yet been devised, unless there are unusual circumstances, some existing walls, ceilings, or floors may have to be penetrated to include illumination not planned at the outset of construction. So far, it is not possible to point and declare "Let there be Light," and have it happen. Therefore, other trades may be required to fill up the holes made by the lighting installer. Of course, all contractors should be cautioned, and then monitored during the progress of the job, not to break into existing areas until given permission by someone in charge. If it is ornamental woodwork, tile, glass, terra cotta, metal, masonry, or paint that has been breached, specialists to minister to the broken segments should be included from the outset to advise on procedures.

Similarly, if the lighting components will interfere with other services like heating, plumbing, ventilating, or air conditioning, those trades must be consulted beforehand. Like any other mechanical and/or electrical system, no lighting is acceptable unless there is ready access to maintain, repair, or replace it. Toward that purpose, establish a strong line of communication to coordinate work among all related parties.

That may not be as difficult as trying to discover exactly what the client wants. Once that is known, it is relatively easy to work backward to select the necessary components and methods to use. In any case, wasted time and efforts of expensive practitioners can be kept to a minimum when the scope of work is clearly defined and the objectives are communicated to everyone associated with the project.

Communication Between Client and Designer/Supplier

Many times, a prospective customer does not give the designer or supplier sketches, photographs, scaled architectural drawings, or even verbal instructions for an undertaking. Yet, without divulging essential details of the objects or areas to be lit, a firm price with a guaranteed performance is expected. It is not unusual to receive a vague telephone message requesting a quotation to illuminate a painting. When a supplier wanted to know the size of the work to be lit and the area where it was located, the caller angrily inquired if the representative "knew his business." The reply was, "Yes, that is why I am asking for details." A few scrawled lines without dimensions on a bit of scrap paper are also not very productive. Both scenarios are tantamount to going to a physician and not telling him or her your symptoms—literally asking the professional to guess what is wrong.

The point is, the customer who endures an "inquisition" to discover all the pertinent facts is amply rewarded by obtaining the best outcome. Many owners of artwork or buildings have actually gained a new insight into their possessions when obliged to investigate them thoroughly. One collector was even saved the cost of cleaning his many large Victorian paintings when he saw them under the mocked-up whiter fiber-optic light, compared to the existing yellow incandescent rays that made all the pictures look dirty.

On the other hand, there are those few self-assured consultants, completely unacquainted with fiber-optic technology, who firmly tell a supplier what materials and methods they want. They announce repeatedly to one and all that "I am the lighting designer!" Once, the staff of a world-famous European museum, full of national self-esteem, not wishing to allow foreign specialists to prepare the bill of material, ordered components on their own from a catalogue. Just as the restaurant patron who, ignorant of French, instead of food mistakenly ordered the manager whose name was listed on the menu, the collection of parts that arrived at the museum were totally unsuited for the job. Swallowing pride, the museum staff then had to allow its neighbors to come over and set the work right. Yes, there was a hefty restocking charge for return of the incorrect equipment.

> *Moral:* Those who serve as their own brain surgeons may succumb to a misprint, while trying to read the instruction book and simultaneously operate on themselves. Fiber optics is not as forgiving as screwing a bulb into a light socket. It really takes practical knowledge of engineering, traditional lighting techniques, construction, architectural history, interior design, and sometimes museum conservation to do it right.

It is no disgrace to be unfamiliar with a technology. If natives discovered by Stanley and Livingston in darkest Africa had been shown a pocket watch and asked what time it was, they would not have been able to answer, not because they were stupid, but because they had never seen such an object before. Bluffing only makes it worse, because gaffs then have to be corrected at someone's expense. A good design professional or supplier will be happy to educate the uninitiated in this subject. Do not be embarrassed to ask—there are no dumb questions about a system that is new to you. The fact that you are inquiring shows that you are seriously thinking about the topic.

Minimum Preliminary Information Needed from Client

The ultimate effectiveness of the illumination, the physical comfort, and psychological impact on viewers and, of course, the price, all depend on obtaining the following basic facts:

1. Purpose of project—task, display, conservation, daylighting, ambient, theatrical, historical

2. Size of area or objects to be lit, including ceiling height

3. Light levels and color of light desired

4. Full physical description of materials composing the space, cases, objects, including colors and reflectances

5. Location of convenient readily accessible location for light sources—in closets, floors, ceilings, walls, furniture, etc.

6. Lighting use—permanent or changing

7. Type of existing lighting, including windows

8. Special requirements—protection against chemicals, children, animals, ultraviolet rays, or electromagnetic interference, wet, confined or hazardous conditions, etc.

9. Special lighting effects—color, motion, dimming, etc.

10. Potential for vandalism

11. Time frame for completion

12. Complete list of the entire construction team already assembled

Sources of Correct Information on Fiber-Optic Lighting

Most reliable information on what unfamiliar technology works and what doesn't comes from peers, colleagues, and the prospective buyer's own eyes and ears. Unfortunately, as of early 1998, there still isn't much reliable reference data. Many times, printed material is inadequate, outdated, or contains exaggerated statements with "enhanced" illustrations, all of which should be taken with a grain of salt. Accomplished architectural photographers can make *anything* look good.

Discover if the initial savings anticipated from a lower-priced system will be offset by an increase in the cost of maintenance. Of course, product durability is a necessity, even for a six-month use. Can it stand up to real-world use as long as required, or, like the proverbial kitchen gadgets that create amazing radish roses in the hands of the slick demonstrator, does it fail to perform once the unfortunate buyer gets it home?

The purchaser should be armed with the best information possible from every source, all the while resisting blandishments from an overly determined seller. There is a difference between salespeople comparing the real properties of different products, and those merely "badmouthing" competitors with patently incorrect facts. The best policy is to "ask the man who owns one." Inspecting recent installations is very instructive. Looking at projects more than three years old will indicate how well the product is wearing, but, because of the constant improvement in materials and techniques, it will not reflect what is currently available.

Myths Swirling About Fiber-Optic Lighting

It goes without saying that incompletely researched statements like "All South American Indians walk single file—at least the two that I saw did," should not be relied upon as gospel by the listener. While one university researcher concluded that "the potential of fiber-optic lighting is tremendous," a colleague, apparently working with very obsolete equipment, categorically declared that "fiber-optics is expensive, very inefficient, and produces inconsistent and unpredictable color." Then, as one lighting designer stated that there weren't "sufficient suitable applications" for the system, another reveled in the wide variety of options available! There are several causes for this dichotomy. One of the main problems arises by mixing up the properties of the plastic version with the glass type of equipment. Another is the general unfamiliarity with both systems, probably caused by a lack of widespread education in this 30-year old technology.

1. *Cost:* Compared to what? You must compare apples with apples. If owners are happy with hot lamps cooking their Rowlandson watercolors, textiles, wood counters, and prospective customers, incandescent or tungsten halogen is certainly cheaper initially. However, in no time, they will have faded sheets of paper and merchandise, dried up wooden furnishings, and prospective patrons fleeing a hostile torrid environment. If the object is to eliminate obtrusive rows of glaring track lights, which usually are never aimed properly and which increase electric bills because of the added air conditioning load, fiber optics is the answer. It will provide discreet, sophisticated illumination. Millions of feet of long-lasting glass fiber are already being made for fiber-optic communications. Once installation and energy costs, maintenance, and conservation of the building and its contents are

accounted for, the price of glass fiber optics (which now matches plastic) is balanced by payback quicker than realtors expect. Some difficult applications cannot be accomplished by anything else but glass fiber optics.

2. *Exaggerated claims and no backup from the seller:* Some suppliers promise too much and then dump the merchandise on the doorstep and run. At first, the manufacturer tells customers yes, yes, yes, they can do everything wanted; but, when help is sought, all of a sudden nobody can figure out how to do the job. With any product, customers should investigate before believing any overly eager salesperson.

3. *Lack of appropriate applications:* If prospective users find that all their clients want to use fiber optics, but the lighting professionals claim "they can't really find an application for which it seems well suited," this signals that perhaps the designer has not done his or her homework and has not kept up with the latest technologies. For those who declare that fiber-optic lighting is "in its infancy," they do not realize that they are referring to plastic only, because glass came first, by decades.

4. *Poor color rendition:* These problems could be related to *any* inferior material, plastic or glass, or plastic that is disintegrating from infrared and ultraviolet rays emitted from the lamp lacking a proper coupler separating the dissimilar materials. Low-quality glass fibers do not do a good job either, or the culprit may be an expiring light source not giving out the light expected. Any reputable supplier will tell the client up front that, if color rendition is important (as opposed to providing emergency light in baseboards just to get the occupants out safely), glass tail lengths of 8 to 10 meters in either direction from the projector are recommended to avoid eventual color shift. Of course the new glass light guides with improved attenuation will substantially change this figure. The fact remains, the combination of good quality glass fibers and the right dichroic lamp will yield bright white light every time, up to 5600 K. Precise color adjustments can be made with glass dichroic color filters for 3200 or 4000 K.

5. *Distortion:* This could be caused by cheap plastic lenses, poor harness assembly, or an inadequate light source, not simply because it is fiber-optic illumination.

6. *Unreliable light sources:* The performance of modern day metal halide lamps is much more stable than when first introduced. They run much cooler than tungsten halogen, use less energy, and last twice as long. Japan and Germany have already come out with very efficient lamps specifically designed for use with glass fiber optics (but they can't be used with plastic). These new metal halide lamps have been used since early 1997.

7. *Inefficiency:* Some plastic can suffer up to double-digit light losses; quality glass does not. However, for *any* fiber optics, if the wrong parabolic reflector is used, or the wrong lamp is employed which scatters rays instead of concentrating them into the harness, the light source will be inefficient. Adequate advance preparation is necessary for proper results.

8. *Need to measure ahead of time:* That is a plus not a minus, and it makes for a less-expensive but better outcome than off-the-cuff lighting lacking careful forethought. Oddly, this conflicts with Myth 15. To wait until the lighting is about to be turned on to cut and run tails on the job is playing Russian roulette with the client's money. The ultimate effects achieved in this "fast-track" approach are uncertain at best. Labor costs will vary greatly according to the expertise of the person cutting and splicing plastic tails in a dirty construction site. Part of the difficulty may be that the client has not decided what is to be illuminated. Not knowing the variables, how can precise lighting be designed?

9. *Need for mock-ups:* While there are those wishing for an instant magic wand to create design, the best designers still use mock-ups on-site. That is the only way to see exactly how the lighting will work in a particular situation, notwithstanding the most sophisticated software programs. Light is so elusive, tables and charts cannot be depended on for outcomes, especially if the sun suddenly pours in the window or someone turns on an existing light in the area.

10. *Interchangeability:* Fiber-optic lighting is a SYSTEM, not a jumble of incompatible components procured from all over. What kind of warranty would there be with five different manufacturers of differing quality? Anyway, the natural laws of physics do not allow mixing up focal lengths and different properties of materials, nor can ferrules

threaded in metric be attached to imperial-threaded fittings. This is not to say that it is not possible to use a well-constructed light source with different makes of glass harnesses with an attenuation of 150 dB/kM or less. It is done every day, because the opening for the common end is usually a standard 30 mm. Glass fiber-optic lighting has always used the universal metric system.

11. *System failure:* Many times, either the electric service or installation is faulty, or extraneous materials have been incorrectly inserted where they should not be. Sometimes there may be a problem with harmonic distortion, voltage drops, or other power quality deficiencies. There is always the possibility of low-quality components being used, or the common omission of providing for adequate dissipation of the heat produced by light. Or, it could be the lamp.

12. *It is difficult to get a very tight focus with glass. You can see the individual threads and dark spots:* Over 20 years ago, early epoxies may have given problems, but not now. Even today, as in any merchandise, if a supplier substitutes from the specs and gives inferior and shoddily made equipment, there will be dissatisfaction.

13. *Impossible to attach ferrules to the raw glass fibers.* Inasmuch as this material is not normally sold unassembled into harnesses, this statement, alleged by one plastic competitor, is obviously intended to dissemble.

14. *Light from glass fiber optics is green:* This is true only if it is very low quality, or from too-long tail lengths where color shift begins, or an expiring lamp. (There has been light emerging from plastic which was positively orange, for the same reasons.) Both plastic and glass will suffer gradual color shift once the immutable physical laws of optics are exceeded.

15. *Impossible to determine the length of glass tails:* Anyone who can't measure from point *A* to point *B* should be in another business. The location of the light source plus where the point of light is needed determine the length of the tails. Obviously, inspection of the interstitial spaces should be made to discover the clear path from projector to where the point of light emerges. This takes a modicum of construction experience.

16. *Glass is outrageously expensive, much more so than plastic:* When the same specifications are used for both, glass is usually competitively priced. Considering the great longevity of glass, it will serve long after plastic has failed. In 1996, a worldwide symposium of museum conservators and curators discussed the eventual decomposition of all types of artwork made from man-made materials, and their inability to remedy the situation. Eventual disintegration of these artificial substances is an inherent property. Thereafter, the client pays double to have the work done again.

17. *Color shift for glass starts at 5 meters (some even say 3 meters), not 8:* This statement arises either from poor quality tails or an overzealous salesperson trying to beat the competition.

18. *The result turned out to be underlit, and they had to retrofit to correct:* By seeking a reduced price, the equipment was equally reduced, so that it could not do the job in the first place. The same effect would happen with any type of lighting system.

19. *Fiber optics can only be used for discos, casinos, aquariums, and exhibit cases:* Not so. Glass fiber optics is eminently suited for *functional* architectural lighting such as task, three-dimensional display, and architectural contours, both interior and exterior.

20. *Light from fiber optics is not strong enough:* Large-size glass fiber-optic light guides can provide substantial light levels at considerable distances. Even coverage over a wide area is also possible.

21. *The glass tails do not filter out ultraviolet rays:* There is a UV filter within the light source that effectively removes these destructive rays. In a test by Frank Florentino, lighting designer for the Smithsonian Institution, Washington DC, with special equipment employed by major museums, this fact was proved. Perhaps there is fear that many fewer lamps will be sold whenever the glass fiber-optic technology is used?

Basic Lighting Methods Are Just Common Sense

The ultimate client should be aware of certain basic lighting techniques, if only to ensure that the professionals brought on the job are following them. Naturally, the entire electric service should be inspected before adding new loads. Benjamin Franklin said, "Guests and fish spoil in three days." Electrical wiring lasts 30 years and should be renewed if it is found inadequate or unsafe for current usage. Defective power systems could cause equipment damage or be life threatening. Like the straw that broke the camel's back, the addition of just one more receptacle could cause failure, especially in older installations.

Some Fundamental Rules for Good Illumination

- Differentiate between ambient and directional lighting. Everything in the space does not have to be at the same light level. Just as heat is not required at the high ceiling of a Gothic cathedral when the congregation is seated near the floor, similarly, the entire area need not be lit throughout at the same brightness. Rather, the equivalent of modulation and syncopation in music should be employed in illumination. In most places, ambient light, sufficient to avoid bumping into the furniture, can be combined with directional highlighting on important features, to produce an interesting effect—contrasting highs and lows. Flat but blinding illumination may have its place, but not everywhere. In fact, on entering a shop, you can immediately tell the quality of the merchandise by the store lighting. The more care given, the higher the value of the goods. Blasting the ceiling with massed fluorescents usually indicates less-expensive items. (See Fig. 2-1.)

- System design should have sufficient flexibility for likely future needs.

- Baffle all light sources so that they do not shine in the viewer's eyes. (See Fig. 2-2.)

- Unless using ornamental fixtures, make an effort to conceal the wiring and lighting hardware so that it illuminates the area and objects without being seen itself. (See Fig. 2-3.)

- Make use of whatever lighting techniques, including theatrical, are necessary to enhance the contours or objects.

- Do not mix colors of different light sources in the same space, unless that is the effect desired.

- Remember that the human eye will accommodate first to the brightest point of light seen. Everything else surrounding that point will appear less visible. Therefore, gradually decrease the light level leading to very low conservation lighting.

Fig. 2-1 Overkill lighting: too many fluorescents in ceiling.

- Do not use the highest light level in the room for ceilings. This will leave the items at floor level in the dark. Even for ornamental ceilings, the contrast should not be drastic.

- Wherever possible, do a mock-up in situ before completing the design and ordering.

- Always make provisions to dissipate the heat from the light source.

- Locate light sources where they are always easily accessible.

- Make all task and/or display lighting as adjustable as possible, because even "permanent" installations change over time. Anticipate near-future needs. Even if this means ordering a few longer glass tails (which can be curled up until needed) or installing a few empty conduits while the walls and floor are open, it is much less expensive than having to do a whole new system later.

- Start with the simplest approach first, and only work up to the more elaborate ones as needed.

- Use sufficient components to do the job. Skimping on one or a few items ultimately wastes the entire amount.

Fig. 2-2 Unbaffled light shining in viewer's eyes.

- At the very beginning of the project, gather all members of the construction team together and acquaint them with the fiber-optic system. This will avoid having the curious take off job time to inspect it. It will also help eliminate accidental damage while it is being stored before installation.

Fig. 2-3 Surface mounted wiring and emergency lights near ceiling.

- Prior to finalizing the specifications, hold sufficient job meetings with the entire team to discuss the fiber-optic installation as it impacts on adjacent trades. Enlist those companies to help decide the best methods to secure the light guides to the fabric of the building. For example, the masons may know the optimum way to attach the light guides to the stone without damaging it.

- In the beginning, spend as much time on figuring out how to get electric power and controls to the system as on designing the lighting. Be sure that workable wiring diagrams are included in the specifications.

- If working in structures over 50 years old, do research on lighting fixtures correct for the period. Using art deco uplights in a Victorian setting looks as incongruous as candlelight in an International-style skyscraper. Also pay attention to the historic light levels that go with the original colors and building materials.

- Investigate what controls and/or special effects might improve the design and/or save operating costs.

- NEVER add or mix dissimilar components without checking with the manufacturer. (See Fig. 2-4.)

- Earmark enough time to focus the lights correctly once they are installed. Poor focusing is one of the chief causes of dissatisfaction for viewer and owner.

- Commissioning, testing, and user training should be included in the lighting package. It is not complete until a

Fig. 2-4 Misfocused light on museum object.

scheduled maintenance program is established and posted on-site. Before leaving the job, the installer should give in-house training in proper operation and maintenance. All lamps should be marked with date of installation and replaced shortly before their expected lamp life expires.

• Establish service contracts and repair procedures, including call-out response times if a fault develops.

Who Does the Designing?

With the parameters given, the next step is design. In some cases, where a proper lighting designer and/or consultant is not engaged, design has been done by the architect, engineer, other consultant, supplier, exhibit builder, curator, conservator, building maintenance, interior designer, or electrical contractor. On one project, the carpenter did the job. The subsequent chain of command can be tightly structured, especially if lighting is being done in conjunction with other building work, or on an ad hoc basis.

Occasionally, the client, thinking there will be savings in professional fees, may simply call in a lamp salesperson who gets a percentage of the number of lamps sold. Without proper training in accepted lighting techniques, said salesperson could very well just load up the job with as many lamps as can be fit into the space, without regard to providing the least expensive but best illumination for the particular purpose. The customer could end up paying more for ineffectual unnecessary lighting and superfluous wasted energy. In an actual occurrence, the fiber-optic quotation given an institution contained such an exorbitant commission for the lamp seller, that the entire project was scrapped.

Or, a friendly electrician may be chosen, who is fine in bending pipe and doing strip lighting in shopping malls, but who may not be au courant with the latest products and methods of selective architectural lighting. In fairness, those electricians who are inquisitive and willing to try something different may accomplish more than those few professional designers who still doggedly stick to their same old methods, no matter what the job requires. Some of these specialists shoehorn their standard plans into every project so that their signature design is readily recognizable. At least, the electrician may be more familiar with how a building is put together, and where and how to conceal the power/control wiring and fiber-optic components. Actually, many of these mechanics are eager to work with this lighting tool and manage to convince owners who depend on them to try it.

What Clients Should Look for, and What Professionals Should Provide

Clients should be sure that they are getting initial information only from those thoroughly knowledgeable in this technology; adequate planning early in the design process; highest quality light guide materials, whether glass or plastic; well-made fittings of a durable material; and competent installers. If all these criteria are not met, there will be disappointments, caused not by the fiber optics, but by those providing it. This is unfortunate too because, once dissatisfied and/or overcharged, the buyer may be very reluctant to try this illumination again.

It is difficult to forget visions of a particular "rush" job, maneuvered by some opportunists just entering the business. Within a few days, they gathered together components from disparate sources. Skinny size-12 glass fibers were hastily thrust into a large size-48 sheathing and powered by a noisy light source that sounded like a coffee grinder. When lit up, this conglomeration produced the most bilious green hue imaginable. It was fast work, but no improvement over the year-old brittle plastic system that it replaced.

Sources of Fiber-Optic Suppliers

Whoever the designer is, a reputable supplier should be consulted to learn what is presently available, and to benefit from previous experiences. Sources include:

- Equipment suppliers, called *factors* by the British, who add their profit to bought-in components, all of which, it is hoped, are compatible. They may also design and/or install.

- Distributors, who are essentially salespeople, rather than engineers or lighting designers. Many times, especially if they carry a large number of other products, they cannot give extensive technical advice beyond what is in the catalogue. They may also not have the ability to customize parts either in-house or quickly at the factory. Dealing with volume rather than personal attention, sometimes they are very difficult to reach when urgently needed. They supply only.

- OEMs (*original equipment manufacturers*), who may have exclusive representatives who have the necessary support from the factory to cater to individualized orders. These people are trained by the fiber-optic maker and are capable of designing and installing, as well as supplying.

- *Rumpelstilskin:* There will always be one-person operations cobbling together components in their basements. They may be a little less expensive than established companies, and their goods may work; but in the end, dealing with them is like playing a game of Russian roulette—only those who can afford to lose should play. When the seller folds the tent and silently steals away, the buyer is stuck without a backup and source of parts, unless another *Rumpelstilskin* is found.

Making It Possible to Obtain a Viable Cost

Chapter 3 covers designing with fiber optics. However created, the specifications, loose or not, have to be bid on by those supplying, installing, and commissioning the equipment. This, too, can be as diverse as calling up a brother-in-law or sending a formal invitation to many consultants and contractors to submit quotations. It is critical that whoever prepares the bill of material includes sufficient data, otherwise it will be impossible to get a meaningful price.

Be sure there is no confusion in terminology between glass and plastic systems. One designer mixed up the tail *dimensions* of plastic with the tail *size* number of glass, confounding everyone. Only consider qualified bidders. Check that their publicity does not exaggerate their expertise.

Glass fiber-optic lighting is not priced by the square foot, or even by the linear foot. Since it is an essentially custom-assembled system composed of three essential parts, all three have to be known and included in the calculations. Similarly, labor costs for assembly involved for plastic fiber optics are also an unknown quantity and must be determined. This means that a customer should not expect a supplier to take a cost figure out of the air quickly, unless the application is identical to one previously done. However, there are so many uses for fiber optics, there is seldom exact duplication. Clients do not benefit by asking for an off-the-top-of-the-head number, because the physical conditions on the job are also a function of the price. This is the reason for a thorough examination of the site prior to preparation of specifications and quotations.

What may seem to be a short, direct route from point *A* to point *B,* could turn out to have hidden obstructions in the ceilings, walls, or floors. This detour will make the light guides much longer than the straight line shown on the drawings. A special fitting may have to be fabricated to solve a problem, or the light source itself may have to be altered to suit its location. Of course, there are published prices for the basic light sources and the stock fittings. However, the harness cost can only be determined by knowing the length and size of the glass tails. If there are one-size-fits-all products, they may or may not provide the illumination expected. Large quantity discounts would further change the per meter figure of the plastic or glass fiber.

Essential Facts Needed to Prepare a Viable Quotation

First-time fiber-optic users are not expected to be able to make all of the selections given in the following by themselves. In fact, it would be better all around if the lighting "wish list," measured drawings, and a description of the area and/or objects were given to the supplier to create the bill of material, in consultation with all the other team members.

1. The light source

    a. Quantity?

        (1) If the harness powered by metal halide exceeds 160,000 fibers (135,000 for tungsten), an additional illuminator must be added.

        (2) If more than one projector, do they have to be synchronized or otherwise controlled by suitable wiring?

    b. Type? Any special environmental conditions—dust, water, temperature, electromagnetic interference?

    c. Kind of light source?

        (1) Metal halide, tungsten halogen, other?

        (2) Wattage and color temperature?

2. The harness

    a. What light levels? Conservation level (50 lux) must be surrounded by low level light.

    b. Size, length, and quantity of light guides (tails)?

    c. Type of sheathing?

    d. Size, type, and material of end ferrules? Threaded, smooth, marine-grade stainless steel?

3. Fittings (lenses and lens holders)

    a. Type? Collimating, diffusing, zoom, framing, downlights, wall-washers, color?

    b. Concave or convex? Frosted, clear, or combination?

    c. Size of lens in degrees?

    d. For what size tail?

    e. Any custom alteration required? Recessed lens, interior painted black?

    f. Finish of lenses and/or holders? Black, white, chrome, bronze, powder-coated?

    g. Method of securing tails and lens holders to the building fabric?

4. Accessories

    a. Motion, color, dimming, or other special effects?

    b. If complex, is a theatrical computer interface needed? If so, what type?

    c. What and how many colors in the color wheel? Speed of change?

    d. What degree of dimming? Speed of change?

5. Additional questions

    a. Scaled drawings indicating where the light sources can be conveniently located?

    b. Detail of existing ambient light in the area?

    c. Complete physical description of area or objects to be lit? Size, shape, reflectivity, material, color?

    d. What provision for dissipation of heat from the lamp(s)?

    e. Are there physical barriers impeding installation of the tails in interstitial spaces?

    f. If joists or other members have to be drilled, has the architect or structural engineer approved the action?

    g. Do the tails need to be protected in some locations (i.e., encasement in flexible conduit)?

6. Further questions specifically required for lighting display cases

   a. Construction of the cases? Wood, metal, glass, other?

   b. If antique, can they be drilled for access holes?

   c. Colors and finishes of case interior? Mirrored back?

   d. Is there space within the case to house the light source? Since heat rises, an upper "attic" is preferable to one below the display area.

   e. If not, where are the light sources to be put?

   f. Do special environmental controls have to be within the case?

   g. Are the mullions wide enough to conceal the light guides along the sides?

   h. Number and type of shelves (transparent or opaque)? Movable or stationary?

   i. Which cases are adjoining, so that one illuminator may be used for more than one cabinet?

   j. Inventory of items to be exhibited?

Caveats for Designers and Users

Inevitably, realizing its tremendous potential, there will be many less-than-competent or, worse, disreputable people suddenly going into fiber-optic lighting. Prospective designers and users should be ever alert for them. Here is what could happen if this is not done:

A private museum employed an architect, lighting designer, general contractor, and a very expensive exhibit-case builder to display an extraordinary and very valuable collection. However, when the quotation for lighting was presented, it seemed high to the administrator. To ensure getting the order, the supplier cut the price in half, but the owner was not told, nor did he check, that, in the process, half the equipment was also eliminated. You may well ask why the client didn't notice the substantial difference in the quantity of material, but sometimes, only the bottom line is considered. When the job was installed, the delicate objects languished in the dark.

An auxiliary lighting plan of fluorescent tubes set in the ceiling of the vitrines only succeeded in heating up the fragile items on the first shelf, still leaving the objects on the lower solid shelves unlit. A further attempt using track lighting around the room's ceiling merely created more heat and glare and did not serve the cases at all. Finally, all lighting was turned off, and visitors have to assume strange acrobatic positions to see the exhibits. The unfortunate museum director has already spent much more than the original quotation trying to rectify the situation, while being bedeviled with both litigation and the angry comments of paying museum-goers. He has learned the hard way that you get what you pay for.

When evaluating competing quotations, watch for performance compromised for cost. As a general rule, the purchaser would do well to throw out the highest and lowest prices and entertain the ones in the middle. If there is a significant discrepancy among quotations, check the bill of material to see what may have been left out by one or expanded by another. Also, throughout the construction, stay alert to make sure you are getting what was specified and not unacceptable unauthorized substitutions.

Now that the necessary details to look for are known, the actual design can be created.

Chapter 3

Designing with Fiber Optics

I n schools of finance, the student learns that, to be successful, he or she should buy low and sell high, but is not told when either limit actually occurs. Similarly, the designer of lighting faces choices of many techniques for illumination, but must make his or her own decisions on what type of design is best suited for the budget and application. There are many excellent books devoted to lighting methods for all types of purposes. The reader is referred to them for further information. Here, only the fundamentals are mentioned, so that Chapter 6, on applications, is better understood.

Some Types of Lighting Techniques

In addition to the usual downlighting, uplighting, and crosslighting, the next four methods are directly borrowed from theatrical practice:

- Grazing = light beam within one foot and parallel to a textured surface

- Backlighting = silhouetting

- Shadowing = light in front of an object projects a shadow on the surface behind

- Modelling = the use of light for three-dimensional effects to create highlights and shadows

    Ambient = the overall general illumination in a space

    Promotional = lighting for advertising

    Building = general exterior illumination of a structure

    Feature = lighting to single out a particular area

    Functional = lighting to enable a task to be performed

    Spotlighting = application of a small area of bright light to single out a specific aspect of the scene

    Highlighting = differs from spotlighting in that it usually involves a larger area lit to a higher level than adjacent ones to give emphasis

    Floodlighting = flat overall illumination without emphasizing a certain area, loosely used to describe large-scale lighting

Since fiber optics is essentially *directional,* it can be used in any of the previously mentioned situations, except general floodlighting. How much light is needed for a task is both subjective and dependent on the relative brightness of the surroundings. An effective result can be obtained in several ways, including illuminating to various light levels and using different colors. There is no need to escalate lighting equipment costs with special high-tech components unless the design is complex enough to warrant it.

And then there is light pollution—illumination that serves no useful purpose or which is glaring and spills over a greater area than what is being lit. This is a visual distraction and may even present a physical hazard to pedestrians and vehicular traffic.

Design Considerations

Many elements can affect the success of the design. They include:

Type of Light Source

Generally, lamps with higher wattage produce more light. Light output could range from 2600 to 135,000 lumens. An exception is the 150-watt metal halide lamp, compared to the 250-watt tungsten halogen source. The long arc of the larger-wattage tungsten halogen lamp makes it less efficient and more expensive to use as a source for this system than metal halide. This is the reason more light can be obtained from a 150-watt metal halide lamp than from a 250-watt tungsten halogen lamp.

Color temperatures also affect the brilliance. Currently available lamps for fiber optics may range from 3000 K (a warmer halogen light) to 5600 K (a medium source daylight).

Reflectivity, Color, and Texture of the Projection Surface

The optimum surface is light-colored matte or textured. Darker surfaces are likely to absorb much of the light and will be less effective. A quick check with a flashlight will show how well the beam is visible on a surface under actual lighting conditions. Shiny glass, mirrors, and high-gloss metals are less suitable than plaster, painted walls, concrete and aggregate, brushed metals, brick, and light woods.

Distance of the Surface from the Light Source

Select a system with sufficient power to cover the desired surface.

Footprint of Light Required

The smaller the image, the stronger the intensity of light. Basically, the trade-off is brightness for footprint size. However, diffusing, wide-angle, telephoto, or zoom lenses can be used to achieve the desired effect.

Color Filters Used

All color filters (gel and glass) absorb light, some more than others. As a rule, reds and blues absorb more light than greens or yellows. When using color filters, to some degree, color is traded for brightness. A white light source (at least 3200° K) must be used, otherwise, the colors will be distorted.

Special Effects

A combination of systems may be needed to set images in motion, have them fade and reappear, rotate, create clouds or water, or produce multiple images from one, using a two- or four-fold prism. If more than three motor wheels are required, a theatrical computer must be employed. More and more equipment originally developed for theatrical uses is now being employed for architectural venues. There is a projector input for the DMX512 protocol, which was first developed just for controlling dimmers. NOTE: Correct control equipment must also be added to send proper signals. Then, the same controls for theatrical effects can be used for other purposes.

Theatrical Lighting in Architectural Applications

Theatrical lighting draws attention and creates realistic settings. Really, the only difference between the former and architectural lighting is the separation between the audience and the space. In the latter, the viewer is inside the space, experiencing the lighting directly.

More and more equipment, originally developed for theatrical uses, is now being employed for architectural venues. The DMX512 protocol, first developed just for controlling dimmers, has 32 channels for more functions like moving light and color changing. Thus, the same controls for theatrical effects can also be used for other purposes, such as to close window curtains for an audio-visual presentation, to bring down a movie screen, or to activate emergency lighting by wiring the light sources to turn on automatically in the event of a power failure. Programming can retain the memory of the previous preset. Easily controllable beams can be produced soft- or hard-edged, colored or patterned. The greater variety of light guide sizes and miniaturized fittings for glass offers a large "palette" enabling the designer to create many more effects.

After carefully studying the architectural drawings and the client's lighting wishes, one approach, familiar to all physics students as "Finagler's constant," is to start with the answer and work backward to determine the equipment needed. Obviously, there is always more than one way to do the job, so suggestions given here are just that—a starting point. The reader is encouraged to find better methods. There are even a few examples given without comment, to entice finding alternate solutions for a logical, affordable, and successful design. One way to learn to produce good lighting is to recognize poor attempts and avoid them.

Bad Lighting Design

To recognize acceptable illumination, comparison with poor choices is helpful. For many reasons, bad lighting can be seen everywhere. If it were good, it would not be so noticeable. It usually reflects a lack of attention to detail. Sometimes it is the fault of careless workmanship or low-quality components. It could be the product of an inexperienced hand, or, perhaps, good old plain common sense was not used. Occasionally, it can be blamed on an established professional shoehorning a signature standard procedure into every application, warranted or not. Here are some examples of what not to do (see Figs. 3-1 to 3-25):

- Fragile Coromandel screens do not do well with hot incandescent floor lights, burning their bottoms. Nor do they show their true col-

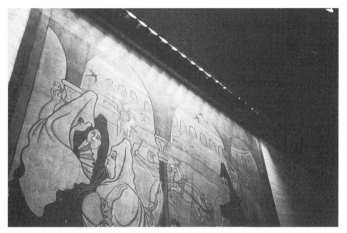

Fig. 3-2 Ugly additional lighting added to period chandelier.

Fig. 3-1 Hot lights on antique theatrical curtain is fading the colors.

Fig. 3-3 Large emergency lights interrupt ceiling decor and cannot be seen if room is smoke-filled.

ors (or even their design) when masked by hot spots from track lights shining on their varnished surfaces.

- Customers who think they will save by cutting the cost of two tails down to one for sidelighting shiny surfaces have outfoxed themselves by obtaining balls of glare.

- Bright spotlights at the bottom of a stair will only succeed in blinding those descending. In historic houses, it could result in a pile-up of prospective donors in a heap.

Fig. 3-4 Hot spot and wrong color light obscuring true colors of ceiling mosaic.

Fig. 3-5 Misfocused track lights intruding in early 20th-century room.

Fig. 3-6 Glaring, hot lights in a museum gift shop.

Fig. 3-7 Spot lights aimed at diners' heads in restaurant.

Fig. 3-8 Cheap contemporary fixture stuck into Victorian medallion.

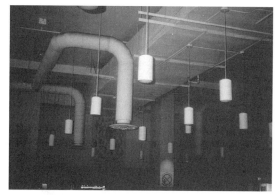

Fig. 3-9 Awful lighting and air conditioning ducts in a restaurant.

Fig. 3-10 Glaring, hot lights in a boutique.

- A corollary is lighting up the treads of a staircase so that it embarrassingly silhouettes ladies' legs.
- Hot lights on hairy wall-mounted stuffed animals will cause the creatures to become bald.
- It does not increase a museum-goer's knowledge when fake windows in a period room are brightly lit to reproduce sunlight, while

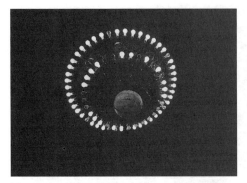

Fig. 3-11 Perennial burned-out bulbs in high-ceilinged chandelier.

Fig. 3-12 Obtrusive lighting nailed onto columns of historic Victorian church.

Fig. 3-13 Infestation of downlights guzzling energy.

Fig. 3-14 Flat fluorescent lighting does not show intricate detail of objects.

Fig. 3-15 Hot tungsten halogen lamps fading 1920's painted silk gown.

(a)   (b)

Fig. 3-16 Huge obtrusive light fixture larger than the object being illuminated (a & b).

the candles in the wall sconces and the central chandelier are blazing with electronic candles. With the price of candles in the eighteenth century, not even the rich would have indulged in such an extravagance during daytime.

- Putting an oversize lamp in a floor lamp just because it was handy is a mistake if it blasts someone entering an otherwise dark hallway with a huge ball of blinding light.

- Selecting the wrong shape, size, and color of bulb for matching torchières standing side by side indicates terminal carelessness.

- In museums around the world, any number of four-poster beds with original hangings are being roasted with hot lights.

- Where marine-grade stainless steel is to be used, someone forgot to order stainless steel screws to match, so that rust stains appeared as soon as the water feature was introduced.

(a)

Fig. 3-17 Track lighting shining on Coromandel screen harms lacquer and throws balls of light onto the shiny surface (a & b).

- In other institutions with highly ornamental or beamed historic ceilings, there may be an outgrowth of strange hooded lighting fixtures, or even whole floating "rafts" dangling from the rafters to contain illumination. This spoils the historic feeling.

- Somehow, track lighting (usually misfocused) and sixteenth-century interiors are just not compatible. The tapestries seem to be fading right before the visitors' eyes.

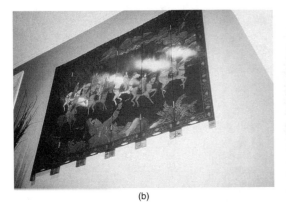

(b)

Fig. 3-17 (Continued)

Fig. 3-18 Too bright a light shining at foot of stairs.

- Then there are the protective Plexiglas screens with light bouncing in every direction, precluding any sight of the artifact behind. Safe lighting should be put within the case to eliminate the glare.

- It is most unfortunate to see valuable antique furniture lit with sewing machine lamps at such close range that the wood is hot to the touch.

- Even worse are library cases of incanabula (priceless earliest printed books), whose leather spines are burning from incandescent lamps almost on top of them.

- Misunderstanding about lighting is not limited to museum displays. One ladies' shoe department in a major store had to redo a recent expensive renovation because the new illumination was so hot, it drove away the customers and bleached the leather.

Fig. 3-20 Show window light shining in viewer's eyes.

Fig. 3-19 Light balding a stuffed animal.

(a)

(b)

Fig. 3-21 (a) Lights fading leather goods in store window. (b) Lights fading textiles in store window.

Fig. 3-22 Hot lights destroying photographs in showcase.

Fig. 3-23 Glaring light in bathroom.

Fig. 3-24 Flat fluorescents in ladies' room give incorrect color for applying cosmetics.

Fig. 3-25 Spotlight on sink faucets, instead of lighting bathroom mirror.

- There have been shop window displays where the lights are shining right into the eyes of the beholder, instead of on the merchandise.

- Other show windows use lighting with unrestricted ultraviolet rays that actually bleach the leather goods or fabrics, so that they cannot be sold even after a short time of exposure.

- A most common mistake is to allow the light source to go unbaffled so that it is not concealed from the viewer's eye. Then the whole illusion is lost.

- There are conservation labs where the light is either too low to see how to minister to the art properly, or so bright, it is ruining what is being restored.

- Restaurant downlighting often is so hot, it cooks the patrons, or it is so weak, a miner's cap is needed to read the menu or see what's on the plate.

- With few exceptions, hotel guest room lighting worldwide is notoriously bad—either hot and glaring, or hopelessly dim.

- Most hotel bedroom lighting precludes reading altogether.

- Eye problems in offices with computer screens have been proliferating because of light bouncing from overhead lay-in fluorescent fixtures.

- The modern lowered ceiling does not contribute to energy efficiency when heat from conventional downlights adds to the air conditioning load.

- Ineffective task lighting on the production line can lead to accidents as well as loss of quality control.

All of these situations could be remedied with fiber optics, which is "cool, man, cool."

Controls for Lighting

Occupants may no longer be satisfied with simple on-off light switches. They may wish to have more control over illumination, which can do different tasks. A control system is an element of a lighting installation, which aims to provide a number of facilities including:

- Functional lighting, which enables people to carry out their particular tasks
- Lighting aesthetics, which enhances the visual quality of the building
- Minimizing equipment and energy costs
- Avoiding duplication or illumination at cross-purposes with existing illumination

Many of these products may have been designed and installed over different periods of time. Good coordination in lighting parameters and, indeed, in all adjacent disciplines, is needed to integrate the newer with the older installations.

Hint: Unless the control system meets user requirements, including flexibility, and is easy to operate, any potential benefits may be lost. Expert advice should be sought before specifying.

There are two types of lighting controllers—switches and dimmers. These can be activated by various means, from simple local manual switches and dimmers, to time-operated controls, motion, and/or heat sensors, to very sophisticated preset and programmable systems. Their purpose could be just for architectural lighting, or for energy management, or for both. Good lighting design should not be affected by whatever mode is chosen. If, because of cost, the client settles for "less" control, what "less" means in convenience and flexibility and the effect on the lamp itself, should be fully understood. Here, again, coordination with all ultimate users should be included before anything is specified.

Hint: For life safety, never turn off lights near stairs, elevators (lifts), or operating machinery.

Electronic controls affect different light sources in different ways. When not needed, turning off or down incandescents (which work without a transformer) does increase their life. There are many types of dimmers on the market for incandescent and low-voltage halogen lamps.

Hint: As with smoke detectors, presence or occupancy sensors should never be placed behind ceiling beams or any other architectural component that could block full operation.

Dimming Metal Halide Lamps

Contrary to popular belief, metal halide lamps can be dimmed successfully without affecting color. The process employs a very early technique, which is nevertheless effective. Except for incandescents, dimming lamps by electronic means generally affects the color temperature and CRI (color rendering index) of lamps using a ballast (except for fluorescents, which can usually be dimmed to about 10 percent of full light output), especially HID (high-intensity discharge) types like metal halide. Since conventional dimming equipment causes this unwanted color change, a mechanical metal dimmer, which interfaces between the lamp and the fiber input bundle, is used. This effectively introduces a physical block to the passage of light.

Solid or mesh, the metal dimming wheel is graded to allow gradual control over the degree of light extinction. This can either be operated manually or remotely from a standard dimming switch via electronic controls. Dimming levels can either go from 0 to 100 percent (for theaters), or stop at selected levels (for restaurants, museums, residential, and commercial uses). Thus, the wheel:

Is lightweight and unbreakable

Is not affected by the heat of the lamp

Does not affect the actual color of the light, particularly important when white light is sought, but of different intensities

If as many as 32 or more different automated sequences are needed, as in an elaborate museum display, then the fiber-optic light source can be modified to accept signals from a more complex control.[1] For example, the standard system would require three channels to control five projectors with operations of color and motion, where a "master-slave" system is employed (only one projector decodes the signals and the other four units move as the master).

Occupancy Sensors

Sensors are mainly needed for conservation purposes and special lighting effects. Please note that they will not save energy on anything but incandescent bulbs. Usages will determine which method to employ. The different types are:

Infrared—sees a heated body and almost instantaneously activates the circuit

Ultrasonic—senses motion within its view

Dual technology—ultrasonic + infrared, to avoid failure and false readings

Ambient lighting photocell—allows for deactivation of lighting when sufficient ambient daylight is available

The circuit must include a time delay to allow people to leave the space safely and to avoid having lights constantly switched on and off.

A case study of a prestigious museum displaying paintings, sculpture, and furnishings in a nineteenth-century town house[2] reports on two main elements of new adjustable lighting. One pertained to the spotlights for the exhibits, and the other was for a central chandelier. A "scene-set" controller provides switching between the following "scenes":

- Display lighting to supplement daylight
- Display lighting for nighttime
- Display lighting combined with the central chandelier when the gallery is used for social functions

Illuminance Sensor–Operated Controls

In areas where there is adequate daylight for part of the time, daylight illuminance sensors (photocells) can be used to ensure that electric lights are not left on unnecessarily. People will often switch electric lights on first thing in the morning when it is still dark, but they are less likely to switch them off later when daylight becomes sufficient, particularly in shared spaces and circulation areas. Illuminance sensors can switch or regulate luminaire light output, but regulation (dimming) will require the appropriate control gear.

Emergency Lighting

During a disaster, when lighting is urgently needed at *floor level* to guide occupants to safety, exit signs mounted near the ceiling are frankly useless, because they can't be seen in a smoke-filled space. Besides, the only available air to breathe is at the floor. Dropping to hands and knees is the only way to maneuver under conditions with zero visibility and a choking atmosphere. A simple nonelectric reflecting sign above an exit is all that is needed to comply with (American) fire codes to indicate the route out during normal conditions. In places of public assembly, glass fiber optics at the *baseboard (skirting) level* is well suited to evacuate occupants in a calamity. Long lengths of tails placed alternately on either side of a hallway create a path to safety that needs little maintenance.

Some portions of a fiber-optic system may be selected to serve as auxiliary illumination. Those components should be wired so that the emergency lighting portion is kept operable and separate from the regular service.

Emergency Power Generation

Commercial and institutional establishments and institutions should provide some sort of emergency generators in case of loss of primary power. In this way, basic operations can continue. The lack of this equipment was clearly noted during the massive power outage in New York City in the 1960s, when the entire city was brought to a halt. In the 1970s, during the nationwide coal strikes in England, as much as 80 percent of normal electrical capacity was provided by alternate means when the main sources were off. This enabled theaters, stores, offices, restaurants, some factories, and hospitals to carry on. At least emergency lighting should be kept in service by this means for as long as possible. The cost of a UPS (uninterruptible power supply) unit is much less than the loss of one day's business profits. Yet, the penny-wise and pound-foolish mentality does not recognize this, even though a facility could be hit by lightning 3 times in one summer, completely incapacitating it for the season.

Computer Drawings and Calculations

In preparation for this book, research was done on computer ray-tracing/radiosity-based visualization systems. The hunt started in 1996 with a friend's son's Ph.D. program at the University of Pennsylvania, then moved to international lighting conferences in Toronto, Canada, and Bath, England. Further clues from an article in a magazine[3] led to a Massachusett's firm, which referred me to a company in California that then

Fig. 3-26 Digital image of lighting program. Courtesy of Lightscape.

sent me to two universities in New York State. From there, I was directed to the illuminating Engineering Society of North America, and finally to a representative in Manhattan. He put me on to the maker of an innovative software program back in California.[4] It seems lighting involves a lot of detective work—not only to discover what lighting is wanted, but what equipment is available, and how to present a design so that the ultimate customer can preview the final product. (See Fig. 3-26.)

In the seventeenth century, scale models, like Christopher Wren's incredible one of St. Paul's Cathedral in London, were built for demonstration and construction. Blueprints weren't used because of widespread illiteracy. Scaled or full-size mock-ups are still used today. In the eighteenth century, Capability Brown used transparent overlays to show his clients the landscaping improvements he proposed for their property. The latest innovation is the three-dimensional computer-produced scene that can be manipulated, even animated, in a variety of ways.

Some of the earlier computer programs were only able to consider straight-line square or rectangular spaces. They could not handle vaulted ceilings or irregular shapes of complex architecture, nor did they show shadows. However, beginning in 1996, software packages[5] were developed allowing designers to produce highly realistic architectural renderings that are often mistaken for photographs.

Neither traditional scan-line renderings, nor high-end ray tracers account for indirect illumination. Unlike these methods which try to "fake" realism, recent software uses radiosity to simulate how light energy is actually distributed in space, as reflected and absorbed by every surface. Subtle, yet significant diffuse lighting effects, such as soft shadows and color bleeding, create representations of reality. The integrated ray tracer adds specular reflections and highlights. Such tools greatly relieve the time and tedium of exploring every lighting possibility manually.

The exact characteristics and behavior of a particular light source (color, intensity, beam spread) can be recreated. Pertinent information, such as the ability to reflect or absorb light energy can be added to the 3D model. The interactive graphics can show the impact of changing from one light source to another, changing the number of fixtures or points of light, or the color or intensity of the source. This enables the speedy exploration of alternative lighting approaches.

The final computerized image is created by defining all components of the space—walls, doors, windows, furniture, fixtures, stairs, etc. Lighting can be selected from existing stock or created specifically for individual projects. Every object in the space will have material properties: color, level of light absorption or reflectedness, how glossy, transparent or translucent. Materials may use scanned texture maps to model complex patterns, and "bump" maps that render complex surface characteristics. Perspective must also be chosen.

Not everyone has the time or the means to change from a former method of designing to this very sophisticated system. When first introduced, the price of this software was high, but it is gradually coming down. However, this path may be worth the cost if an important project can be expedited proficiently. An alternate route is to engage a computer specialist in this field who will take on a project for a fee so that the one responsible for the lighting design does not have to go to the expense of acquiring the advanced hardware, software, and training in-house.

Even with these space-age techniques, lighting remains one of the more elusive elements. A paint sample in the drafting room may, when viewed under lighting at the site, look quite different, proving that there is still no substitute for a designer's training, experience and design sense. The fact remains, whether done with pencil and paper, or computer, the same type and amount of details have to be defined, analyzed, and decided on in order to arrive at a satisfactory conclusion. There are no shortcuts to good lighting design. It is not all glamour—it's still the hours of methodical attention to myriad minutia that produce excellence.

Final Details to Be Included in Lighting Specifications

Sometimes, because of circumstances or personnel, it is just not possible to follow all of the ensuing suggestions, even though they are the most logical way to proceed. Nevertheless, the following items should be included in the specifications. Since most specifications are rarely read through, it might not be a bad idea to call the entire crew together at the outset and discuss these points:

- Before preparing the final fiber-optic bill of material, reconfirm the dimensions shown on original drawings, as well as the latest position of other systems, like existing or new conventional lighting, heating, ventilating, air conditioning, and life safety. If any of these items are added or moved at a date after that of the drawings in the lighting designer's possession, the fiber-optic design may not be in synch with the actual conditions. This is particularly true when communication among team members is less than perfect.

- Assign someone to create adequate protection for existing architectural features and furnishings, which cannot be removed during construction. In addition, all floors, windows, and ornamental components must be properly covered before any work commences.

- As soon as equipment is delivered, the shipping receipt should be signed "subject to inspection for concealed damage." Don't wait months, until ready to use, to ask for missing or damaged components.

- Safe, clean, and sufficient space should be provided to store materials and equipment until needed. Protection from theft should be included.

- A defined route for workers into and out of the building, if it is large and/or complicated, should be clearly indicated. On offshore oil rigs and at busy railroad stations, actual building models have been constructed for this purpose.

- Before adding any additional electrical load for lighting, check the condition and capacity of the existing electric service.

- Switchgear and emergency generators, especially if they operate life-safety equipment, should never be located below grade, where uncontrolled water from man-made or natural disaster can instantly disable them.

- If emergency lighting is included in the design, provide an emergency generator or UPS system to ensure that this illumination is available to lead occupants out safely. Separate wiring to this segment must be provided.

- Provide a working sketch of all configurations of tails for the installer to follow as the light guides are fed through the floors, ceilings, or walls.

- Do not delegate any aspect of design to installers or others on the job, unless convinced of their ability.

- Construction conditions may not allow a direct path for the tails behind walls, ceilings, and floors, so alternate routes will have to be found. Because this may alter the length of tails, careful inspection of the site should be made before tails are specified.

- Decide the location for the light sources, what kind of access will be provided, and where they are to be located before the space is finished off.

- For multiple projectors in the same area, devise a safe configuration for them so that the heat from one does not reach its neighbor.

- Do each portion of the work in sequence. This means that the lighting installation should not have to wait until after the rooms have been completely decorated and furnished. The fiber-optic installers are not furniture movers. There will be increased labor costs and possible insurance claims for property damage if this out-of-order procedure is followed.

- Do not schedule delivery of fiber-optic equipment on the job site until all other heavy construction has been completed and the area is broom clean. Like fire alarms and other such sensitive systems, if allowed to sit unprotected, dust and dirt will be introduced, which will require careful cleaning and may affect future performance. If the area will be normally dusty, specify an appropriate type of light source for that environment.

- Confirm the colors and finish of the fittings before manufacture. Otherwise, the installer will have to spend expensive time hand-painting them, which will not produce the most professional approach, but will increase labor costs.

- Require the manufacturer to mark projectors and harnesses clearly so that there is no confusion on-site which are to be used together.

- As soon as it arrives, unpack all fiber-optic equipment to check for breakage and correct quantities and types. Then repack carefully and store until needed.

- Do not specify nonwatertight projectors in locations where they may be subject to water or heavy condensation.

- Be sure to specify watertight connectors and other means of sealing off unwanted water entering the light source, if it is under water. Also ensure that corresponding screws or other fasteners are stainless steel.

- Before the fiber-optic harnesses are installed, protect the glass at the common end and at the end ferrules from accidental scratches. Painter's tape, which does not deface surfaces, may be used, or any suitable wrapping. Do not use ordinary masking tape.

- Wherever dimming or other controls are attached to the projector, ensure that the exhaust fan motor in the light source is wired separately so that it continues to run at full speed at all times when the light is on. Otherwise, heat build-up will automatically turn off the fan.

- If the harnesses will be placed where they may be damaged (as in spaces above the ceiling where they may be stepped on), specify a method of protection for them. Suggestions include flexible or rigid steel conduit (PVC conduit will defeat the purpose of the environmentally safe Megolon™ sheathing), or even split Greenfield.

- Always use some type of fire stop material wherever there is a penetration of wall, floor, or ceiling.

- Clearly indicate who is to furnish and install all panelboards, controls systems (dimmers, etc.), conduit, wiring, and associated fittings. The project electrical contractor who also provides scaffolds and/or lifts, ladders, etc., normally provides this. Specialist contractors brought in exclusively for the fiber-optic installation are not expected to do routine electrical work.

- Specify that all preliminary wiring for power and controls are completed before bringing in special fiber-optic installers on-site. This will eliminate lost time. If the project electricians are also to put in the fiber optics, work can be done simultaneously, with one team doing the conventional electrical wiring and the other fishing the tails.

- Specify active coordination of all trades adjacent to fiber optics. This includes mechanical trades, masonry, carpentry, plumbing, flooring, and all decorative finishes.

- Adequate and safe work lights (not tungsten halogen) should be provided. In display cases, question what color the protective glass will be, so that color corrections can be figured in advance to achieve the final color seen by the viewer. Green-tinted glass will distort true colors of the objects exhibited behind it; therefore, suitable color filters will have to be added, either within the illuminator or at the tail ends.

- Initially, it is very important to check the service voltage at each location (floor/area). There could be considerable differences existing even in the same building, which would change the performance and durability of some lamps. In such a case, the illuminator's transformer may then have to be altered to suit the conditions.

- When changing lamps, always wear white gloves, or at least use a piece of clean material to handle them. Oils from the skin remain on the lamp, and fingerprints are magnified many times in projects. Lamp life is also reduced if touched by bare hands.

- Remind the client that at the same time lamps are replaced, the boss of the projector should be gently dusted. In case of an unusually dusty environment, monitor the condition for possible additional dustings.

- A workable wiring diagram for all needed controls must be provided, especially if more than one light source is involved.

- If color, dimming, and/or motion are to be produced simultaneously by a number of illuminators, these light sources must either be ordered synchronized at the factory or wired accordingly on-site.

Business negotiations for quotations on labor and material and financing are the next steps.

Chapter 4

Economic Considerations

Since the end of the World War II, the United States has led the world in getting used to very high wholesale light levels that are really energy wasteful. Therefore, an improved understanding of where light is really required, and how to deliver it, can do much to reduce energy use, while actually improving illumination. Whole rooms full of same-level light will then be obsolete, replaced by task-oriented *directional* light paired with a suitable *ambient* type. Whereas a developer of speculative structures is usually only interested in initial construction costs, the subsequent occupants are very concerned with ongoing overhead. Therefore, the architect, engineer, and lighting and/or interior designer should have some idea of the ultimate usage of the space to plan ahead, not only for adequate electric power supply and access for the proper lighting application, but for *affordable* operation.

In the United States, the national Energy Policy Act (EPACT) of 1992 legislated the phased discontinuation of fluorescent and incandescent lamp types that didn't meet specified lpw (lumens per watt) and CRI (color rendering index) standards. It offers lighting users the opportunity to take a fresh look at their lighting systems and select new cost-cutting options. Other countries have followed the same limitations. Considering the eventual depletion of oil and other natural resources, efficient systems like fiber optics and light pipe offer a viable solution.

Relative Costs of Glass Fiber-Optic Architectural Lighting

Requests for quotations become the "chicken-or-the-egg" question—which comes first, the bill of material developed from a design based on all the details, or a budget price? The costs of the standard light sources and fittings are established. However, the sizes and lengths of the light guides composing the harnesses have to be known BEFORE an actual bid can be prepared. Since the length of the tails constitutes the major portion of the price, every effort is made to keep them as short as possible. Therefore, there has to be at least a rudimentary layout with measurements on which to base a meaningful figure. One of the first questions to answer is where the light sources will be placed. The second is how far from the projector will the light have to emerge? What kind of light is expected? The following is a rough idea of the range of 1996 component prices of standard items:[1]

Light source:	about $250 to over $2000
Prism light guide (light pipe):	about $10 to $150 per foot
Plastic side-emitting:	about $7 per foot for the largest size
Glass fiber:	starts at about $2 per meter ($0.66 per foot) and up

Obviously, without knowing the composition of the harness, the application, the physical environment, the percentage mark-ups, and quantity discounts, these numbers do not indicate much. It is not possible to use a general area-based figure, such as square foot, or one depending solely on the tail lengths.

However, there are some known facts. There is a direct saving in changing *low-voltage* lamps to fiber optics. The 150-W metal halide light source consumes 172 W. If you replace 8 × 12 V, 50-W lamps with this unit, you will remove 420 W of energy (includes energy from lamp and losses in transformer[s]). The direct saving is therefore 420 − 172 = 248 W, or 31 W per fitting. This is a saving of 60 percent on tungsten low-voltage lamps. Since one lamp source can power multiple points of light, the more fiber optics used, the greater the energy saving. As many as 1000 objects in a museum exhibit could be individually lit with only 13 projectors and lamps.

Also, by not introducing additional heat normally produced by conventional light into the area being lit, the load for air conditioning is lessened considerably, pleasing electric utilities' Demand-Side Management departments.

The other significant saving is in maintenance. The rule of thumb is that metal halide will last 6 to 8 times longer than low-voltage lamps, which also burn hotter. The actual cost of lamp replacement is difficult to define. However, if you consider the cost of personnel, plus the lamp value, disruption of space and business, and possibly scaffold or lift rental, the price is higher than most people think. This is especially true if the lamp changer is directly employed, because those costs are lost in the overhead figure and show an artificially low labor figure for this operation.

Because the glass tails will not stiffen, suffer color shift, or disintegrate from heat and ultraviolet rays emanating from the lamp source, they can be reused. With reasonable care, they will last for decades.

A further advantage of glass fiber-optic functional architectural lighting is that once installed and focused, the integrity of the design remains unaltered. This is important to all display people who know that as soon as conventional lamps require replacing, there is a good chance that the wrong beam, wattage, and/or color will be installed, thereby spoiling the overall, expensively designed "look." To avoid mistakes, lamp manufacturers should use a rejection feature, similar to that in fuses, to avoid the possibility of using the incorrect size, style, and color of lamp, or of burning it in the wrong position (up, down, horizontal).

The cost of fiber optics, either plastic or glass, has become competitive. In fact, as usage increases, it is on a downward spiral, much like the situation with early television sets. Depending on the sophistication of design, payback on this portion of the initial investment is a length of time much shorter than the 10-year period anticipated by building managers for other construction costs. After retrofitting with fiber optics, customers would owe about one-fourth the previous amount for subsequent monthly electric bills.

An added advantage of this system is the elimination of destructive heat and ultraviolet rays normally produced by artificial light. Life of the items displayed will be substantially extended. This task lighting is also more comfortable to work under, possibly even increasing sales and production.

Example of Cost Saving with Fiber Optics

Suppose an existing lighting load is 12,000 watts. Replacement of equipment with glass fiber optics would reduce the load to 2960 watts, a saving of 9040 watts. If you assume that the facility is open for 2000 hours per year, and the cost of electricity is $0.09 per kilowatt hour, then the original cost per year is $0.09 × 2000 hours × 12 kilowatts = $2160 annually. If the area has air conditioning, then it will cost about 2 to 3 times that amount to operate chillers. This total could be from $6480 to $8640 per year.

The new fiber-optic system would require $0.09 × 2000 hours × 2.96 kilowatts = $532.80 per year. Considering air conditioning, it would then become from $1589.40 to $2130.40 annually. This is a saving of between $4890.60 and $6509.60 per year. This amount does not allow for multiple conventional lamp replacement costs, which will certainly be more frequent for tungsten lamps than for metal halide—generally 3 to 4 times more. The figure also does not include the labor cost for relamping, scaffolding, etc., in high or inaccessible areas.

Since conventional fixtures could not accomplish this particular task, the building manager requested only plastic and glass estimates. The bids were about the same, but with the difference in longevity of service and a 5 percent cash discount extended by the particular glass supplier, the glass had the edge. Payback for this project could be obtained in four years.

Business Negotiations

The majority of people act in good faith. They have the courage to say "no" if they don't want something; and if they say "yes," they have the ethics to abide by the terms of the agreement. However, there are also those few purchasing agents who know all the ways of putting the seller on the defensive. They list a long string of alleged dissatisfactions with the product and squeeze the salesperson with tales of competitors' much lower prices, which may or may not exist. Dangling a prospective order, they get knowledgeable representatives to act as lighting designers and consultants without fee, just as some in the general construction industry exploit salespeople in place of engaging professional architects or engineers. At the outset, these buyers may appear to be sharp, but often, they outsmart themselves, because two can play the game. Some equally unethical suppliers, heavy into unauthorized substitutions, will give them an underdesigned, low-quality, poorly installed and difficult-to-maintain system that is very short-lived.

By pitting glass against plastic vendors, a few people try to beat down the price and even inveigle "freebies" thrown in for good measure. A "free" item is usually either already included in the price, covered by lower-priced substitutions, or subsequently added on to the next order. There is really no "free lunch." Occasionally there are special circumstances where the commission would be so prestigious that gratis equipment may be given because it is more productive than money spent on general scattershot advertising. However, not every job falls into that category.

Experienced purchasing agents expect all vendors to give their best prices the first time around, without haggling later. And, reputable buyers do not divulge prices to competing bidders. If the seller is pressed to keep dropping prices under pressure, who knows when the right price is reached?

A Master Plan Is the Most Economical Approach

No matter what type of project is contemplated or how long it will take, some final goal has to be in sight. However, lack of agreement among those in charge of the undertaking may preclude achieving it. This occasionally happens in some nonprofit institutions, where financial advisors, administrators, conservators, curators, maintenance crew, and an exhibit department may be working at cross-purposes. Consequently, there is no master plan concerning illumination, including suitable display light levels and scheduled maintenance, both essential to create a unified, affordable, and user-friendly environment for occupants and objects. Chronically seeking financial support, these organizations may take decades to complete improvements. In fact, by the time the money is in hand, the price for the work may have escalated.

Usually, the absence of a master plan occurs when there is no firm hand in charge, or when various departments are jockeying for power, so that each group vies for available allotments without regard for priority. The overall results may never be unified. With disunity and one-upmanship in each section, one faction might denigrate another's selection of lighting, with the most powerful winning. Some sectors are more adroit in pulling strings to get money ahead of others. Until the last minute, everyone seems to be in the dark about items and spaces to be lit, even for permanent exhibitions. These nonactions could lead to indifferently fashioned illumination that will probably be ineffective and energy guzzling.

Imagine a hypothetical museum. Visitors enter a long, wide, high-ceilinged hall with sunlight streaming in and are at once blinded by misfocused high-beam lamps shining in their eyes. These conventional lights are placed so close to the ceiling, heat build-up causes them to burn out prematurely. More often than not, the maintenance crew carelessly knocks the rest out of focus, hence the "third-degree" effect for those coming into the place.

Once inside, many displays are found in the dark. Without consulting the exhibit department, which favors high light levels to please viewers, conservators run around surreptitiously turning off the overly bright case lighting because the delicate objects within are being roasted.

At the far end of a long hall will be a new exhibit, which is expected to remain in place for 30 years. Against the back wall is a stupendous installation of early massive machinery. It could be seen as a wondrous "cathedral of power," uplit like sculpture or a Gothic church. Instead, two lights are focused on the ceiling of the back wall behind the equipment, leaving the artifact in the gloom and totally ignored by the patrons.

Removing all those bright but useless ill-focused lamps in the ceiling in this great hall would gradually get the viewers' eyes used to lower light levels as they proceed toward the new exhibit area. In this way, the eye can see better, even in lower light. Because these same monster ceiling lights are shining on the murals above new floor cases, higher-than-necessary light is needed in these cabinets below. Retaining the conventional lighting system, there would be two different light sources, colors, and light levels in the same space. With the human eye automatically closing for the brightest light, no one would be able to see the exhibits.

Suppose six months elapsed without making decisions, leaving very little time to get the lighting material and install it within the one-month deadline for opening. Although the lighting for this permanent installation was expected to last for decades, the superior longevity of glass fiber was confirmed after discussion with several previous users; the price and delivery of glass was right; the design for light levels for both cases and the paintings above was finally balanced with help from the glass supplier; and even the request for a "free" segment was matched—the choice went to plastics instead of glass.

The full explanation for this decision was not stated, though it was thought that the plastic tails could be cut, just days before opening, while they made up their minds about what objects were to be included. They were also impressed that a "firm 15-year" warranty was given for the plastic (while glass would last at least twice that time). Why weren't all the previous months spent in determining the contents of the cases and how they could best be presented? This action left the in-house installers, unfamiliar with any of these procedures, having to learn to cut and assemble the tails in the field, amid the chaotic atmosphere of the deadline. The resultant illumination was of the "to-whom-it-may-concern" type—flat, general, and without the spark to make people stop and linger on special features gently highlighted. Clearly, this story has less to do with lighting than with administration and internal politics, but they are all inexorably intertwined. The dénouement was that, after the installation, the successful supplier subsequently switched from using plastic to glass.

There is another scenario destined for failure. This may occur where certain consultants, who have managed to build up a reputation within the museum community, are called in to write a grant proposal for some work. There may be some disciplines in which they are specialists, but lighting is often not one of them, if they recommend 1950's materials taken from an obsolete catalogue and are blissfully unaware of recent developments. The unfortunate institutions who continue to engage these practitioners are obliged to keep trying to find money for improved illumination, while the collections in their care are suffering from accelerated disintegration.

In an attempt to save money on energy, low-pressure sodium lamps (the awful orange ones) were used to illuminate a beautiful mosaic ceiling. The true colors of the decoration were lost, and hot spots obscured the elegance of the space.

Additional Caveat

Always bear in mind that light is not the only destructive element in architecture. Unbalanced temperature humidity levels can cause as much damage as overly bright and hot illumination. If neither the building nor the display cases are climate controlled, the building and its contents are not well taken care of, especially during extraordinary conditions. Where a single display case may contain environmental protection, what happens if the power fails and the hot, humid atmosphere of the building seeps in?

Another insidious factor is lack of scheduled maintenance. This is the most expensive *inaction* to take because, instead of remedying a small problem promptly, it leads to large, unnecessary capital expenditures later. Therefore, even after employing the most skilled design professionals and mechanics possible, false economies may doom not only the lighting, but the entire operation of any undertaking, commercial or not.

The next step is selecting a team for installation of the fiber optics.

Chapter 5

Installation of Fiber-Optic Lighting

Need for Total Coordination and Communication

This concept cannot be repeated too often. After deciding on a scope of work, obtaining a design, and creating plans and specifications on which price quotations are based, there is yet another essential item to be added. That is, the creation of a competent team to execute the work. Candidates might include those who participated in the preliminaries. Almost everyone understands that an orchestra needs a conductor. However, when it comes to construction (and lighting is included in that category), strong coordination and communication sometimes are lost. It is just as important to have someone in charge of every project, large or small, as it is to have a leader to make harmonious music. Otherwise, the job "grows like Topsy," and there may be much backtracking and/or expensive change orders involved. In other words, every team needs one person responsible to see that the job gets done on time, on budget, and in accordance with expectations. What could have been straightforward projects become littered with awful mistakes made by minor miscommunication within the team. This indispensable commander may also have to referee dissention within the troops to achieve the common goal.

Whoever does it, the proper power and control wiring must be provided for the installer. "Nearly all problems encountered by DMX512 users and installers are due to simple cable faults, poor cable layout or interference. There are also a few products on the market which do not conform exactly to the DMX512 specification. DMX512 lines should be kept away from power cabling, particularly load cables from dimmers, and should not be run in conduit or trunking with power cables or cables carrying large currents, as this could cause interference and errors."[1] With some glass fiber-optic illuminators, you have only to connect the three wires to the lamp and plug in the DMX signal.

The problem of jurisdiction concerning who should install fiber optic lighting may arise, as it has in the past about electric heat. While it would seem to be fairly obvious that the latter should be in the electricians' province, in some areas, it is claimed by the carpenters. Granted, they are an essential part of the construction team, but they are not usually specialists in mechanical/electrical services. Only professional electricians or those properly trained to provide electric power and controls for any type of lighting—conventional or fiber optics—should make that portion of the installation, because of life-safety factors. Once familiarized with the fiber-optic components, they are also capable of getting the tails through the building or display cases. However, sometimes, since there is no electricity involved, the exhibit builder, lighting designer, or even museum curator may be called on for this process.

There are great similarities in the installation of glass and plastic systems; therefore, the following procedures may generally be used for both types. Still, the manufacturer's suggestions for handling plastic should be carefully followed.

Checklist for Installation of Glass Fiber-Optic Harnesses

- Undo the carton carefully, taking care not to pull or stretch the harness. Untangle and separate the tails into the individual lengths. The easiest way to do this is to stand several feet above the floor (on a large toolbox or ladder), hold the harness by the common end, and let the tails dangle until they hang straight.

- Count all fittings and components and compare with quantities ordered.

- Check the dimensions to establish which tails are for each function. If they are not already marked, label them, along with fittings, for the corresponding projector and location.

- Stretch the tails out on a clean flat surface and shine a flashlight through the common end of each harness to check that light is emerging from each tail. If not, make a freight claim immediately.

- Repack and store the projectors, harnesses, and fittings in a clean place until ready to be installed.

- If multiple tails are to be placed in one conduit, stagger and tape them together 1 foot (0.3 meters) from the ends.

- When pulling tails through a conduit or any other channel, DO NOT exert excessive force. This is glass, not copper wire. Excessive twisting will damage the individual glass fibers and reduce output. If the tail will not pull without undue force, then reroute or enlarge the access.

- When the tail is in position, DO NOT screw the ferrule at the end of the tail onto the lens. Instead, hold the tail steady and screw the accessory onto the tail.

- When inserting the common end into the projector, take care that the tails are not crushed or compressed in the immediate area of the light source.

- The common end has a small amount of adjustment when being fitted into the boss. Ensure that it does not touch any special-effect wheels that may be inside the projector. Normal white light projectors do not have these wheels.

- For submersible projectors, allow an additional 9 in for the length to accommodate the incoming harness. Allow 3 in all around the depth and height of the box. This unit is fan free. It will NOT require any ventilation system.

- If a normal light source were used in a waterproof access pit, then a 4-in vent would be required.

- Always wear white gloves when handing lamps.

- All changes and/or additions to lamps or filters must be compatible and must not impede heat dissipation. Check with supplier before adding to, or altering, any equipment.

- Remember to use watertight connectors or marine-grade stainless steel accessories where necessary.

- Light sources must be put in permanently accessible locations.

DO NOT

- For personal safety, do not remove the end ferrules. Otherwise, stray glass fibers can enter the flesh and be very uncomfortable.

- The glass tails cannot be shortened, lengthened, or otherwise altered in the field. Special factory equipment must be used under clean environmental conditions to do this.

- An individual glass tail cannot be replaced within a harness. The entire assembly must be returned to the factory for service.

Hint: If one tail in a harness is less bright than the others, first check to see if dirt, dust, or paint is on the lens. If a break can be located, patch with monofilament polymer.

- When pulling tails through a conduit or any other channel, DO NOT exert excessive force on the ferrules by applying draw wires or pulling directly on them or the silicon sleeving.

- NEVER twist, crush, or otherwise deform the tails.

- When the tail is in position, DO NOT screw the ferrule at the end of the tail onto the lens. Instead, hold the tail steady and screw the accessory onto the tail. Such mishandling will break individual strands and reduce output.

- Do not bend the fibers beyond 90°.

- Do not allow the glass ends of the fibers or the common end to be scratched or abrased.

- Do not hang any weight or fittings onto unsupported fibers.

- Do not leave harnesses unprotected prior to final installation on a building site where there is a possibility of pedestrian or vehicular traffic running over them.

- Never add or substitute IR and/or UV filters originally provided within the light source without ensuring that the new filters agree with required criteria.

- Do not leave the projectors unprotected on a dirty floor covered with sawdust, nails, etc.

- Do not put two or more projectors adjoining so that the heat from one goes onto the other. If necessary, use some flexible clothes-dryer exhaust pipe to connect up to the vents, sending the heat upward, away from adjacent light sources. Alternately, place them at right angles to each other.

- Do not cover nonwaterproof projectors set outdoors in a wet environment with plastic or other materials so that heat cannot be dissipated. The lamp will automatically turn itself off.

- Do not install the light sources in locations inaccessible for maintenance. Provide catwalks, etc., if necessary, or use angle-iron brackets to hold them for wall mounting.

Special On-Site Tips

- Make sure the completion date is correct. If it isn't, last-minute overtime may be necessary, escalating expenses.

- If the path for the harnesses is not clear, consult with the person in charge of the project about penetration of the structure or ornamental surfaces. Do not make holes that will decrease the structural soundness of the drilled beams or joists.

- If it is known that repair of decorative features damaged through penetration is beyond the expertise of the fiber-optic installer's capacity, the person in charge should make prior arrangements with the specialists in those fields.

- Do not put buckets, tools, etc., down on carpeted floors or other furnishings.

- Do not use furniture, empty cartons, etc., in place of a safe ladder.

- Protect all existing furniture, floors, and decorative features—glass, woodwork, metal, terra cotta, masonry, etc., during construction.

- Food and drink should be consumed off-site. A spilled soda in the wrong place can mean an insurance claim.

- Wrappings and packaging should be thoroughly searched before being discarded DAILY. Debris causes a fire hazard and chance for personal injury. NEATNESS COUNTS.

- If the project is historic, smoking and hot work (open flame) should be banned on-site unless special protective measures are taken.

- If working in finished areas, have a sufficient supply of CLEAN drop-cloths, plus a clean vacuum, dust pan, and brush to tidy up.

- Unless a painter is available, in already finished spaces, have a few small artists' paint brushes on hand. Get some touch-up paint OF THE RIGHT COLOR ahead of time and keep it handy.

- A drop of silicon adhesive will hold the tiny "sparkle" lenses on tails used for a constellation effect in the ceiling.

- The larger the active diameter of the transmitting bore, the greater the bend radius that is required to avoid stress and damage to the fibers. See Appendix C for typical bend radii.

Division of Labor

The labor for the actual installation can be divided between the conventional provision of power from source to system, and the placement and focusing of the glass fibers. If there are already commercial electrical contractors on the job, they should first provide the electric power and any additional systems, like life safety, security, plus dimming or other controls, so that everything is ready for the fiber-optic installer brought in specifically for that task.

A word of caution, the glass tails are best handled and concealed in interstitial spaces by those experienced in traditional (pre-1940) construction methods and the best ways to fish wires through a structure. If the construction team does not have such mechanics, the fiber-optic supplier should be able to recommend names of competent people.

Focusing can be done by the lighting designer and/or installer, closely advised by the ultimate users responsible for illumination. Moving the light guide just $\frac{1}{16}$ inch one way or another can make a drastic difference. Do not forget to baffle. Fittings installed in cases or for items on floor, stair, or wall display should always be placed so as to avoid glare from any angle.

Once properly focused, secure the fittings in place so that they cannot be moved by vibration, gravity, or careless maintenance.

Dissipating Heat Created by Light

Of course, as with all types of illumination, adequate space around the light source must be provided to eliminate the heat produced by light. Most fiber-optic illuminators expel the heat with an integral silent fan within the container. If this heat is not properly disposed of from conventional systems, several things will happen:

1. Lamp life will be shortened considerably.

2. Black spots will appear around where light emerges.

3. If a serious amount of heat accumulates, fire could occur.

These problems are absent with fiber optics because no heat is introduced into the area being lit. For standard glass fiber-optic light sources, only about 3 in of space surrounding them is needed for ventilation.

Foreign Configuration of Plugs

Fiber-optic light sources can simply be plugged into a receptacle. Until worldwide conformity happens, it is helpful to know the configuration of the various plugs needed to activate the equipment. Even within one country, there may be several configurations in operation. Besides using plugs, other methods to get power to the lighting include wall switches, through other control devices, wired directly from a breaker in the panelboard, or through a controlling computer. And don't forget to check the voltage in each area. (See Fig. 5-1.)

> Hong King uses the same plug configuration used by the United Kingdom and Singapore.
>
> The United States, South America, Japan, and Taiwan use another style.
>
> Europe, Russia, and the Middle East have another.
>
> Australia and New Zealand have yet another.

Effects of Harmonics and Poor Power Quality on Fiber-Optic Lighting

The electrical contractor should ensure that sufficient safeguards are taken to overcome the effects of harmonics caused by the nonlinear loads

Fig. 5-1 Foreign plugs.

of electronic transformers, variable-speed motors, computers, etc., on the same circuit as the lighting. Not to adjust the power supply accordingly would create heat build-up and could severely damage equipment. Even though wire sizing was originally installed in accordance with existing codes, the neutral (earth) wire may have to be increased, or other measures taken, if the possibility of adverse harmonic reaction is present. General power quality of the entire electric service should always be checked by the electrical contractor and improved, if necessary, before installing lighting.

Lessons Learned from Empirical Experience with Fiber Optics

These procedures should be followed for both glass and plastic:

- It goes without saying that the building's structural soundness must be ensured first before any other construction begins.

- Benjamin Franklin said that "guests and fish start to spoil after three days." Electric wiring may do the same after 30 years, so adding just one more extra fitting to an ancient overloaded or defective service might cause trouble. Confirm the serviceability of the electric service first.

- Moreover, until the physical law governing the fact that water runs *down* is repealed (highly unlikely), all switchgear, emergency units, and other vital systems should be placed at grade level or above. Otherwise, expensive, sophisticated power equipment will be rendered useless within the first 30 seconds of a catastrophe. The New York World Trade Center explosion in 1993 illustrated that point very well.

- It is very important to check the voltage at each location to be illuminated. Considerable differences could exist, even in the same building, which could change the performance and durability of some lamps. The transformers in the light sources may then have to be altered to suit. For example, if a 250-watt ELC photographic lamp is used as a light source, here are the differences in lamp life and temperature at different voltages:

$$\text{At } 24.0 \text{ V} = \ \ 50 \text{ hrs @ } 3470 \text{ K}$$
$$\text{At } 19.7 \text{ V} = 360 \text{ hrs @ } 3120 \text{ K}$$
$$\text{At } 18.5 \text{ V} = 675 \text{ hrs @ } 3040 \text{ K}$$

- If the work is expected to be performed over a considerable period of time (subject to availability of funding, for example), there should be a master plan in hand from the very beginning of the project. This is the only way the outcome will be of one piece and not finish in a hodgepodge of unrelated efforts. There is that awful vision of two teams digging a tunnel under the river from either side. When each finally reached the middle, one segment ended up 2 feet above the other.

- If you arrive on the site for the first time and smell fresh paint, it is much too late in the day to do any significant lighting cost effectively. Urge those in charge to include illumination early in the planning stage.

- The installer must be firm in insisting on being involved in the construction of the areas to be lit to simplify the installation of fiber optics. Many a "Rube Goldberg" contraption can be avoided by conferring with the general contractor up front.

  On one project, just before completion of a 2-year renovation, it was decided to include some fiber-optic lighting. The supplier installer was not given the names of anyone else on the job, no matter how hard he tried to get this information. Consequently, the tails had to be extra long to compensate for a very awkward location allocated for the projectors. In fact, the whole task was like scratching the left ear with the right hand. It was not until the opening party that the supplier finally met the general contractor, who said that, if he had known about the existence of the fiber optics, he would have done the job differently, allowing for a much easier installation! All that extra effort and money could have been saved with one telephone call.

- As soon as the equipment is received, it should be checked for quantity, type, and breakage, so that when it is ready to be installed, there will be no delays.

- Once inspected, the equipment should be carefully repacked and stored in a CLEAN place away from construction dust and dirt.

Before bringing on-site any sensitive equipment for lighting, life safety, and fire detection, the storage area should be broom clean, so that alien substances do not infiltrate and adversely affect future performance and warranties.

- Suitable wiring diagrams for both lighting and controls must be furnished with the design. Determine the type of controls and their location before starting power and control wiring.

- Close communication and cooperation among all the trades is essential, because the lighting impacts on all adjacent services.

- Strict attention to details, such as stainless steel screws to avoid rusting surfaces and waterproof connectors for wiring under water, is critical.

- Create a logical job schedule. Don't lay new carpet BEFORE digging up the floor beneath it.

- Always do mock-ups on-site. Do not rely solely on tables and graphs, because existing lighting conditions can change in an instant.

- Metal halide lamps can only be dimmed using a motorized metal wheel. This can be controlled by anything from a simple on/off switch to a sophisticated DMX512 computer.

- Do not use a light source of below 3200 K with color filters, unless the colors are adjusted to the lower color temperature.

- If light has to transverse more than one medium (air, water, air), consider whether dimming is necessary.

- If multiple light sources are intended to work together (for color, motion, dimming, etc.), they must be synchronized either at the factory or suitably wired on-site.

- Red and blue filters are less successful colors than lighter ones. The former cut down the amount of light emerging.

- Never insert incompatible parts into a projector without checking with the supplier.

- Never cover an indoor-type projector while it is running. It will automatically turn itself off when heat build-up occurs.

- Never bend glass tails past 90°. This may break individual fibers, reducing light output.

- Never twist the tails while installing end fittings.

- Introduce the existence of glass fiber-optic lighting early on at the job site, so that everyone is aware of it. This saves time wasted on curious looks at the material.

- If the premises are historic, specifications should require that all architectural features and furnishings left on-site be carefully protected. Likewise, eating, drinking, and "hot work" with open flame (except under special supervision) should be forbidden.

- No penetration of original fabric, including decorative materials, should be made without consultation with and permission from the person in charge of the project.

- Use the same lighting techniques following the physical laws of optics as used with conventional systems.

- Always be flexible, ready to adjust to sudden, unexpected changes in construction.

- Permanent access to the remote light sources must be ensured. How do you relamp when an immovable display is in front of the closet door where the projectors are placed?

- Unless there is a reason for doing otherwise, coordinate light levels and color temperatures among different types of light sources. Otherwise, the divergence is physically confusing to the human eye.

- If protective case glass is used, question what color it will be (usually green tint), so that color corrections to the lighting can be figured in advance. If this is not done, the objects and surrounding area behind the glass will not be seen in their actual colors. Clear, nonreflecting glass is preferable.

- Always wear white gloves when handling lamps. Oils from the skin remain on the lamp, and the images of fingerprints are magnified many times in projection. Lamp life is also reduced if bare hands touch the source.

- The specifications should include a workable wiring diagram for all the lighting power and controls. The client should select locations for those controls before the wiring begins.

- Once all components are installed, precise focusing must follow.

- Provide instructions for scheduled maintenance.

Plastic Fiber-Optic Installation Only

- The illuminator should be placed as close as possible to the design. At all times, the plastic must be protected from the heat and ultraviolet rays of the source.

- Special couplers to insulate the tails from the light source must be used.

- The illuminator should be placed to allow the optical bundle to exit straight for 18 to 24 inches and to allow the straightest possible optical bundle entry into the design.

- The loosest possible bends and turns should be used in the optical bundle throughout the design. Plastic is less flexible than glass.

Glass Fiber-Optic Installation Only

If color rendition is critical, test where physical color shift occurs with tails longer than 8 to 10 meters coming out of the projector in any direction. High-quality glass can usually perform at longer lengths.

Preparing Instructions for the Installer

After a successful mock-up in either full or reduced size has been made, clear directions have to be communicated to the installer:

1. Start with a clean, accurately dimensioned floor and/or reflected ceiling plan, which indicates objects to be lit. If the area is large, divide it into manageable sections. Determine location of light sources. Overlay a transparent sheet for notations.

2. Refer to photographs or other notes describing both the area and/or objects and what kind of illumination is needed (conservation level of 50 lux [5 footcandles], historic, etc.).

3. Devise symbols to indicate the various sizes of fibers to be used. Color coding is useful. Use corresponding labels for each piece of equipment.

4. If it is not already done, mark which light source powers which harness. Example: FOP-1A = fiber-optic projector 1A; FOH-1A = harness

1A; FOF-1A = fiber-optic fitting 1A. Also indicate quantities of each component on drawing.

5. Use solid lines for straight-on beams and broken lines for upward or downward beams. If the light is to create a pattern (like a constellation), provide a sketch of where each tail is to go.

6. Try to find the shortest path for tails from light source to where the light emerges, considering the actual construction conditions. Check that the route of the tails through the building's interstitial space is not impeded by construction components. Also choose a path free of potential damage (from nails, heavy traffic, etc.) to the light guides.

7. Best results for accurate color are from a glass harness with maximum attenuation of 150 dB/km and with tails between 2 and 8 meters. If color rendition is critical, have all tails lighting the same area of the same length. Curl up excess length in accordance with the bend radii limit for the particular size tail.

8. If excavation has to be done (as for a garden), coordinate it with other trades, so that the earth does not have to be dug up more than once. ALWAYS check the respective utility company first for all buried electric, water, gas, and telephone lines.

9. Before leaving the job for the last time, instruct the maintenance staff how to relamp and dust the projector.

10. All work should be documented with drawings and photographs for future reference.

Example of a Fiber-Optic Installation[2]

An early 1997 project serves as a compendium of many of the points to be considered in employing fiber optics. Knowledge of older construction methods, general lighting techniques, engineering, and even architectural history, was involved. (See Fig. 5-2.)

Modernist architect Mies van der Rohe's landmark Seagram building in New York City was erected some 40 years ago. Since its opening, the main floor has contained an elegant restaurant designed by Philip Johnson. Entering the lobby, the visitor comes upon a 12-ft-high theatrical hanging done by Picasso in 1912. To the right is the Grill Room, containing the central bar. To the left is the Pool Room, with a white marble surface pool in

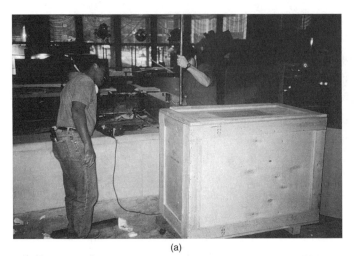

(a)

Fig. 5-2 Progress shots of installation at the Four Seasons Restaurant, Seagram Building, New York. (a) Unpacking the 340-pound crate. (b) Using gravity to hang out the harnesses.

(b)

the center containing gently turbulent water, surrounded by four life-size trees that are changed with the seasons, hence the name, Four Seasons. At the windows, the metal beaded "curtains" that move with the breeze, and the thin metal "stalactites" over the bar, are other distinctive features.

However, over the years, the large openings for the uplights in the tree planters had become receptacles for debris, and the underwater fixtures were corroded and a problem for maintenance. For this reason, although all other original lighting was to remain, the pool and trees were fitted with the latest invisible technology—glass fiber-optic architectural lighting, a system eminently suited for historic architecture. After two demonstrations with actual equipment in the pool, it was determined that this was the only illumination that could satisfy all of the client's requirements, uppermost of which were longevity of service and minimal maintenance. The client expected to go for at least another 40 years with the new lighting. Flexibility of color was also desired to provide cool, discreet illumination to suit the sophisticated decor. What finally convinced the lighting

(c)

designer to recommend glass fiber optics was the fact that the supplier was willing and able to guide the team throughout the exercise and did not just make a sale and disappear.

For some strange reason, the very thought of using fiber optics, that "space age" material, sometimes brings fear to American construction managers, so that their normal methods of operation are unnecessarily altered. Some first-time users are even at a loss to know how to bid such work. In this case, a not-to-exceed formula was suggested. Unfamiliarity makes "nervous Nellies" telegraph their anxieties to the whole team, reducing normal efficiency and productivity. As in skiing down a mountain, there has to be some element of faith that it can be done. Calm heads, common sense, and a well-thought-out design—plus guidance by an experienced supplier—are the most effective ingredients to do the first-time job on time, on budget, and with the fewest headaches.

(d)

Fig. 5-2 (Continued) (c) Checking quantities and types of components. (d) Corners of the marble pool removed to contain the tails.

Fig. 5-2 (Continued) (e) Uncoiling the flexible conduit that will encase the pool tails in the trench. (f) Drawing three tails each through the conduit. (g) Filled conduits with tail ends protected, stored inside pool. (h) Sawing the tail stainless steel retainer to size. (i) Installing the metal band under the lip of the pool. (j) Helper assembling the custom-hooded pool fittings prior to installation.

(k)

(l)

(m)

(n)

(o)

Fig. 5-2 (Continued) (k) A projector sitting at the bottom of the planter until the metal stand was made. (l) The flexible conduits coming up from the trench into the pool. (m) Tails emerging from the protective conduit into the pool. (n) The wooden partition for the signature tree and the two projectors. (o) Pulling the tails through the holes in the retainer.

(p)

Initially, the Pool Room commission appeared very simple—just upgrade the obsolete lighting in the central water feature and the trees surrounding it. Gradually, the design evolved from "plain vanilla" to a *croquembouche* (a tall pyramidal arrangement of cream puffs covered with caramel). Moreover, there were strictures. One was that everything had to end up looking exactly like the original design, which was sacrosanct. Second, the job had to be done within two weeks. In addition to the pool and tree illumination, the final scope of work included replacing the entire

(q)

(r)

Fig. 5-2 (Continued) (p) One side of the pool illuminated, and electricians working in the planters. (q) The pool lit. (r) The eight adjustable lights in the planter focused on the tree. Progress shots by G. W. Kay.

large professional kitchen, a new electric service, installing improved pool plumbing controls, and adding new marble pool cladding. At all times, it was essential to protect all existing historic decor from damage.

While it is normally a straightforward task to attach glass tails under the coping of a pool, this project was a textbook case of the need for extremely close coordination among all the trades and disciplines to compress the construction efficiently into the time allotted, while retaining architectural integrity. All the adjacent trades—floor, marble, plumber, carpenter, electrician—had to work together to conceal the glass light guides as they ran from the four planters, under the channeled floor, and up through the new double marble pool facing. Here, the "knee bone was connected to the thigh bone" as stated in the old song.

The fiber-optic team included the managing partner of the restaurant; the architects with their own interior design staff; mechanical and electrical engineers; the construction manager; lighting designer; plumbing, floor, marble, and electrical contractors; the fiber-optic supplier; and the manufacturer. Also involved was a specialist just to handle the paperwork for codes, licenses, landmarks' conformance, etc.

As soon as the 340-pound crate containing the lighting equipment was opened, each harness was uncoiled in a straight line on a clean part of the floor and a flashlight shined through it to see if there was any damage. All the parts were properly marked at the factory. Then, all the fittings were counted. One projector was opened, studied, and energized. To keep construction dust and dirt from entering the light sources, after checking, everything was then carefully returned to the crate and recovered until electricians were available to install it later. While both the manufacturer and supplier were on-site from Friday to Wednesday waiting for components for other trades to arrive, they showed the electricians the easiest way to proceed.

Obviously, the restaurant kitchen had priority on manpower, so the fiber optics got attention sometimes by a single electrician, and then only whenever time was available within the 14-day period. Nevertheless, the electrician subforeman was up to the job and cleverly figured out many of the items that had not been previously addressed, even how the float switch for the drain was to be handled. Just two days before reopening, work on the planters hadn't even begun. (It was done in time, when another electrician was finally provided.) This was a real working-by-the-seat-of-the-pants project, with design problems often solved on-site by the craftsmen.

Concealed in each of the four large planters around the pool are two light sources, one for one-quarter of the pool and one for each tree. To begin with, the floor contractors created a trench from each planter to the pool. This was to hide the tails coming from the bottoms of the planters. Meanwhile, the marble setters cut into the four corners of the original marble pool sides to make room for the light guides. They would later add new vertical cladding to cover these recesses. The carpenters built four heavy wooden protective partitions to be inserted within the planters. These were to allow removal of the seasonal plantings, which are set in heavy concrete bases, without disturbing the light sources. Electricians assembled slotted metal supports to keep the illuminators at a convenient height for relamping beneath the planter cover. The removable top, covered in wood chips to look like it held a live tree, had to be in small enough pieces to be handled easily. Adequate space to dissipate the heat from the light sources within the planters also had to be allowed.

For protection while in the trench, six sets of three tails each were fished through six short pieces of 1-in flexible plastic conduit. To expedite getting the triple bundle of light guides through the conduit, the first tail had a second one taped a foot away from the end, and the third was taped yet another 12 in down. The glass at both the common end and at each tail end had to be kept from being accidentally scratched. Lacking painters' tape, which would not leave a sticky residue on removal, the apprentice suggested using a small wirenut to protect the ends, being careful not to let the metal part touch the glass. The larger common end was "gift wrapped" with bubble wrap until ready to be inserted into the light source. Once the installation started, the safest storage space for the harnesses, partially encased in flexible conduit, was in the empty pool (at least until the plumber worked, when the coils had to be moved out of his way as he progressed around the corners).

It was a tense moment when the general contractor spied a floor man (a specific person) who was making the trenches between planters and pool, JUMPING on the glass tails laid in them to even them out for the layer of sand and then concrete. Contrary to what was expected, the glass fiber is very sturdy and survived the handling and constant moving about. Twisting is actually the most harmful treatment to the fibers. Although all the original crew had been told of the fiber optics, the personnel kept changing, with many out with the flu. When daily substitutions were brought in, they, too, were advised of the equipment.

There was a custom stainless steel metal band, drilled with 68 holes, which was to be attached around the underside of the pool to support the glass tails. However, its dimensions did not take into account that each pool wall was handcrafted slightly differently, so that when the band arrived, considerable adjusting, including sawing off ends, was needed. The marble setters worked right alongside the electricians, so that as each end of the pool was fitted with the fibers, they inserted the new slabs. All the while, the plumbers were also in the pool (dry) with their blow torches, putting in the new pipes and controls, as the floor workers were covering up the four trenches.

Although the lighting concept had been initiated in April, 1996, all activity on the project stopped until late October. The two job meetings concerning the fiber optics were not held until December, 1996, and actual work didn't start until January 1, 1997. This effort, with an outcome as fascinating as a detective story and employing the expertise of many, was the first large commercial use of glass fiber-optic lighting in a major historic site in New York City. Here are some practical procedures discovered by these first-time users of fiber-optic lighting:

- Spend adequate time discovering exactly what the client's lighting wishes are so that the right equipment is provided. Is dimming really necessary when light has to travel through several different media—air and water and air? Will the six-color wheels be used more than several times a year? The color filters have to be tested underwater, which was not absolutely clear. Darker shades of red and blue will not be perceived as they appear in the air. This means that lighter hues should be selected to be visible in the actual color of the water.

- Design was based on two preliminary mock-ups on-site. Timely and accurate drawings enable all participants to assess their roles in the process. Planning should include input from the respective contractors where a number of crafts are involved. Particulars, such as how the glass tails are to be held up around the pool, should be decided on as soon as possible, so that components can be fabricated to be ready when intended, without causing delay in the timetable.

- As soon as all the players are selected, provide each with the names and numbers of all the other members of the team so that preliminary discussions can be held with them to facilitate installation. Do not wait until only a few days before work begins to bring in the electrical contractor who has not had the benefit of previous job meetings. Allow enough manpower and equipment for the fiber optics, especially if other contracting segments are being done simultaneously.

- Establish a central point of command that will send prompt, steady communication to all participants throughout the life of the project. Early on, decide who does what so that the proper tools can be on hand when needed. For instance, who punches the holes in the stainless steel retainer band—the kitchen supplier or the electrician?

- On the first day of construction, introduce all members of the team to the fiber-optic system. This will eliminate the curious stopping work to investigate it on their own. As personnel change, new members should be acquainted with the presence of these components. If the project is a historic site subject to landmark restrictions, inform the entire crew of this fact also, so that accidental damage to irreplaceable components is avoided.

- If the job is in an existing structure with significant architectural features, plus decoration and furnishings that cannot be removed during construction, securely protect everything with plywood flooring, dust covers, etc. Costly insurance claims can be avoided that way. The restaurant owner was not amused when he saw dusty work boot prints on his hitherto unprotected expensive Italian black leather seating.

- To avoid dilemmas cropping up, include *all* details, large and small, for general discussion at job meetings. For example, if adhesives are to be used, will they mar or discolor the masonry? It turned out that the better way to secure the fiber-optic components to the white marble pool was with the stainless steel band with holes for each fiber tail. Who designs and furnishes it? Were stainless steel screws specified for use in the pool? Will the position of the plumbing pipes interfere with the pool lighting? Who prepares the wiring diagram—the lighting designer, the electrical engineer, or the fiber-optic supplier? Where should the lighting controls be located? If foreign objects like wood chips are likely to fall on top of the light sources and create a possible hazard, specify a metal mesh screen under the planter cover to catch them. Will there be sufficient space within the planters to dissipate the heat being exhausted by the silent fans?

- To avoid duplication of work or the need to undo and redo items out of sequence, create a logical work schedule—do not lay new carpet *before* trenching the floor.

In spite of the initial anxiety felt by everyone about working with glass fiber optics, the job actually entailed nothing more than:

Fishing 72 pool tails (4 were spares), 3 tails apiece, through pieces of flexible conduit cut to reach from a planter to over the edge of the pool

Inserting the pool tails in the retaining band

Attaching the 68 hooded lens holders

Providing power and control wiring

Making eight slotted angle platforms to support two projectors in each planter

Leading eight tails up through the interior to shine on each tree

In short, it was just like any other electrical lighting job, including replacing the electric service and providing control wiring. It was the lighting designer's task to focus the adjustable tree lights that were positioned at the outer edge of the planter covers. Alternate tails were aimed at the bottoms of the trees, while the others were directed toward the tops as far as 25 ft up.

This was the first major glass fiber-optic architectural lighting installation done in an historic building in New York City. It proves that this technology is well able to provide functional illumination. Chapter 6 gives examples of other applications of fiber-optic lighting.

Chapter 6

Applications

It is difficult to know how to separate the various categories of applications, because there is a lot of overlap in usage. Thus, an office with many computer terminals requiring glare-proof task lighting might also display a valuable art collection. Industrial plants and institutions usually contain restaurant facilities. Every type of activity requires adequate lighting for necessary business operations of record keeping and accounting. Historic tourist attractions often have gift shops. Just like museums, retail and wholesale companies may have to protect textiles, leather, books, and other fugitive organic materials from damage from light. Many use display cases. All types of transportation facilities require lighting for multiple purposes, from task to hospitality. Museums, art galleries, and private collections have many illumination requirements similar to both retail establishments (display) and historic properties (conservation). Keep in mind that fiber-optic lighting techniques are interchangeable and not restricted to any one arbitrary category of a commercial, institutional, industrial, residential, or historic nature. Consequently, readers might find it helpful to go through all the examples of applications to find ideas best suited for their particular requirements.

There are many more uses for fiber-optic lighting that haven't even been thought of yet, but to illustrate the range of applications, one manufacturer listed some of the projects recently completed:

Special projectors for the British Crown Jewels in the Tower of London

Lighting a bridge over the Thames River

Great country houses

Libraries

Underfloor lighting in the British Broadcasting (BBC) Studio

Lighting in a vehicle climatic test room with temperatures from −20° to +100°F

Task lighting in a special treatment room with a magnetic field. Emergency lighting also included

Supermarket display cases

Caviar, champagne, perfume, chocolate, and through-the-ice fish displays (see Fig. 6-1)

Paintings and sculptures in offices and homes

Large-display fish tanks

Exclusive shops for clothing and leather goods

(a)

(b)

Fig. 6-1 (a) Caviar and champagne chilled display, Harrods' Food Halls, London. (b) Closeup of the lighted ice.

Light Pipe™ at One Liberty Place, Philadelphia.

A spectacular sign.

Flat fluorescent lighting does not show intricate detail of objects.

Pulling the tails through the holes in the retainer at the Four Seasons Restaurant, Seagram Building, New York.

One side of the pool illuminated, and electricians working in the planters.

The eight adjustable lights in the planter focused on the tree.

Caviar and champagne chilled display,
Harrods' Food Halls, London.

Closeup of the lighted ice.

New 35-ft counter filled with ice and fresh fish. There are 22
projectors below the ice. The ice does not melt as quickly
as before, and alternate lights sparkle to call attention to
the display.

The lighted ice.

The ventilated space under the counter for the projectors.

Plastic lighting for perfume.

Glass lighting for perfume.

Theo Fennell Jewels, London, showing free-standing cases and wall displays.

Storage for the projector under the free-standing case.

Typical show window for Dior.

Retrofitting low-voltage lights in **BBC 4** restaurant ceiling.

Porcelain display: Fiber-optic heads just visible at the ends of each shelf. Special holding arrangement at each head, giving local adjustment. Projector beneath case.

Objet d'art: A 5-ft 2-in tall gold caparisoned elephant. Waddeston Manor, England.

Silver collection, Victoria & Albert Museum, London. Note points of light in ceiling of case. There were also "shepherds' crooks" delivering light at midcase from the floor of the cabinet.

The Turtle Law, Ft. Lauderdale, Florida.

Institut des Frères Lumière. Note that only the roof uses fiber optics. Conventional floodlighting is used elsewhere.

Campo de Las Naciones, Madrid, Spain, courtesy Philips Lighting, The Netherlands.

Art deco.

Shakespeare in Stratford-upon-Avon.

Model of dynastic Egyptian throne room.

Lighting the Mappa Mundi.

Single lamp reflecting in case, making Ghengis Kahn display difficult to see exhibit.

Color is flat.

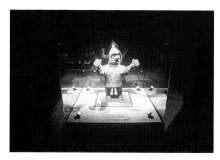

Same collection shown under glass fiber-optic lighting at the Auckland Museum.

Sample lighting in vitrine at the Nelson-Atkins Museum, Kansas City, MO.

Life-sized mounted armored knight.

Special ivory exhibit at Detroit Institute of Art.

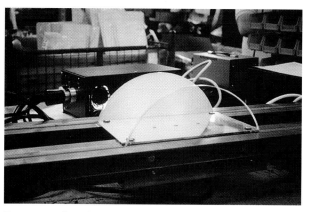

Factory test for edge-lighting for a Durban, South Africa, hotel.

Vandal-proof lighting on a bridge over the Thames at Docklands, London, England.

Cathedral at Nantes, France. (Top and bottom photos.)

Musée de Cluny, Paris, France—the Unicorn tapestries.

The Sea Horse fountain, Country Club Plaza, Kansas City, MO.

The larger dots of light are for dimmable ambient light. The star effect works independently from the room illumination.

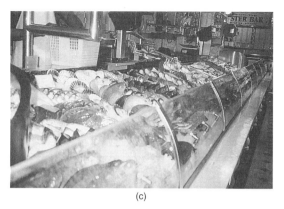

(c)

(d)

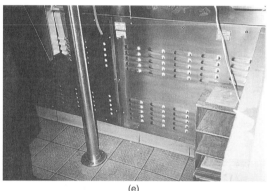

(e)

(f)

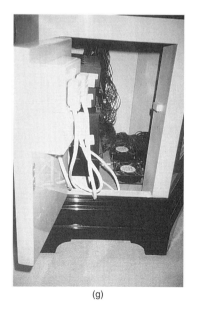

(g)

Fig. 6-1 (Continued) (c) New 35-ft counter filled with ice and fresh fish. There are 22 projectors below the ice. The ice does not melt as quickly as before, and alternate lights sparkle to call attention to the display. (d) The lighted ice. (e) The ventilated space under the counter for the projectors. (f) Theo Fennell Jewels, London, showing free-standing cases and wall displays. (g) Storage for the projector under the free-standing case.

Jewelry displays for gems and gold (see Fig. 6-1)

Simulation of nighttime sky effect in homes, restaurants, and shopping centers

Swimming pools

Hotel lobbies, bedrooms, and restaurants

Water features—fountains, water theme parks

Edge lighting of etched glass in a specialty shop

Museums

Signage

Railroad passenger coach lighting

Cruise ships

Retail store show windows

All of the following case histories illustrate if, when, and how to use fiber-optic systems most effectively. When this manuscript was completed, all of the jobs had not been executed. However, the thought process leading to the manner of designing and installing can be used for commissions similar to those discussed. Although some examples may be less detailed than others, they do show how fiber optics gives the designer more flexibility, precision, and control over the end result, and may serve as ideas for the employment of this lighting system. Wherever possible, the particular lighting requirement and its solution will be stated in the words of the person submitting the material for this book.

Some accounts kindly given by manufacturers, lighting designers, or clients, are from 1992 on and were done with earlier components fabricated before more recent technical improvements. It has not been physically possible to inspect all of these installations around the world to see if they are still in full operation or have subsequently been replaced by more up-to-date equipment. Readers should check for themselves to determine how well the equipment is currently operating. Notice that sometimes a balance of conventional and remote source lighting serves the purpose best, because nothing in this business is carved in stone.

In order not to give the impression that fiber optics is the cure-all for all lighting challenges, some case histories contain a few illustrations of less-than-successful attempts, or projects that never went ahead at all, for reasons totally unconnected with the technology.

SECTION 1. COMMERCIAL

For-profit ventures are in this category. However, there may be some crossover, such as community theaters and hospitals.

Retail Stores

Obviously, the primary purpose of store lighting is to sell merchandise. If interior lighting makes the display counters hot to the touch, the buyer will not linger long. A more energy efficient and practical way to sell is to employ several levels of illumination, all with true color rendition and including the imaginative ideas of the display director. The first is the ambient lower level to allow safe passage through the space. Another is to highlight specific locations where goods can be found. A third draws attention to special offers. All of these requirements can be met with cool fiber optics. In addition to the usual display lighting (which might be adjusted for both busy and quiet trading levels), retail stores may also need illumination for cleaning and restocking, and office work.

A RETAIL STORE CHAIN[1]

A chain of jewelry stores wanted to change the lighting in their selling space. Being in a very hot climate, they were mainly interested in reducing the air conditioning load from existing downlights, as well as providing more up-to-date illumination at the entrance.

The existing chandeliers with PAR38 90-watt lamps were to be reused alongside the new fiber optics in the front room. The fluorescent lay-in fixtures in the balance of the premises would also be retained. The owner was aware that this meant three different lamp color temperatures.

The fiber-optic *ambient* light was chosen so as not to compete with the brighter accent lighting in the cases and wall shelves, because a marked contrast was desired between the two. Miniaturized glass fiber-optic adjustable downlights were arrayed in a grid pattern in the ceiling for greatest flexibility with changing displays. The grid contained 16 size-24 glass tails powered by six 150-watt metal halide illuminators. The accent was provided by 96 size-12 glass tails with adjustable fittings. The effect on the jewelry could be striking.

SMALL DEPARTMENT STORE

At the entrance are two show windows, each with two levels. Strong sunlight floods in, washing out lighting in the windows and in the front of the store. To begin with, an opaque strip on the front windows was suggested to block out the 6-in bare spot between the awning and the metal security gates. The client was particularly interested in changing the 12 floodlights in the 35-ft-high ceiling just inside the door because of difficulty in relamping. He wanted BRIGHT, but in spite of selling $5000 evening bags, he had a very low construction budget. However, with his excessively large electric bill from the many lighting systems accumulated over the years, which were still lit, it was obvious he had to do something to reduce overhead.

For the front windows, two 150-watt metal halide light sources could be placed above the front door, each powering a window with these glass tails: three size 48, six size 36, and three size 12.

The tails could be inserted in the egg-crate louver at 10 ft 5 in above the floor of the lower window. The windows, crammed with merchandise, are changed monthly, so adjustability is critical. The fiber optics would also eliminate the need to get into the window and disturb the display to relamp.

Three 150-watt metal halide projectors, each with four size-96 glass tails, replaced the 12 powerful conventional downlights and solved that relamping problem. There was one more item: Six-foot-high ledges on both sides inside the front entrance contained four life-size mannequins. Two 150-watt metal halide illuminators, each with eight size-48 glass tails did that job. The resultant plan offered better definition of the goods, simple maintenance, and most welcome savings in electricity.

WINE SHOP

Following problems with conventional lamps heating the display shelving in the fine wine department, a fiber-optic design fitted size-12 glass tails discreetly into each shelf. They provided 1200 lux output from four 150-watt metal halide projectors. Originally, the client only wanted two light sources, but after doing a mock-up, realized that they would be inadequate.

Housed out of sight on top of the units, the projectors illuminate six 1200-mm-wide bays on two levels. The tails are fed into the pricing rail through a purpose-made reflector, throwing the correct amount of light on the back storage racking. The installation, in the words of the client, "has reduced maintenance time, energy consumption and relamping. Any disruption in the store is drastically reduced, as the lamp changing can be carried out with the display in place."

Hint: The heat of even fluorescent lamps below can adversely affect expensive liqueurs displayed on glass shelves, especially if the bottles are half empty. The resulting waste can be avoided by using fiber-optic illumination.

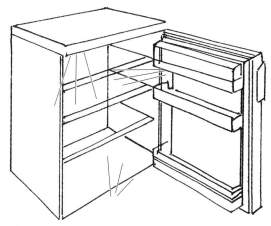

Fig. 6-2 European cold-storage lighting, courtesy Schott Fiber-Optics, Germany.

SUPERMARKET COOLERS[2]

Unpredictable cold weather ballasts have always presented a problem in food display and storage. It is estimated that grocery store operators in the United States alone may be spending as much as $1 million annually to operate the present undependable lighting systems in the cases and coolers. To get around this waste and inconvenience, following pioneering work in Sweden, glass fiber optics is being introduced (see Fig. 6-2). Bulk lumen output after attenuation, Fresnel reflections, and typical incident lumens/mm^2 from metal halide illuminators confirm the practicality of this step. The ballasts are located within the light sources outside the cold environment, and only light rays are brought into the space to be lit.

Here is the bill of material for several walk-in refrigerators:

Produce walk-in

    2, 100-watt metal halide projectors

    2, 12-tail S24 glass harnesses

    24 fittings with glass cover

Energy consumption:
    280 watts = 3870 lumens

Bakery prep walk-in

    1, 100-watt metal halide projector

    1, 6-tail S36 glass harness

    6 fittings with glass cover

Energy consumption:
    140 watts = 744 lumens

Service meat walk-in	Energy consumption: 280 watts = 4021 lumens
Same as produce	
Freezer walk-in	Energy consumption: 280 watts = 3349 lumens
Same as produce	
Dairy cooler walk-in	Energy consumption: 280 watts = 3349 lumens
Same as produce	
3, 7-ft-square walk-ins	Energy consumption: 140 watts = 1374 lumens

The three 7-ft walk-ins could share a projector with the bakery prep walk-in only if they are close together. This would require only one projector, but the harness specification would change. This is the only situation where a single light source can operate in more than one case. If it is adjacent to the bakery prep case, the material would be:

1, 100-watt metal halide projector

1, 12-tail S24 glass harness

12 fittings with glass cover

If the bakery case is not close enough, then two projectors will be required for the three 7-ft walk-ins:

2, 100-watt metal halide projectors

2, 12-tail S24 harnesses

24 fittings with glass cover

PERFUME WINDOW DISPLAY[3]

This illumination is designed to function within the confines of a glass presentation case where excess heat would constitute a safety hazard and ultraviolet rays might discolor the objects displayed (see Fig. 6-3). The projectors are built into special compartments in the cabinet for easy access. Components are:

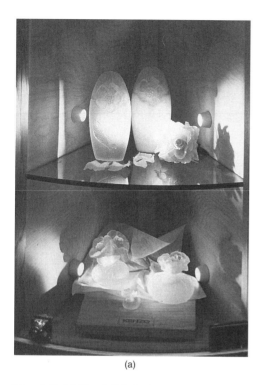

(a)   (b)

Fig. 6-3 (a) Plastic lighting for perfume. (b) Glass lighting for perfume.

4, 50-watt 12-volt light sources cooled by forced-air ventilation

4 harnesses, each with 4 plastic tails 1 m long, sheathed in fireproof material

16 recessed mounted white terminations with an outside diameter of 30 mm providing four 23° light beams per window and generating approximately 900 lux at 40 cm

A more recent installation employed glass fiber optics in a number of vitrines containing scents.

LARGE DEPARTMENT STORE[4]

Problem:

A center city flagship store covered nine stories and over 1 million square feet. The Ladies' department filled an entire floor. Like a veritable museum of lighting, it had examples of every type of light fixture since the 1950s, all left in place in the ceiling and still lit. When exiting from the elevator, the shopper was greeted with a nondescript haze. It was like going through a maze, because no sections were differentiated, and it was not only difficult to find shoes, blouses, or dresses, but impossible to make out the color of the items. The same garment looked red in one location, purple in another.

Antiques, part of the company's extensive collection, were mounted above the cases but were very difficult to make out. The energy bills were exorbitant; nothing was displayed to advantage; and sales were plummeting. The shoe section, with a lower ceiling, had such hot lights, no one went near it. Salespeople tried to hide in the cooler stockrooms.

Solution:

A few departments were selected as pilot projects to try glass fiber-optic lighting. The decorative antiques were highlighted so that their intricate details could be seen. Figures, dressed in the apparel sold in each area, were mounted on pedestals to indicate where the goods could be found. They were spotlighted as beacons for the purchaser. The merchandise in the racks below the indicating models was illuminated with enough ambient light to make the true colors visible. Rather than go to the trouble of removing all the superfluous hardware in the ceiling, the management simply turned off most of it.

There was such a drastic change in appearance. Although nothing but the lighting was changed, shoppers thought the entire floor had been redecorated. The dropped ceilings made the transformation a mere matter of bringing the thin glass tails through small holes drilled in the tiles. There was plenty of room in the void above to place the illuminators. The cost for the new lighting was less than the high monthly electric bills the store had been paying for years.

- Women's shoes—to accommodate 5 vignettes against the walls

   1, 150-watt metal halide projector

   1, 10-tail size-12 glass tails + 10 collimating lenses

   Room in the harness to light up adjacent tables with 8 size-36 tails

- Children's Shoes—to light 8 adjacent cabinets with 16 lights

  1, 150-watt metal halide projector

  16 size-7 glass tails with fittings

  There was also room to add 14 size-24 glass tails

- Women's Sportswear—for each display

  2 size-48 glass tails on figure

  2 size-36 glass tails on artwork

  2 size-36 glass tails on merchandise below shelf

- Women's Sportswear—for mock-up of two adjoining sections

  4 size-48 glass tails

  4 size-36 glass tails

  8 adjustable fittings

  There was room to add 4 size-36 tails (This one existing circuit used 540 watts. With fiber optics, this would be replaced by 172 watts.)

INTERIOR DESIGN SHOP-CUM-RESIDENCE[5]

A large, three-story Edwardian house had been converted into the showroom, offices, and residence of an interior designer. Almost every piece of furniture and artwork was for sale, so extremely flexible lighting was needed when one article was replaced by another, perhaps of an entirely different size, shape, color, and material. Although many of the objects were antiques, the client wanted as high a light level as possible. The existing illumination was not only unpleasantly bright, but also very costly to maintain.

Trying to get accurate dimensions and further instructions on access to locations for light sources, was like climbing a hill of sand. The designer's staff was too busy to stop and measure, and the principal was away traveling most of the time. Only with the lighting consultant/supplier's site visit with an engineer, electrical contractor, and architect in tow, was it learned where it was possible to gain access through the floorboards. The carpet could be lifted to thread the glass tails into the ceilings of the floors below. Once spaces for the projectors were found, the lengths and sizes of the light guides could be determined. By carefully apportioning light guides to the closest illuminator, the number of light sources was kept to four to cover all three floors:

Fig. 6-4 Three-floor stairwell.

Light source 1—in ceiling of closet, third floor north

Light source 2—in middle of closet, third floor south

Light source 3—in floor of closet, third floor north

Light source 4—in ceiling of closet, first floor

An assortment of fully adjustable lenses, from pinpoint zoom to framing projectors, was supplied to take care of the ever-changing displays.

When lighting stairways, light should not shine in the eyes of those ascending or descending. Graduated sizes of glass tails (96/48/36) with downlights in the third-floor ceiling provided light down the three-story stairhall (see Fig. 6-4). An alternate method would be side lighting at the riser, but that proved too labor intensive in this case and, besides, would have meant cutting into the handblocked wallpaper.

A SPECIALTY SHOP SHOW WINDOW

Problem:

High-priced leather handbags and shoes were being baked and faded under the intense window lights. Even sturdy khaki military uniforms were bleached white from light. The now-distressed goods could no longer be sold. Moreover, some of the window fixtures became unfocused from vibration of passersby and ended up wrongly facing out toward the viewer. This made it impossible to see past the glare to the merchandise on display.

Solution:

Once an opaque awning to shield the windows from direct sunlight was added, the lighting could be changed to glass fiber optics to keep the objects both visible and saleable after removal.

A CHAIN OF LUXURY BOUTIQUES[6]

Prior to Christmas 1996, white vertical panels fitted with masses of decorative glass fiber optics were ordered for all of the company's shops from

Paris to Japan. These were placed in the show windows behind the displays of fashions or perfume (see Fig. 6-5). The critical point here was that voltages and electric services were different in every country. Light sources had to be made to conform to each locale, ready for shipment simultaneously, and provide the same effect everywhere.

A SPORTING GOODS STORE

In addition to conventional store illumination, plastic fiber-optic light guides are concealed on the ledge near the ceiling around the perimeter of the shop. Three bundles of these side-emitting fibers are twisted around each other, each bundle glowing a different color to create a gradual color change. Glass side-emitting fiber optics could have been used similarly.

MUSEUM SHOPS

Even in the finest institutions, there are few gift shops that have good lighting. Perhaps not as much thought or budget is given to this income-producing segment as to the main facility. Consequently, hot, overbright lighting can literally drive prospective customers out the door.

Fig. 6-5 Typical show window for Dior.

A CHINAWARE MANUFACTURER[7]

Problem:

A wholesale showroom for china and crystal had a wonderful first-floor and lower-level midcity location. However, the lighting was not only difficult to maintain in the high ceilings, but oppressively hot, and it left much of the merchandise in the dark. When the halogen lights were burned out, they could only be changed by high-priced employees provided by the landlord. At night, because of the dim illumination, the interior displays could not be seen from the street through the wraparound show windows. The client wanted new lighting to be long lasting, but he did not want to attach anything to the rented property. He only wanted to light his own display cases.

Any energy savings from improved lighting went to the owner, rather than to the tenant, because the high rental included electricity. Nevertheless, it was obvious that lighting had to be changed because buyers for an upcoming trade show did not linger long to make selections in the space because of the excessive heat thrown by the lighting.

Solution:

For the first floor, eight mobile black ash-enclosed 150-watt metal halide units were specially designed to fit under the corresponding four-shelved glass vitrines behind the show windows facing the street. Light from a 15-tail size-18 glass harness would shine up through the shelves. The effect on the crystal was spectacular. Extra long cords allowed these wheeled rectangular wooden boxes to be moved wherever needed for changing exhibits. Now the displays within were visible through the large panes of glass.

For the lower-level, 16 illuminators served 16 pairs of tall, vertical shelved cabinets with 20 size-12 glass tails and lenses. A seventeenth unit lit another full bay plus a corner display with 15 size-12 glass tails and lenses. The tails were easily concealed in the sides of the display cases and could be taken to another location.

The offending hot lights were turned off and just left in the ceiling. Optional size-7 tails could also be included for highlighting of special offers.

SPORTS SHOE STORE

Problem:

The show windows facing the main walkway in a shopping mall featured three levels of shoe display. The hot halogen lights in the windows were actually melting their surroundings and fading the brightly colored shoes. In addition, they burned out quickly because heat could not be dissipated fast enough.

Solution:

The top level of shoes could be lit by glass fiber optics directly within the ceiling void. The second shelf would have lighting attached to it. The bottom level could have light sources in the window bed to keep the tails short and the cost down (see Fig. 6-6). An attempt to illuminate the lower level from the main ceiling would cause severe shadowing and subsequent loss of intensity. The bill of material was:

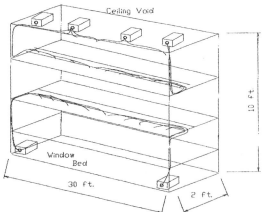

Fig. 6-6 Sketch showing deployment of glass fiber tails in shoe store.

6, 150-watt metal halide light sources

2, 15-tail S12 glass harnesses with adjustable fittings

4, 15-tail S12 glass harnesses with adjustable fittings

Hospitality—Hotels and Restaurants

Food service is provided in both commercial and institutional structures. Lodging can be found in universities and other nonprofit institutions; therefore, this particular application has a separate heading.

BBC CHANNEL 4 RESTAURANT[8]

Problem:

This large 24-hour facility was on three levels with expansive wraparound windows. The clients did not want to continue using the existing low-voltage fittings due to the difficulty and frequency of relamping the 324 fittings in the area. The ceiling height varies in three steps between 4.5 and 3.4 meters. They also did not want to undergo extensive and lengthy renovations, putting the staff dining room out of operation for any length of time.

Solution:

The only alternative to compact fluorescent was a glass fiber-optic version of the 12-volt dichroic lamp. Originally, the architects showed the clients downlighters that were very low maintenance but did not produce any highlight or sparkle. An engineering company involved in the mechanical/electrical design of the building mentioned glass fiber optics to the architect. It would give long lamp life via the 150-watt metal halide projectors and has the appearance of a dichroic lamp. A sample was produced, received immediate approval, and was installed.

There are now 32, 150-watt metal halide light sources (as opposed to 324 original lamps), all placed with purpose-built access panels within the ceiling. The retrofit used a MR16 50-mm dichroic lens assembly glass reflector with 26° convex clear lens. This is used where replacement of 12-V/35-W dichroic lamps is required, and it will fit most existing downlights (see Fig. 6-7).

DOWNLIGHTING TABLE PLACE SETTINGS

Another use for fiber optics would be miniature downlights over each place setting on a table. Being cool and without glare, they could provide

Fig. 6-7 Retrofitting low-voltage lights in BBC 4 restaurant ceiling. Richard Rogers Partnership, architects; engineers: YRME, England.

light adequate to see the food, yet keep the intimate ambiance of the room. The fittings would be adjustable in case several tables were put together for a larger group.

RESTAURANT SIGN[9]

A large chain of moderate-priced department stores wanted eye-catching signs for their fast-food eating places. Having previously used neon, they now sought something requiring less maintenance and offering greater longevity of service. Each sign was composed of one 100-watt metal halide projector with four-color wheel and 75 ft (25 m) of 7-mm-diameter side-emitting plastic fiber with insulating coupler.

COVE LIGHTING IN A CAFETERIA

The latest side-emitting glass[10] product produces a continuous band of light. There is also a "broken" tail that really needs to be viewed directly, rather than used in cove lighting. Both of these light guides will eliminate the maintenance problem encountered with other types of materials.

For a sample cove area ¾ in deep, three glass tails per run were specified, hence a six-tail harness 6 m long would be required with a 100-watt illuminator. Overall diameter is 5 mm (¼ in). The fixing can be easily carried out on-site using tie-wraps, etc. (see Fig. 6-8).

RECYCLING AN HISTORIC HOTEL

Recognizing the economic benefits of employing structurally sound properties erected prior to 1940, "boutique" hotels are now being created out of underused building stock. As quoted in *The New York Times* Real Estate Section,[11]

> Developers say the re-use of sturdy skeletons and foundations in these buildings keeps costs below those of new construction, even with extensive renovations, and takes about half the time required to erect a new one. Charging a lower price than large newly built convention hotels, this innovative form of accommodation offers personal service and revived decorative features lacking in many modern buildings. Since the mechanical/electrical services have to be completely redone anyway, here is an opportunity to include more advanced but low maintenance systems like fiber-optics.

Another concept is to take an underused art deco hotel and convert it into a "budget" category, or recycle industrial properties into inexpensive office/research and manufacturing space for start-up companies. All of these uses need lighting.

HOTEL GUEST BEDROOM

The design[12] of a typical rejuvenated-hotel guest bedroom includes fiber-optic illumination. A 150-watt metal halide 6000-hour light source can be housed in an accessible location behind the bed. Frosted lenses are specified to prevent any possibility of a "hard" edge to the lighting. These cool reading lights are attached to each bed. They come with an iris attachment to switch off. It is composed of a light source (MR16), two 24-in-long flexible arms, with an additional 50 in per arm of Megolon™ sheathed glass fiber fitted into the common end, and the iris and cowl, ready to be fitted to the headboard. The light source end of the arm is threaded for fixing directly to the headboard. There is also an optional rectangular cover plate from which the arms can be mounted off the headboard. Where there are low-ceilinged hallways, the fiber-optic lights avoid throwing heat on the occupants' heads.

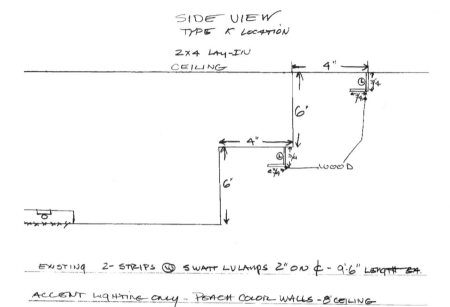

SIDE VIEW.
TYPE K LOCATION

2X4 LAY-IN
CEILING

4"

6'

4"

6'

WOOD

EXISTING 2-STRIPS @ 5WATT LULAMPS 2" ON ¢ - 9'-6" LENGTH EA.

ACCENT LIGHTING ONLY - PEACH COLOR WALLS - 8' CEILING

(a)

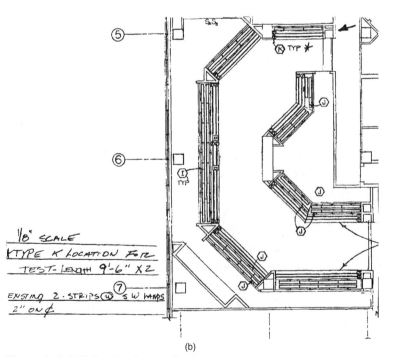

5

6

⅛" SCALE
KTYPE K LOCATION FOR
TEST-LENGTH 9'-6" X 2

EXISTING 2-STRIPS @ 7 5W LAMPS
2" ON ¢

(b)

Fig. 6-8 (a & b) Sketches for cove lighting.

Display Case Lighting

In addition to museums, this illumination is also employed in residences, retail stores, offices, and many other venues. Often, it is not enough to use just downlights in a case, with light bouncing off the top of them, especially if the objects are three-dimensional or have unusual features which should be seen in toto. A bit of experimentation with various sizes of tails from different angles and positions should be done. In a week, even a beginner could test at least 500 individual items with fiber optics to find the best combination. The right choice will be immediately obvious. Be sure to include some smaller tails in the harness to illuminate the darker areas of the cabinet and eliminate multiple shadows cast by the primary lighting.

If it is difficult to conceal the light guides in a display case (mullions too narrow or nonexistent, for example), one suggestion is to make a "sandwich" of a shelf. The tails and fittings can be laid into the bottom part, and the top put back. Little clearance, 2 in (50 mm), would be needed for this created interstitial space.

Relying on funding sources or gifts, museums often have to make do with existing exhibit cases that may not lend themselves to providing sufficient light. This makes it very difficult for the institution to take the best care of the items placed within it. One patron donated $20,000 to build a 5-ft case to display rare eighteenth-century musical manuscripts, but not a penny to light it properly. The museum could only afford a single fluorescent lamp to put in it. Once deposited in this unfriendly environment, the paper started yellowing and getting brittle at once.

ELABORATE ANTIQUE VITRINES

Two very elaborate antique vitrines contained small objets d'art in a great house operated by the British National Trust.[13] The lighting designer determined that, with the delicate cases and the collection, glass fiber optics had to be used. This work received the 1996 Lighting Design Award for interiors. The fibers were run unobtrusively outside, rather than within the historic cabinets, to avoid making holes in them. The thinness and flexibility of the tails made this possible (see Fig. 6-9).

JOHN SOAMES MUSEUM CASES

Some years ago, exhibit cases in the John Soames Museum[14] were fitted with glass fiber optics to be as unobtrusive as possible within this early nineteenth-century interior.

(a)

(b)

Fig. 6-9 Waddeston Manor, England. Photographed by Jeremy Cockayne, York, England. (a) Porcelain display: Fiber-optic heads just visible at the ends of each shelf. Special holding arrangement at each head, giving local adjustment. Projector beneath case. (b) Objet d'art: A 5-ft 2-in tall gold caparisoned elephant.

WALLACE COLLECTION, LONDON

Several galleries in the Wallace Collection,[15] London, have had glass fiber optics for some time. The latest installation is in gallery 4, the ceramic section, where there are tall, elegant metal cases, which are brand new but look antique. They contain important pieces of china. The glass fiber optics was chosen particularly because it could render the brilliant colors most clearly.

In gallery 6, the finely carved details on the medieval triptych are now visible (see Fig. 6-10). For the ornamental plaster ceiling in gallery 22, one roundel is lit by two fiber-optic tails, one on each side. The other section has no additional lighting. In the conservator's words, "You can see how a small amount of lighting can make a big visual improvement."

Fig. 6-9 (Continued) (c) Original cases of 1880. Previous internal lighting by 10-W bare filament tungstens. Overheated the air so that when it cooled off at night, the drop in temperature reduced the pressure, and outside air with water vapor got drawn in. Not good for enamels on metal. Tails are on outside, in steel tubes sprayed with gold flock, so that antique vitrine did not have to be drilled. Conduits are on frames, hinged, for folding back.

Fig. 6-10 The Wallace Collection, London. The new custom-built cases have mirrored backs that reflect the light, distracting from the display. Another approach would have been to have small individual mirrors behind each piece, avoiding the glare.

AN ANTIQUE JEWELRY EXHIBITION

A display of eighteenth-century jewelry, with a few pieces each placed in custom-built cases, was lit with a large number of conventional MR16 lamps arrayed along the top of the cases. The lights were only semi-baffled, so were visible enough to compete strongly with the diamonds. The sparkling gems could have been shown to greater advantage with concealed fiber optics. Certainly the pearl-embroidered textiles would have been better protected from the heat and ultraviolet rays thrown from the conventional illumination.

DIAMOND EXHIBITION

Another diamond exhibition reused existing cases that were almost too low for even a child to look down on comfortably. The unbaffled fiber-optic tails stuck up vertically with fittings mostly askew, so that they missed the object completely and instead were shining in the observer's eyes. Other light guides that were not misfocused, were not working altogether, probably disabled from previous harsh handling. The color temperature of the light source, instead of being a clear white, was yellowish, diminishing the brilliance of the gems. A generally insufficient amount of light succeeded in making the real stones look like dull paste.

CASES CONTAINING CHANGING EXHIBITS

Problem:

After working two years with a world-famous architect, a museum called in a fiber-optic consultant to light a large (25-ft-long × 8-ft-high × 6-ft-deep) sealed exhibit case[16] not originally figured in the major renovation. The exhibit director was willing to try fiber optics to provide an evenly lit background and to highlight changing items as needed. The fact that the fiber-optic supplier was not put in touch with the architect or the general contractor complicated the project. This meant that, without benefit of consultation with other team members, the only location provided for the light source was in an adjoining closet to the extreme right, instead of logically in the middle of the ceiling of the display case. This position required much longer tails than would have been used if the projector could have been placed in the center. Previously, the architect's lighting designer, unfamiliar with fiber optics, ordered a "belt-and-suspenders" arrangement, where old-fashioned track lights were installed within the exhibit, "in case the new fiber-optics system didn't work." What was not taken into account in the overall design was that there were now three different lighting systems in one room, thoroughly confusing the human eye. Not only the light levels, but also the colors of the light were tripled in this one space. One was very harsh and bright (the tungsten); one was yellowish (the old incandescents); and the third (glass fiber optic) was a soft, white glareless glow.

Solution:

For this long platform area, seven groups of three size-12 glass tails were placed vertically behind the "picture frame" front of the case, to provide even conservation-level lighting (50 lux) for each of seven 40-in-wide panels of photomontage. Additional tails in a horizontal row across the top highlight the changing exhibits in front, such as a grandfather clock, two tables with silver objects, and a sofa and another piece of furniture upholstered in rich Victorian hues.

Note: If higher than a 50-lux level is desired, the tail sizes could be selected accordingly.

Days before the grand opening for 500 important museum benefactors, the special German case glass arrived broken. Someone was dispatched to Germany to escort back a replacement. Unfortunately, all that was available had a blue cast, so that the once vividly colored objects in the case took on a decidedly ghostly hue. Corrective color lenses were hastily inserted in each tail end.

On the next floor, there is a very ornate 9-ft-tall Victorian wood and marble piece of furniture in its own glass-covered niche. The top section of the highboy has a mirrored back, needing close-up cross-lighting. The wood is very dark and heavily carved, calling for highlighting. One 150-watt metal halide light source powers tails all around all four sides of this recess, plus tails for legends on the wall on either side of this niche, as well as four adjustable downlights in the ceiling around the corner illuminating a 5½-ft-wide list of items contained on that floor. Of the four size 7s at the bottom of the alcove, two light up the bottom carving, and the other two eliminate the heavy shadows in the corners.

Unfortunately, multiple reflections of the EXIT signs on the wall opposite could be seen in the case windows, resulting in a rather surrealistic combination of Victorian furnishings and red EXIT letters. Emergency lighting with glass fiber optics should be at the baseboard where it can be seen if the space is smoke filled. Permission was obtained to change the EXITS from red to green, but they still shine right into the mirror back of the piece of furniture, tripling the images in the glass case. At least the fiber-optic installation in both places is invisible, thanks to the width of the mullions holding the glass. In fact, guests at the opening party stretched their necks to find where the invisible source of light was coming from.

MUSEUM GALLERY RENOVATION

A museum was renovating some of its galleries. It had a large collection of wax miniatures placed in 1930s exhibit cases around the room. There was one fluorescent tube at the top of each cabinet containing vertical boards slanted slightly backward, on which were fixed the little portraits. These fabric-covered slats were placed at the top of the cabinet base, flush up

Fig. 6-11 Silver collection, Victoria & Albert Museum, London. Note points of light in ceiling of case. There were also "shepherds' crooks" delivering light at mid-case from the floor of the cabinet.

against the glass front. They leaned back at a 20° angle. The light at the top of the case was much too hot for the wax. By the time it reached several feet down to the bottom of the case, it had fallen off to practically nothing. The reflection of the ceiling chandelier was visible in the case glass wherever observers stood. Returning from a trip abroad, where he had seen it in operation, the department curator agreed to try glass fiber optics. Previously, he was under the impression it was only for discos.

The museum director, heads of lighting and exhibit, and chief curators and conservators were assembled for a demonstration. The first thing the fiber-optic consultant asked was if the slanting boards could be recessed 2 inches, so that there would be room for the narrow light guides. The answer was no, so lighting could not be done from within the case. Second, the frames for the miniatures were so deep, only light shot straight on could hit the actual miniature at all. The raised surface of the frame kept light coming from the side from reaching below it. That would mean focusing some large (size-96) tails directly onto each glass section from the center of the ceiling. That, too, could not be done because the place had just been painted, and the new wood flooring was scheduled to be installed immediately. The construction timetable could not be altered.

Although the conservators lobbied for the new illumination, nothing was done. Soon after this phase of work was completed, the resident lighting designer departed.

MUSEUM COLLECTION RELIGHTING

The entire silver collection at the Victoria & Albert Museum in London was relit with glass fiber optics (see Fig. 6-11).

LABELING IN DISPLAY CASES

Exhibits filled with fugitive materials can be labeled with fabric woven with fiber optics, so that the entire silk-screened legend glows. In this way, the viewer can read what is in the vitrine, and the objects are protected from heat and light.

NEW DISPLAY CASES

A private library needed two sets of recessed cases (48 in wide × 10.33 in deep × 57 in high) in the entrance lobby where they would show changing exhibits. The objects displayed were papers over 200 years old and had to be illuminated at conservation level (50 lux). The exhibit builder's responsibility was to include lighting. The entranceway was brightly lit, both by chandeliers and by the surrounding windows admitting sunlight. An unobtrusive shade over the glass of the front-viewed cases was suggested to shield the low-level light inside from the higher levels above and outside the cases.

With custom-made cases, room could be provided in the upper portion to house the light source. Since no one knew what would be exhibited, even illumination was requested for the cases. For objects that should be gently accented, it is only a matter of adding an adjustable lens. Seventeen size-12 glass tails arrayed along the sides and in the top of each case could be flexible enough to take care of almost any combination of artifacts. The case mullions baffled the light guides so that the viewer did not see the fittings. Equipment was four 150-watt metal halide illuminators.

ANOTHER EXAMPLE OF EXHIBIT CASES FOR CHANGING DISPLAYS

This structure had been under construction for over a decade. Shortly before opening, the curators rejected the original lighting for the custom-made special exhibition cases. They categorically refused to put their valuable collections into such hot environments. Several million dollars were allocated to research how to solve this and other serious problems plaguing this long overdue completion.

It seems that groups of fiber-optic light sources without fans were placed in the bottom of these cases without proper insulation. The resultant heat rose to fill the exhibit spaces intended to hold paper and leather, so vulnerable to infrared rays. In addition, the containers had been made so deep, it would take a giant to be able to see to the back of them. Moreover, an insufficient number of light guides had been provided to cover the entire case interiors.

The solution was to remove the fanless illuminators altogether and replace them with smaller but more powerful light sources fitted with exhaust fans. The light sources were relocated to recesses below the floor, where the heat could be dissipated. If there were projectors adjacent to each other, they would be vented to carry away the heat so that one would not automatically turn off its neighbor when a certain temperature was reached. This was happening constantly with the original lighting equipment. Enough glass tails for total flexibility of service were also added.

What could not be remedied was the edict that the engineers and lighting people could not communicate with the curators. Perhaps this had been done to avoid having one of lesser authority make decisions, but in the end, it precluded reaching the best illumination, which could only be accomplished by interaction among the disciplines. It was almost like an ancient Chinese doctor working with a small ivory statue of a woman, instead of examining the patient directly.

Outlining Exteriors

TIME SHARE RESORT AND SHOPPING CENTER[17]

Shopping centers worldwide are beginning to use fiber optics and light pipe mainly for the low-maintenance feature.

While fiber-optic lighting today is used to meet all sorts of intricate installation requirements and ambient environmental conditions, this time it also had to meet "The Turtle Law" (see Fig. 6-12). This law states that

Fig. 6-12 The Turtle Law, Ft. Lauderdale, Florida.

direct lighting cannot be used on structures directly across from or facing the ocean, because such light attracts sea turtles to the land.

In this installation, lower output illuminators and lower density fiber-optic tubing were paired to create a softer, more subtle form of light, comparable to the indirect and cove lighting employed on the Beach Place buildings themselves. By affixing aluminum U-shaped channels underneath the leading edge of the stairs, the lighting designer created a cove-light effect. The fiber-optics yield even more luminosity without glare, simultaneously providing definition and direction for people accessing the stairs to or from the buildings, while being compliant with the law. Concurrently, the fiber-optic tubing serves as both an architectural and a decorative element. Its parallel lines are programmed to illuminate with different colors each night of the week.

Equipment included 19, 150-watt HID illuminators with 2500 ft of side-emitting plastic tubing.

Large-Scale Ground/Floor Lighting

EUROPOLE BUSINESS CENTER, PLACE ROBERT SCHUMANN, GRENOBLE, FRANCE[18] (see Fig. 6-13)

(a)

Fig. 6-13 The Europole Business Center (a, b, & c).

(b)

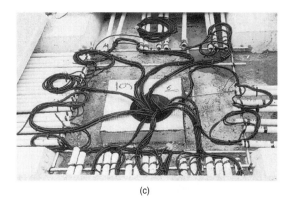

(c)

Fig. 6-13 (Continued)

Visitors to this business center no longer have to look up at the sky to see the stars. When night falls on the vast esplanade that fronts the buildings constructed in 1991, a constellation of 767 lights embedded in the pavement stretches out at their feet. This feat is no heavenly miracle, but the visible tip of a complex underground fiber-optics lighting system providing a contemporary effect for the 4,000 square metre area, reflecting the style of the building complex. The brief was to create something monumental in scale yet discreet and elegant in form. Conventional ground-level fixtures were unacceptable because they would be too visible by day and pose an obstacle to pedestrian traffic. In addition, they would increase overall maintenance costs due to their constant exposure to the elements.

Instead, 767 miniature luminaires were embedded in the pavement, protected by unbreakable lenses and wired to a vast network of underground cables. By day, the tiny spheres, measuring between 2 and 10 mm in diameter, appear to be no more than a decorative motif on the 4 m^2 paving stones. By night, however, they produce a spectacular constellation effect across the esplanade.

PAVERS[19]

In a shopping center, one 150-watt metal halide light source was used to power each of four 60 × 60 cm pavers, with sandblasted and reinforced glass measuring 25 × 25 cm. Size-48 glass tails with 12-mm ferrules are 6 to 17 meters long. (Note that because of the high-quality glass, acceptable color was obtained from much longer than the 8-meter limit suggested.)

In fact, this designer stated that "in all my projects, the arguments to use glass fiber optics or light pipe are the advantages of remote lighting, safety in use, low maintenance, electricity saving, uniqueness and beauty, and especially longevity."

Fiber Optics in Flooring

The project was a meeting area in the new headquarters for a television station.[20] The architect wanted to create an unmistakable space with a version of the station's logo. Customized parabolic spinnings were fitted below the 200-mm-diameter glass discs in the floor void. These housed concave frosted lens assemblies to provide an even illumination of each glass disc. The architect was concerned that the emergent light did not show as "shafts" of light, which could act as a deterrent to people. Neither did he want to repeat the gaff of shining up ladies' skirts, as done on a staircase in Hong Kong. He wanted more of a gentle "glow," which would be welcoming. There are four light sources at floor level around the outside of the outer circle.

Another option had the benefit of not having to dig up the floor to lay fibers underneath it: Large circles of light (6 to 10 in in diameter, depending on the ceiling height) can be thrown onto the floor from fibers concealed in the ceiling. White discs are inlaid into the floor of the exact diameter of the beams of light shining onto them. The optic beams are on tight focus, while a very slow color change was introduced so that patterns of light gradually appeared to swirl like clouds drifting across the moon. The floor circles appeared to be glowing from within, but the light was actually shining from above (see Fig. 6-14).

Fig. 6-14 BBC 4 floor lighting.

Exterior Illumination of Buildings

CANOPY ENTRANCE AT SOUTH QUAY, DOCKLANDS, LONDON, ENGLAND[21]

An entrance canopy was fitted with 144 sparkle lenses with white bezels at the end of small glass tails. These are connected to one 150-watt metal halide external-rated projector/harness combination mounted within the canopy. The sparkle effect is also visible during daylight hours. Many points of light can be easily installed in hard-to-reach places, for spectacular effects.

INSTITUT DES FRÈRES LUMIÈRE[22]

If there is one building in Lyon, France that deserves to have its name in lights, it is the Château Montplaisir. Formerly the studios of pioneer cinematographers August and Louis Lumière, it now houses the institute in which their historic work is preserved. The challenge was to design new lighting to highlight the building's unusual roofing tiles—laid in groups of five to form a cloverleaf pattern—while adding to the sense of magic that surrounds the site (see Fig. 6-15).

The fiber-optic solution proposed consists of 496 roof-mounted luminaires divided into two groups. The first group lights each cloverleaf with a beam directed at its center, while the second consists of lights of varying intensity that are projected towards the ground to create a sparkling effect.

Fig. 6-15 Institut des Frères Lumière. Note that only the roof uses fiber optics. Conventional floodlighting is used elsewhere.

Hidden in the eaves of the building, the system's generators are equipped with 40 dichroic halogen lamps with a color temperature of 3000°K. 35 harnesses, ranging from 4 to 15 metres in length, are reserved for the tiles themselves. Each carries 12 cables containing 30 optical fibers. The other 5 harnesses, of 4 to 6 metres in length, feed into the lights that are turned groundwards. Each of these carries 9 to 33 cables.

Places of Assembly—Large-Scale Architectural Lighting

CINEMA IN A SHOPPING CENTER[23]

In a shopping center in Rishon L'Zion, Israel, 400 size-1 glass tails powered by a 75-watt halogen source provided interesting ceiling lighting. "In appropriate sites, traditional lighting with low-voltage halogen luminaires can be replaced by a fiber-optic system, with considerable savings."

CAMPO DE LAS NACIONES CONVENTION CENTER, MADRID, SPAIN[24]

To the 2,000 visitors seated in one of the two auditoriums at this convention center, the ceiling soars so high that the stars themselves seem to be shining overhead. In reality, the 1,340 lights arranged in geometrical formation over the 2,400 M^2 structure are only the visible part of the design to fit the hung ceilings. The designer felt he could create the ideal effect by placing a large number of low-intensity (20–30 lux), warm-colored lights at regular points in the ceiling structure with fiber optics (see Fig. 6-16).

Because of the dimensions of the auditorium, the lighting system would have to be placed in an almost inaccessible location—as high as 16 metres (48′) directly over the seating area in auditorium A. A primary concern was to keep maintenance costs from going literally through the ceiling. Instead of conventional high-temperature, high-maintenance lamps, central light sources were installed on the metal catwalks located over the ceiling, where they can be easily serviced and adjusted. The generators are cooled by high-performance forced-air ventilators and equipped with a short-arc 200-watt metal halide lamp (13,500 lumens at 5900°K). To ensure a color temperature of 3500° K at the lighting end of the tails, the projectors are equipped with dichroic color correcting filters. The tails are a 1-mm polymer (PMMA) fiber protected by fireproof sheathing 11 mm in diameter. Each harness contains 181 cables, each containing 4 to 8 optical cables measuring 7 mm in diameter. Tails are protected by a fireproof sheathing. The total length of light guides is long enough to stretch all the way from Madrid to Barcelona! The points of light are placed in groups of four, one at each corner of the 2.5×2.5 metre tiles that compose the hung ceiling. The effect is a geometrical array of starry points, providing an optical performance that begins long before the lights go down.

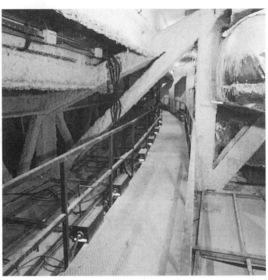

(a)   (b)

Fig. 6-16 Campo de Las Naciones, Madrid, Spain, courtesy Philips Lighting, The Netherlands.

Art Galleries

With one foot in the historic category and the other in an income-producing mode, the decision was made to include this type of usage in this section on commercial applications.

HISTORIC ART GALLERY[25]

The previous lighting scheme for a permanent collection in a gallery in a former castle was inappropriate. The 36 portraits, all of a different size, were completely flattened by the combination of daylight and artificial light with little tonal contrasts. The new fiber-optics illumination gives each painting a strong dramatic, even mysterious air, especially when the room is used for candlelit dinners. The lighting enhanced the building's features without destroying its antiquity.

No light was to fall on the frames or the surrounding green paneling. Rather than using a miniature framing projector, each fitting contained a *gobo* (templates of special design allowing only selective light patterns through) to shape the light beam to the size of the respective picture. The designer studied the subject of each portrait to determine where to aim the light on the planes and facets of the face. At first, the resulting beam was far too small, which resulted in an almost ghostly solution, with the heads of some of the paintings seemingly floating off the walls.

By experimentation, the gobos were made larger, but not too large so as to allow spill light onto the frames, or create veiling reflections. Thought also had to be given to placing each optical tail between the person looking at the picture and the wall. This ensured that people do not cut across the beam when viewing the pictures.

Six projectors were used, each with 6, 6 metre plastic tails. The light source was a 4000°K 150 W metal halide lamp. The warmer version lamp was tried, but did not produce the required image quality. The new lighting brought the pictures to life without the eye being conscious of the lighting method employed.

Exhibits for Trade Shows

Problem:

Everyone has attended trade shows in convention centers and perspired under the heat of the booth lighting. Worse, the usual high-wattage metal halide lamps blazing in the ceiling can wash out any kind of display below, so that the viewer can't really see what is being presented. It is not only the visitor who has difficulties. Exhibitors encounter them, too.

Solution:

Those companies who exhibit at many trade shows might consider having glass fiber-optic lighting built right into their traveling displays. Then, the equipment has only to be unpacked and plugged in on arrival. In addition to avoiding the need to hire people to do the special lighting in each place, the cool light is inviting for show attendees to approach in comfort, in contrast to the hot lights normally encountered in this type of presentation. Of course, booth design to shield the excessive overhead lighting is still needed.

At one international event, three separate exhibitors obviously rented identical booths, all of which had a row of veritable automobile headlights shining right in the viewers' eyes, literally keeping them away from the demonstration. Their three-day electricity bill must have been astronomical.

A TRAVELING EXHIBIT[26]

Glass fiber optics was planned for a miniature façade of a vintage theatre and surrounding kiosks. Side-emitting loops in lengths of up to 75 ft ran around the theatre and were fed at both ends from a projector. The white light source (150-watt metal halide) powered two different colored bands. The glass tails are very flexible and able to survive the anticipated rough handling from city to city. The color rendition remains crisp, even when a few fibers break, creating a sparkling effect.

General Lighting

EUROPOLE'S UNDERGROUND PARKING GARAGE[27]

Seventeen 200 watt metal halide fiber-optics projectors powering 726 tails are installed in this parking garage where they can be easily serviced. The light guides with protective metallic sheathing are threaded like ordinary electrical cable through pipe sleeves laid under the esplanade. The tail end has an anodized cap that screws into a fixure embedded in the pavement and is protected by a shock- and scratch-resistant lens (see Fig. 6-17).

Offices and Boardrooms

COTEBA CORPORATE BOARDROOM, CLICHY, FRANCE[28]

To allow board members of this corporation to take notes and consult documents during audio-visual presentations, each seat at the 1.5 by 4.2 metre (5' × 13.8') conference table is equipped with an individual fiber-optics tail. Mounted on the end of a flexible 60 cm wand, the light can be positioned as desired. Components were:

2 projectors with 50 W 12V 24° dichroic lamps.

2 harnesses, each with 7 tails, 1.4 m long.

14 thread and fittings guided by a 60 cm flexible attached to a fixed, extensible mini-spot.

Additional controls may be required to open and close curtains, lower a movie screen, dim lights and other functions.

A SKYLIGHT IN AN OFFICE BUILDING[29]

Assuming that the light sources can be positioned locally to the feature, the calculations show that at desk height, assumed at 2 ft 6 in, the light level would be approximately 500 lux

Fig. 6-17 Boardroom.

(50 footcandles), and at floor level, approximately 439 lux (43 footcandles). An average harness length of 3 meters was chosen. For any length in excess of that, reduce the predicted light levels by 3 percent per meter (per 3.3 feet). The illuminated area on the floor would be an approximate 3.6-ft-radius circle about the center of each point. Bill of material:

8, 100-watt new type metal halide light sources

8, 4-tail, S36 glass harness

32 white 13° shallow mounting convex clear lenses + holders

BANKS OF COMPUTER TERMINALS

These can be lit with fiber optics so that there is no glare on the screen.

Lighting in Theaters

While this topic is a whole other subject for many books, some mention should be made here about the myriad applications possible. Creating something like a starry sky can be done easily with fiber optics, because all those little bulbs do not have to be replaced piecemeal.

ACTUAL THEATRICAL LIGHTING

Among his many commissions, theatrical lighting designer, Jules Fisher,[30] New York, multiwinner of the Tony Award for Broadway lighting, did *The Will Rogers Follies* (see Fig. 6-18). As he puts it,

> The concept for the production was that the entire show would take place on this giant staircase (14 steps × 40 feet wide). Thus, the steps had to provide great variety of visual effects. It would be impossible to use standard methods of lighting steps, such as vast arrays of colored light bulbs, because of heat, space and electrical limitations. Only fiber-optic or optical light film techniques would work. This "simple" solution embodied one 450 watt lamp at both ends of each step, with a color scrolling device. Thus, every step could glow with an infinite range of intensity and hue.

Mr. Fisher was also the lighting designer for the Julie Andrews' musical, *Victor/Victoria,* which had unusually elaborate sets. One scene was two levels, depicting hotel rooms on different floors. The lights in the low first-floor ceiling were distracting and hot for the actors to work under. Fiber optics were considered to eliminate the heat and glare.

Fig. 6-18 Will Rogers Follies.

THEATER INTERIORS

In those cases where the original auditorium lighting is to be recreated, a fiber-optic version of rows of clear carbon-filament bulbs would eliminate the need for continual relamping.

The urge to add more lighting than necessary to create the period effect should be curbed. Much brighter modern auxiliary lighting should not be used, because it would make the historic portion pale in comparison and, in fact, become almost invisible to the human eye, which is accommodating to the higher light levels. Spotlights are meant to be aimed at the stage, not at the audience.

A PERFORMANCE CENTER[31]

It was decided to gently light the crown placed in front of the Royal Box (see Fig. 6-19). Since this huge Victorian structure can seat almost 8000 people, it presented quite a problem to get lighting to this 2-ft wooden object installed between two levels, four stories above the floor. Spotlights from other parts of the hall could not reach it and, even if they could, would be very unwelcome to the patrons. Incandescent lights placed too near it would burn up the wood and velvet components. In any case, because the crown was in such an inaccessible location, constant relamping with conventional bulbs would be not only damaging to this nineteenth-century object, but hazardous to the staff trying to reach it.

Only an outlining glow was desired, which could be adjusted to the level of the house lights during and before performances. During a mock-up, after having the house lights turned up and down, a 75-watt light source was deemed sufficient. Because all of the boxes were privately owned, there could be no glare in anyone's eyes.

Two maintenance employees of the Hall, the house electrician, the fiber-optic supplier, and the installer were all hanging over the edge of the balcony trying to reach this elusive object. Finally, a ladder was produced and placed in the box below, so that sample tails could be held up for the architect and interior designer—equipped with binoculars and walkie-talkies and seated blocks away across the auditorium—to communicate the effect seen. One other person was dispatched to monitor above at the next level to ensure that no errant light rays would emerge.

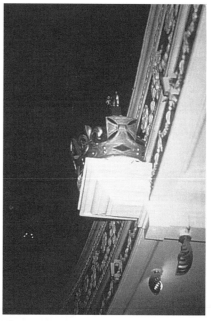

Fig. 6-19 Insignia in front of theater box.

A combination of 50 size-1 glass tails, to provide the outline of the crown, and size 12s, to delineate the pearls and lion atop it, were taped in place. Next, the original plans of this monumental nineteenth-century building had to be looked at to see where the hollow portions in the floor and walls were to conceal the tails. Only the smooth part of the heavily ornamented balcony surround could be penetrated.

Several ways of securing the tails in place were considered, including a narrow metal band punched with holes for the tails. The crown had to be refurbished, including regilding, which would make a considerable difference in the lighting, once the shiny surface was renewed. The best way to find out how to introduce the light guides was to do mock-ups on the actual artifact, before it was restored. Certainly, the red velvet interior could be one solution for concealment.

The next problem was where to house the light source. After much discussion, including asking permission of the owner, it was decided to put it in the antechamber, above the entrance to the Royal Box, within a container designed to match the historic moldings already existing around the ceiling. While this initial site visit was challenging to decide on lighting procedures, it was not half as stressful as having to endure a simultaneous dress rehearsal of a rock band, which had the sound turned up to such an unbearable volume that the building felt as if it would vibrate right off its foundation. But, it is all part of the job.

Transportation

Transportation Centers

- In a subway (the underground), fiber-optic lighting used with glazed tile surround can be cleaned just by hosing it down.

- In a roadway tunnel, 11,800 ft of Light Pipe[32] replaces linear fluorescent luminaires, providing uniform light with lower maintenance costs. The lighted guidance tube (LGT), which is the leakage light

Fig. 6-20 Callahan Roadway tunnel, Boston, MA. Maintenance costs reduced by up to 75%. Designed to withstand roadway vibrations. Sverdrup Civil Inc., engineering consultants; Fay, Spofford & Thorndike, Inc., design engineers.

from a prism light guide, helps drivers traveling through hazardous roadways. The LGT is mounted on guard rails or concrete barriers to provide a continuous line of light (see Fig. 6-20).

THE RAILROAD STATION

Once upon a time, people would do almost anything for a job. In a train station with a 100-ft ceiling, workers used to be willing to clamber over a cargo net to change the incandescent bulbs in the decorative ceiling. Employees started losing their nerve when the almost 100-year-old netting began to unravel. Because the huge waiting room is busy 24 hours a day, it is not feasible to erect scaffolding to change lamps that high up, and there were no catwalks above the ceiling. A simple solution would be first to erect catwalks and then to provide a fiber-optic system. Circus-type performers would no longer be needed to relamp. Care must be taken that the brilliance of each point of light is not so strong as to appear like a searchlight, rather than a decorative star.

THE CLOCK AT THE ENTRANCE TO A TUNNEL[33]

Illuminating an exterior metal clock in the archway above the mouth of a tunnel could be accomplished by two 6-tail size-36 glass harnesses powered by two 100-watt metal halide projectors. Two light sources are needed because the total number of fibers exceeds the maximum of 160,000, which can be served by one HID lamp. The fiber does not have to rely on the reflectivity of the back of the clock's five-minute indicators. Neither the summer heat nor winter weather will affect the glass components.

Vehicles

The Society of Automotive Engineers (SAE) graciously provides voluminous pages of references to papers on the use of fiber-optic illumination in all modes of transportation—planes, trains, automobiles, and ships.

- Since about 1986, the consoles of some German automobiles have been lit by fiber optics, eliminating the need for sockets, wiring, and frequent replacement of individual burned-out bulbs. With about 75 points of light, this mode of lighting is a decided improvement.

- Almost every new cruise ship built features both task/display and decorative fiber-optic systems in restaurants, bars, nightclubs, and for major staircases. One ship even has its name emblazoned on the side in fiber optics. Because the glass being used is so thin and flexible, it can be easily installed in the shallow recesses of the marine ceilings, where conventional components might not even fit. The following quotation[34] states:

As more and more cruise lines install state-of-the-art lighting, sound, and rigging systems on their new vessels, land-based theatre technicians often find themselves working "at sea" because of the different kind of electric power on ships. Most major cruise ships are equipped with 3-phase "delta" power, as opposed to the 3-phase "wye" power in the land-based facilities. For safety and practical reasons, these two systems should be understood.

3-Phase Wye Power:

This consists of three phases (hot legs), a neutral and a ground. The neutral is actually bonded to earth ground at the point where the power enters the building, or at the main transformer if there is one inside the facility. Branch circuits or dimmers each have a single-pole circuit breaker, since one side of the circuit, the neutral, is actually grounded.

In the United States, the common system is 208/120 volts, with 208 volts between any two phases and 120 volts between each phase and neutral. In a 208/120 volt wye system, the power available on each phase at 120 volts is generally indicated by the rating of the main circuit breaker.

3-Phase Delta Power:

In a shipboard installation, it is generally not possible to ground the neutral of a 3-phase system. On board a ship, "ground" is actually the ship's steel. Grounding the neutral would result in "eddy currents" in the ship's steel, which would eventually cause severe corrosion problems. To avoid this, the neutral is eliminated completely, and the delta system, which has only three phases and a ground, is used.

In a delta system, the three phases "float" above the ship's steel. This means that each dimmer or branch circuit must have a two-pole circuit breaker, so that when the circuit is shut off or a fault occurs, both sides of the circuit (known as *I.1* and *I.2* instead of *hot* and *neutral*) will be disconnected from the power. It is this two-pole requirement for safe operation that often eliminates a land-based dimming system from shipboard installation. This is why rental lighting systems on board ship should be properly engineered for marine use.

A delta system also has different voltage and current relationships. In a 120-volt delta system, there are 120 volts between each of the three phases. Likewise, some European ships use a 220-volt system, with 220 volts between each of the phases.

Calculating the available current can be tricky: a 120-volt delta system with a 200-amp three-pole main breaker does not have 600 amps available at 120 volts, as it would in a wye system. Rather, the available current is calculated by dividing the sum of the breaker poles (600) by 1.73 (the square root of 3), which in this case shows that the 3-pole 200-amp breaker allows the connection of 347 amps total at 120 volts.

Basic rules for delta power:

1. All equipment needs two-pole branch circuit breakers.

2. Use the 1.73 dividing factor to calculate the available current.

3. Don't install land-based lighting equipment onboard ship without engineering help.

- The number of train buffs in the world is very large. There are people everywhere rescuing, restoring, and running old railway carriages. Glass fiber optics can be used to provide general illumination in the ceiling and adjustable reading lights under the overhead luggage racks. Both can be at historic light levels, matching the age of the vehicle. The crack modern Trans-European Expresses also employ fiber optics.

- In 1997, British Rail and Dutch National Railway began considering glass fiber optics for the bar and restaurant areas, and for reading lights in the first-class section. The light sources require antivibration mountings and can be housed within luggage storage areas and in certain parts of the ceiling, where space is available.

- British Airways advertises that its newly upgraded first-class cabins have fiber optics at each seat (see Fig. 6-21).

Task Lighting

It is much more pleasant and productive to read or work under cool, clear light than under light that is uncomfortably hot and glaring. Hotel bed lamps, ambient glare-proof lighting near computer terminals, and work lights on production lines are just some of the uses for fiber optics in this category. The lights can be placed on flexible extensions for maximum maneuverability. They can also be made portable for either plug-in or battery operation.

Design of any task light begins with an analysis of the task itself and its visual requirements. Prototypes tested in the actual workplace are essential. Criteria for lighting all types of workstations are:

(a)

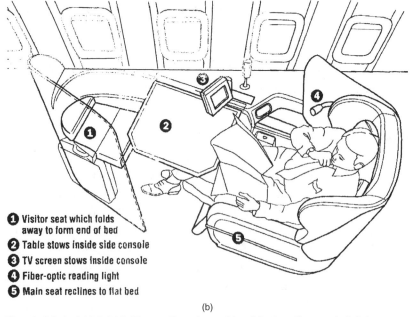

❶ Visitor seat which folds
   away to form end of bed
❷ Table stows inside side console
❸ TV screen stows inside console
❹ Fiber-optic reading light
❺ Main seat reclines to flat bed

(b)

Fig. 6-21 (a & b) British Airways first-class cabin with glass fiber-optic lighting.

Even and ample illumination over an adequate range of the workstation

No glare

Cool area to work under

Capacity to move the light in multiple directions as needed

Hazardous Locations

In addition to the usual commercial, institutional, industrial, and residential uses, there are many special applications that this type of nontraditional illumination is well suited to do. Examples are paint shops, grain elevators, offshore oil rigs, or solvent storage, where the ability to locate illuminators remotely and seal off potential spark-producing incandescent or discharge light sources can be crucial. Sensitive testing equipment like computers or magnetic resonance imaging (MRI) areas are also candidates for this technology because of the absence of interference from other electrical systems.

In a hospital operating room, a failed light could have very serious consequences. Using fiber optics could eliminate frantic relamping of individual bulbs. Other suggestions include under- or on-water, dynamic signage, dust-filled mines, high-humidity conditions, cold rooms, corrosive environments, emergency lighting and portable airfield lighting.

A PETROCHEMICAL PLANT[35]

Lighting was required inside 29 chemical reactors and filtering systems. Because of the physical nature of the reactors, normal tungsten hazardous-area fittings were either unsuitable for the lux output needed, or just too large physically. In one case, an aperture of just 30 mm diameter × 200 mm deep was available in which to introduce lighting. Twelve light sources were sited in "safe" areas up to 17 m away from the reactors in adjacent buildings. Harnesses of 8 or 12 size-12 polymer fiber tails (4 mm diameter) were used (totaling over 2.4 km). (In theory, S12 glass and S12 polymer will not produce the same light level unless the length of the polymer is very short. For a glass tail of over 17 m, the attenuation percent loss would be 51 percent, i.e., 49 percent emerges. The loss of polymer would be 76.5 percent, i.e., 23.5 percent emerges.) Special equipment was manufactured so that the tails could be held in the desired position.

In most of the reactors, an area 260° horizontally and 120° vertically was illuminated. To enable the operators to see to the bottom of the reactors, three of the tails were made to shine directly downward. All of this was fitted within an aperture of just 80 mm diameter × 300 mm deep. The routes of these reactors were tortuous. There was a surrounding maze of pipes carrying all kinds of hazardous chemicals, solvents, air, steam, and water. Control cables and monitoring equipment of all shapes and sizes were also present, making the installation more complicated. However, close cooperation with the clients, consulting engineers, and other trades made the job easier.

Some of the reactors are heated internally to 105°C, and at this temperature, polymer fiber is likely to melt. To overcome this problem, cool instrument air was introduced into the lighting aperture to cool the fibers to below the danger point of 80°C. The enclosures used to house the light sources were also cooled with instrument air. The main reason for this was the possibility of the ambient air becoming charged with acid particles, which would necessitate a complete washdown of the whole area. (The guess is that the instrumentation in this highly volatile environment would have been operated by air pressure transducers to eliminate the risk of electrical sparks.) The instrument air, at 6 bar (= 6 times the air pressure on the ground), allowed doing away with ventilation apertures, which, under normal circumstances, would have allowed water to enter the enclosure.

Levels of 300 to 600 lux have been reached, depending on the size and type of unit lit, better than could have been achieved with conventional equipment under such demanding circumstances.

CHEMICAL STORAGE ROOM

An explosion-proof lighting system was needed that did not require maintenance within the hazardous area of a chemical storage room. The client did not yet have the racking layout for storage, a detail that is necessary for the actual location of light output lens holders. Lacking this information, a general layout providing approximately 500 lux (50 footcandles) at 1 m (3.28 ft) above the floor was submitted. Megolon™ sheathing offers an additional safety feature. Equipment used was eight 150-watt metal halide projectors located outside the hazardous area and eight 8-tail size-48 glass harnesses with lenses.

SECTION 2. INSTITUTIONAL

In this category are included museums, historic houses, governments, libraries, schools, and other nonprofit entities. Some of the period structures are shown in Fig. 6-22. Examples of where to locate the light guides and projectors are shown in Fig. 6-23.

Illumination for Historic Structures

Fiber optics is eminently suited for historic places, where lighting anachronisms, intrusion, and unnecessary penetration of original fabric cannot be allowed. Its discreetness is especially welcome, as is its elimination of destructive infrared and ultraviolet rays. Fugitive organic materials like wood, paper, textiles, ivory, lacquer, feathers, and leather are very vulnerable under light of any kind. Many original lighting fixtures can be retrofit with fiber optics. Historic light levels and color can be recreated. Components appropriate to the particular function can be fabricated so that the designer is not limited to a small variety of stock items.

One feature of structures erected prior to World War II with traditional construction methods is that they usually have more interstitial spaces within which to conceal new lighting systems.

Buildings dating from the 1960s and 1970s may be nothing but solid concrete floors and ceilings, necessitating expensive diamond drilling to chase out space in which to insert tails. They certainly will not have high enough ceilings to allow dropping a few inches to contain equipment. The throwaway character of these properties, with their limited life span and

(a)

Fig. 6-22 Typical historical styles that can be lit with fiber optics. (a) 15th-century half-timbered.

(b)

(c)

(d)

Fig. 6-22 (Continued) (b) Mid-19th century. (c) Early 20th-century arts & crafts. (d) Art deco.

(a)

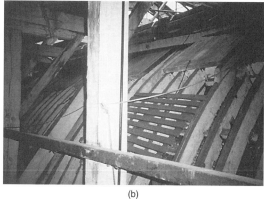

(b)

(c)

(d)

Fig. 6-23 Examples of locations available to conceal equipment. (a) Along heavy timber beams in 18th-century mill. (b) Space above vaulted ceiling in mid-19th-century assembly hall. (c) Fishing through a 1920's ceiling. (d) Ample space beyond terra cotta building blocks in 1930's planetarium.

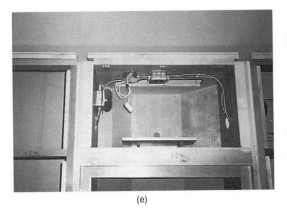

(e)

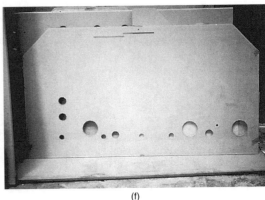

(f)

(g)

Fig. 6-23 (Continued) (e) Attic provided at top of display cabinets. (f) Plywood template drilled with holes to contain glass fiber-optic fittings in ceiling. (g) Holes drilled in chandelier canopy for glass fibers to play on paintings around wall.

lack of decoration, further accentuates the value of recycling the prewar buildings. The latter usually have the three most important features of successful real estate—location, location, and location. In addition, without instruction, the public is instinctively drawn to them because they are user friendly. These structures, if well maintained, are usually fully occupied and thriving and, so, are in a position to upgrade lighting. The ensuing quote is a comment on this particular segment of illumination pertaining to cultural heritage:

Lighting for Historic Buildings[36]

No matter what the age of a structure, in order to provide the best illumination, there is a need to understand every building, its style and function. Also, differences between day and nighttime lighting must be recognized.

World architecture developed under daylight, and architects and builders learned to understand its geometry, to use its variability, and to create buildings which, at first for functional, and later for decorative purposes, were influenced in their plan and section by the introduction of natural light.

The decorative quality of artificial sources of light, associated with the manner of their support and containment, was discovered at an early stage of man's development. An interest was shown first in the candles and candelabra, lamps and chandeliers from which the light was derived, leading on to the design of wall or ceiling to which these might be fixed, the one reacting to the other. Fiber-optics can simplify replication.

The whole development of interior design relates to knowledge and understanding of the laws of light; the laws of reflection transmission and refraction, its geometry and color and its capacity to provide information by means of light and shadow.

Daylight and the alternative means of "fire" light, when thought of in terms of architectural form, remained entirely separate until the development of electric light, and the immense increase in the efficiency of modern light sources. The buildings considered "historic" demonstrate this separation.

The later buildings of the 20th century display a tendency to integrate, the form of the building being designed to use the functional qualities of natural light during the day, in association with those of electric light both during the day and at night. Natural light and electric light were used together to achieve a functional whole.

The National Trust in England has very kindly given "some examples where fiber optics (glass) has been used, very successfully, to provide good lighting at conservation levels":

- *Calke Abbey, Derbyshire.* To illuminate a magnificent 18th century State Bed with silk embroidered hangings: The great flexibility of these light sources to illuminate with no heat or ultraviolet light, awkward places such as under the canopy, is well illustrated here. The bed is displayed in a "glass box" which has conditioned air passed into it from the adjacent room, which also houses the fiber-optics light source.

- *Chartwell, Kent.* This was the home of Winston Churchill. Fiber optics is used to illuminate wartime uniforms in a special "museum display."

- *Beatrix Potter Gallery, Hawkshead, Lake District.* In the home of the creator of Peter Rabbit, fiber optics lights a display of her water-colors.

Here are further examples:

THE REYNOLDS ROOM, CASTLE ASHBY, NORTHAMTONSHIRE, ENGLAND[37]

This stately home now is a visitor attraction. It was not possible to obtain photographs of the spaces before the new brochures were issued; however, a plan of the room with each painting shown in position follows, with sizes and angle of the light for each (see Fig. 6-24).

The light sources are mounted on the floor of the King William room above. They were made with oak covers to blend the units into the furnishings. All the paintings are cross-lit by two glass tails with recessed framing spot downlighters. Some of the art had not been seen as clearly for many years. The total value of the paintings in this room, all by Sir

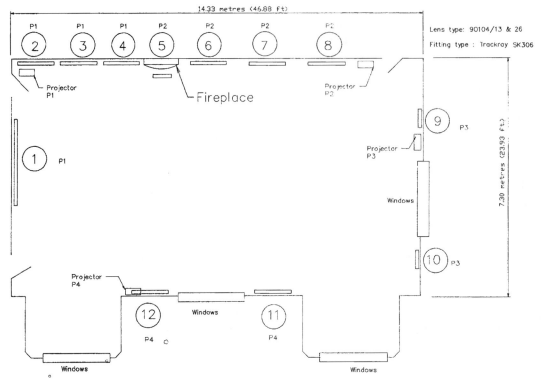

Fig. 6-24 Lighting plan of Castle Ashby.

Joshua Reynolds, exceeds £10,000,000, an excellent reason for careful illumination.

SHAKESPEARE'S BIRTHPLACE, STRATFORD-UPON-AVON, ENGLAND[38]

An early proponent of glass fiber-optic architectural lighting has been employing this system wherever appropriate in his commissions. Unobtrusive lighting in this sixteenth-century cottage was specified for this very popular tourist attraction (see Fig. 6-25).

A MEMORIAL HALL[39]

Problem:

A late Victorian Memorial Hall contains a 30-ft-wide chapel with a dark ceiling about 70 ft high. Two 10-in-diameter "wagon wheel" chandeliers in the center of the transept provide rather dim ambient light. Along the dark walnut-paneled walls there are plaques 6 ft apart. These 4-ft-square

white marble memorials have gilt incised letter-
ing on them. They are hung starting 7 ft above
the floor going up to 20 ft, and have to be lit
softly, yet brightly enough to read by. Existing
illumination was a row of very bright spotlights
that were very glaring and disturbing to the rev-
erent ambience of the space. The architect
thought that glass fiber optics would provide
the permanent light required without damaging
the interior.

Solution:

Because penetrating the walls would not be per-
mitted, the architect, experienced in working
with historic properties, suggested that the glass
fiber-optic light sources be placed on the chandeliers to keep all the historic fabric of the building intact and greatly simplify maintenance.

There were two choices for a base to hold
the light sources in a flat plane—either transparent Plexiglas or a black mounting base
(metal or fire retardant wood) placed across the
spokes of the chandeliers. The boxes containing
the light sources and the fittings would be matte
black, to be as invisible as possible. The black
version was selected.

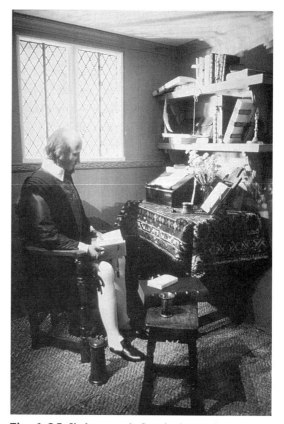

Fig. 6-25 Shakespeare in Stratford-upon-Avon.

After careful calculations, it was determined that 54 size-48 glass tails
with 2-in lenses could be powered from three light sources mounted on
each of the antique lighting fixtures. (A few spare tails would be used for
final light balancing.) Beam angles would vary, depending on tail location
on the chandelier. For fine on-site adjustments for even light, there was a
dimming system on each lens holder. With this dimmable lens, there
would be good control over beam size and light level.

From previous projects, it was known that for the long throw distances, from a minimum of 18 ft to a maximum of 28 ft, more than one
tail was necessary to keep the light level of the entire area more evenly balanced. One size-48 tail will deliver approximately 120 lux (12 footcandles) at 16 ft. Up to 2 m (maximum) of tail length was allowed for three

light guides out of each 9-tail harness, so that they could be run around the chandelier to wherever required.

Zones were designated for each light source, and the tails were apportioned between the six projectors. With the added weight of three light sources and the platform on which to mount the projectors, each chandelier had to carry an additional load of 150 to 200 pounds, plus whatever weight would be exerted on the fixture by the person relamping. To keep the hanging fixtures steady and to further support the additional load, a series of guy wires were attached from the dark ceiling.

FOREIGN EMBASSY—DRAWING ROOM AND LOBBY

A very famous architect designed a foreign embassy in the 1920s. To protect the valuable loan collection of art which changed with each ambassador, and also to provide a permanent yet flexible residential style lighting system with reduced maintenance costs, glass fiber optics were selected for the main drawing room and lobby (see Fig. 6-26).

Windows on three sides opened onto the garden, reducing available wall space. There were no adjacent closets, pieces of furniture, or any other recesses in which to place the illuminators. Luckily, original architectural drawings were found, which indicated the interstitial spaces usually present in pre-1940 structures. They could indicate where the equipment could be concealed without penetrating decorative features. If discreet holes had to be punched into ornamental plaster surfaces, only the smooth portions would be chosen, because that would be much easier to patch. The following equipment provided sufficient illumination to make out the colors in the paintings, and the details of the furnishings:

Drawing Room (A)

2, 150-watt metal halide projectors

2, 8-tail size-36 glass harnesses

16 adjustable recessed fittings

Fig. 6-26 Decorative ceiling where fiber optics is to be installed.

Lobby (B)

> 1, 150-watt metal halide projector

> 1, 5-tail size-36 glass harness

> 5 adjustable recessed fittings

BEAUX ARTS–STYLE EMBASSY

Problem:

A 100-year-old embassy in beaux arts style contained two grand reception rooms with elaborately painted ceilings. The object was to illuminate this art gently and evenly, and also provide sufficient ambient light for receptions. Penetrating the historic fabric was to be kept at a minimum, and all new lighting was to be as discreet as possible. This property was located in a seismic area, so all installations had to be very secure and as environmentally safe as possible under disaster conditions.

Solution:

The original scheme for room *A* was for 8 to 10 projectors, but restricted funds reduced that amount to 6, which would have lowered the light level proportionately. However, six of the new 100-watt metal halide light sources provided brighter illumination, even with fewer projectors. Since the project was located in a foreign country, the first thing to be done was to check the electric power to be sure the voltage of the light sources was made compatible (see Fig. 6-27).

Room A: Seventy-two size-24 glass tails with a 36° lens in a reduced bezel lens holder with deep lens mounting were spaced at 300 mm behind the deep cornice molding around the room. The light guides were held in a retaining band attached behind the heavy cornice, prepierced (like the Four Seasons project) to accept white lens holders. Since this was a place of assembly, Megolon sheathing was used for life safety.

Room B: In contrast to room *A,* which had a flat but beautifully painted ceiling, room *B* had a vaulted ornamental painted ceiling. Equipment here included eight conventional projectors powering six 13-tail and two 20-tail glass harnesses of size-24 fiber. The same type of fittings were provided as in room *A.* Only an installer specially trained in working with highly decorated historic structures should be used in attaching the metal retainer behind the plaster. Here is a case where the

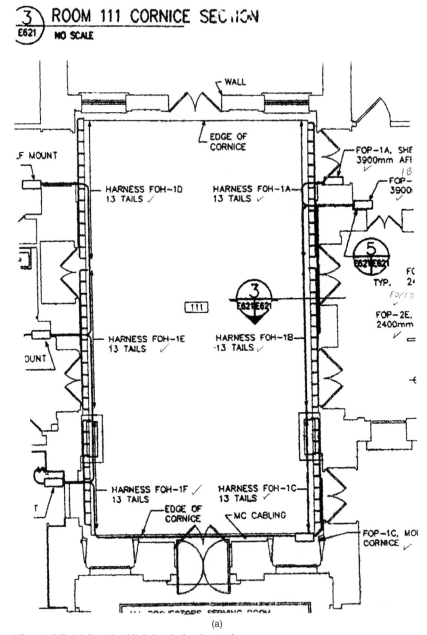

Fig. 6-27 (a) Sketch of lighting in foreign embassy.

(b)

Fig. 6-27 (Continued) (b) View of one room.

most careful design and suitable material could be negated by careless installation.

HISTORIC MASONIC TEMPLE

Requirements:

A small Masonic Temple administered by dedicated volunteers sought to have special lighting effects but with reduced maintenance. There is a concave plaster-on-metal lath ceiling painted dark blue with pierced holes for constellations. They wanted to:

1. Create a glass fiber-optic constellation in the ceiling. There are two 12-in bridges 8 ft apart above the ceiling where the light sources can

go. Requested specialties included star formations like Saturn and Jupiter to light up in the same order as they appear in the sky. There are painted clouds at both ends of the ceiling imitating a twilight sky.

2. For the half-hour Masonic ceremony, a sunset-to-sunrise effect was to be recreated from the 8-in-deep trough lighting around the perimeter, above the cornice. This was currently being done with incandescent lamps controlled by an ancient and very noisy rheostat.

3. Retrofit wall sconces for ambient light in room to gain same color lighting throughout the space.

Solution:

Dividing the drawing of the "sky" into quadrants greatly simplified the design. It then became a matter of grouping the tails into positions for a selected time of year. Ample room above the ceiling houses the light sources. Synchronized mechanical dimming and color wheels create the sunset-to-sunrise illusion. The sconces, high on the wall, having solid arms, can be retrofit with clear tails discreetly attached on the top side where they cannot be seen from those standing under them.

Architectural Models

NAPOLEONIC ART SALON

A 1-in (25-mm) = 1-ft model[40] of a Napoleonic art salon is used to teach glass fiber-optic lighting to both undergraduates in architectural/engineering programs and professionals in continuing education courses. Complete with black-and-white marble floors, custom-built period furnishings, a collection of master paintings, mantle garniture, and a 1-in-long crystal chandelier, this little room is a tool to show how to light a complex interior design. The intent was to show contours, color, or translucency. Many types of lighting techniques were employed, with varying intensities and colors, according to the properties of the particular object. Included was cross-lighting for contours, lighting up through translucent material, downlighting for flat pieces, and spotlighting. Holes in the ceiling were drilled at an angle for easy insertion of the tails. Each was numbered with the size tail to be used in it. It took six specialists one day to prepare the little room.

Hint: One thing learned at once was, high levels of overhead illumination would wash out whatever lighting was in the model.

It was only after the open side (what would be the fourth wall) was shaded by an overhang, that the discreet lighting within could be seen. This is the same problem existing in exhibit halls with very bright ceiling fixtures.

Another trick was to recess the tail slightly in the lens holder and paint the inside of the fitting black. This made the point of light almost unnoticeable. The same methods could be used for antique dollhouses, or for that matter, full-sized spaces.

ARCHEOLOGICAL MODEL[41]

A large archeological museum had a "look-in" model of an ancient Egyptian throne room. Built in the 1920s for school children to see, the interior's bright wall paintings were covered with very high gloss varnish to keep fingerprints off. Lit with a few incandescent bulbs, it did not present this exact replica to its best advantage. People could look in from both the south and east sides, making it difficult to light from within without having glare in someone's eyes.

The exhibit designer obtained a glass fiber-optic demonstration kit and, with the supplier, started to experiment with different tail sizes from changing angles (see Fig. 6-28).

Fig. 6-28 Model of dynastic Egyptian throne room.

Exterior Illumination of Historic Buildings, Structures, or Ruins

This process has to be carefully done with concealed components and power wiring. Everything has to be easily reversible. Already vulnerable to theft and vandalism, these structures should not suffer irreversible damage to original fabric due to insensitive lighting techniques, installation, or inadequate security. Sometimes, if access is not available on the object itself, it may be possible to get permission to use other buildings or ornamental bollards, fences, directional signs, or specially designed dual-purpose lamp posts, from which to attach and focus light.

Although kind volunteers are useful for many chores, the administrators of historic sites should employ only experienced professionals who know where to place the lighting hardware to enhance architectural details. Above all, do not overlight, or unknowingly employ, too many different colored lights.

House Museums

House museums can be as grand as Versailles or as humble as a log cabin. The lighting for all elements of cultural heritage must ensure the continued existence of the structure and the interior, while making it possible to see them as clearly as possible.

VICTORIAN COUNTRY HOUSE MUSEUM

A Victorian country house, now a house museum in honor of the founder of an important botanic garden, wanted to try out glass fiber optics in one room. Figure 6-29 illustrates how the number of tails was determined. Because of the antique fabrics and furnishings, conservation level (50 lux = 5 footcandles) was chosen.

1680 SWEDISH BRICK HOUSE

A senior class architectural project was to measure a 1680 Swedish brick house and use glass fiber optics to light it with period illumination. Since it was long empty and there were no drawings extant, their adjunct professor had to guess about the appropriate furnishings to show the students where light would have been used (see Fig. 6.30). Unfortunately, half way through the work, the city came without notice and pulled the building down.

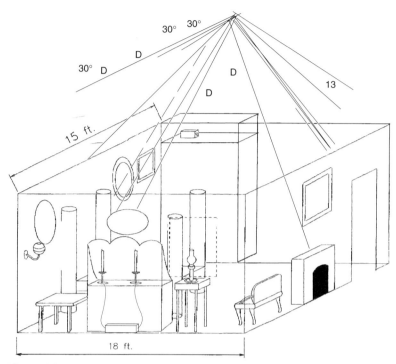

Fig. 6-29 Sketches of lighting design for St. Louis Botanical Gardens (overlay). Courtesy of architect W. Philip Cotton, Jr.

AN EARLY NINETEENTH-CENTURY FARMHOUSE-MUSEUM

A very simple American Midwest timber-framed farmhouse was being readied for visitors. Only general lighting was requested, because the types and location of furniture were not yet known. Nevertheless, wherever possible, adjustable fittings were specified, just in case. Room above the rafters was found to conceal the light sources.

For the gift shop, one 150-watt metal halide projector with an 8-tail S12 glass harness was specified. In the bedroom was a similar system. The room with changing exhibits had a light source powering a 16-tail S12 glass harness. The period toilet room (a novelty at the time) called for the projector with a 5-tail S12 glass harness (see Fig. 6-31).

A WORKING HISTORIC MUSEUM[42]

Problem:

An eighteenth-century mill was to be turned into an industrial archeology museum. The client's subassistants and raw interns sent the fiber-optic

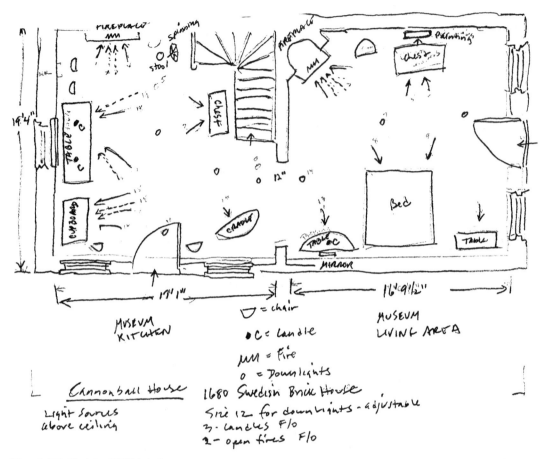

Fig. 6-30 Sketch of 1680 interior.

consultant barely legible faxed line drawings with numerous deletions and additions penciled in. Unless the lighting designer was familiar with the architecture and original workings of a mill, it would be difficult to visualize what was happening. There were three levels, each containing a selection of original machinery and exhibits of related artifacts.

One of the first questions always asked is, where would it be convenient to put the light sources. Lacking any interstitial space in this structure, it was finally learned that light sources and glass tails could be put exposed on the underside of the timber framing. The (American) National Electric Code permits drilling a small round hole in the center of the timber members to fish the tails through in a direct path, thus shortening their length.

For the archeological excavations at the bottom, they wanted low-level light. Several phone calls later revealed that the pits were approximately 2

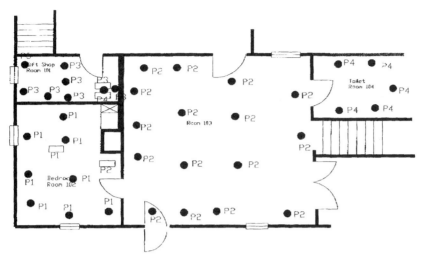

Fig. 6-31 Lighting sketch of 19th-century house museum.

× 8 ft, and there was a 4 × 8 ft vertical wall showing original construction, which also had to be lit at low level. The only object on the ground floor which was to be brightly lit was the machinery with three wheels and the shaft, which continues up through the entire building.

Later they added two metal mesh sections 6 ft high by 12 ft wide placed at right angles to each other, just outside the room partition on the first floor. They will hang 1 ft from the ceiling and 1 ft from the floor. Changing objects relating to milling will be attached to these sections. There will be a description at the top. The architect didn't know if the light should be even on these panels, because there may be flat photographs and fabrics (like sacks) at the top, and three-dimensional objects on the bottom. They want natural light coming from the windows, and fiber-optics just where it is dark.

Solution:

More telephone messages and faxes went back and forth and, finally, a beginning point for a design appeared, despite some areas "to be determined." On the ground floor, two light sources provided low-level light for the archeological remains pits, and higher intensity for center machinery, gear shafts, and wall surfaces. A selection of sizes 12, 24, and 36 glass tails with varying size lenses was used.

The first floor contained wall panels for artifacts, millstones, machinery, and the separate corn sheller room. Three light sources powering size-24 tails did this section. The second floor had bins, bolting reels, and gear machinery, illuminated by size-12 and -24 glass tails from two 150-watt projectors.

Often, the specifier has to make large guesses in presenting a scheme, to provide a point from which the customer can begin to express the lighting "wish list." At least, a definite yes or no is obtained on some points, and then there can be progress to determine exactly what is wanted.

HISTORIC MILL CONVERTED TO CORPORATE OFFICES[43]

This heavy timber-framed late-eighteenth-century stone structure was being turned into corporate offices for a large manufacturing firm. It was a very complicated project, because of the combination of historic and office features. The owners liked the panache of being in a period building. They were also taking advantage of the (American) federal 20% Investment Tax Credit for rehabilitating income-producing properties over 50 years old, which required careful attention to original architectural fabric and design. They particularly wanted glass fiber-optic candles lit every night in all 57 windows. (Unless for a very special occasion, that would never have been done by the original tenants.) Clearance throughout was very tight, and distances were great. The clients themselves served in the roles of architect, engineer, and interior designer.

Although the lighting wish list was known, a bill of material had to be made to price the work. A solid week of calculations, site visits, and conferences between the electrical contractor and the fiber-optic consultant/supplier followed. After considerable study and discussions, a lighting design was prepared that allowed for glass fiber optics to do the candles, internal lighting in offices and board rooms, baseboard emergency lighting, and even the security lights over the various external exits. Only lighting the stairs in the basement was left to conventional methods, because only a single incandescent bulb was needed there.

To keep the tails as short as possible, two copies of the eighteenth-century triangular corner cupboards, similar to the original one found in the kitchen, were built on the second floor to house the light sources as indicated. As a safety measure, all of the projectors that control the candles and emergency baseboard lighting were connected to one UPS (uninterruptible power supply). In the absence of definite information on the final position of furniture and wall hangings, the exact location of tails remained a mystery until the very end. Here is how the bill of material was created:

Because of the many floor levels and the size of the spaces, the plans were divided up into segments to be more manageable (see Fig. 6-32). First, all the required points of light were marked on the drawing. Afterward, the location of a light source was picked. Working backward, requirements of each light level led to selection of the size of light guide. Then, the shortest route for each tail from the projector was sought. This entailed actually walking through the spaces, because this was a two-building complex of different heights, both greatly changed over the centuries. Nothing was built square or identical, even on opposite sides of a room, so accurate measurements were critical. Investigation behind the walls was also important, leading to many surprises.

It was always important to keep track of the maximum fibers used before another projector would have to be added. Where lenses were required, the right type had to be picked out. In many instances, illuminators had to serve several rooms or floors, to keep the number of light sources as low as possible. Of course, a computer program could have expedited this complicated task by exploring all the alternatives, but it could not take the place of visual inspection of the premises.

First-Floor Dining Room—Annex

2, 150-watt metal halide light sources in lower-left closets of second-floor lounge

Glass tails for three window candles + four candles for second-floor lounge powered by this projector

For the table: 12 size-24 with adjustable downlights

For walls: 10 size-24 glass tails

For fireplace: 6 size-24 with adjustable downlights

For stairs: 6 size 7

For baseboard at entrance door: 1 size 7

For outside vandal-proof downlights: 2 size 36

First-Floor Main Building

1, 150-watt metal halide projector in north central basement

• Northwest quadrant

3 candles west side

West stair hall: 8 size 7

West fireplace: 1 size 24 with adjustable downlight

3 candles east side

Outside: 2 vandal-proof downlights size 36

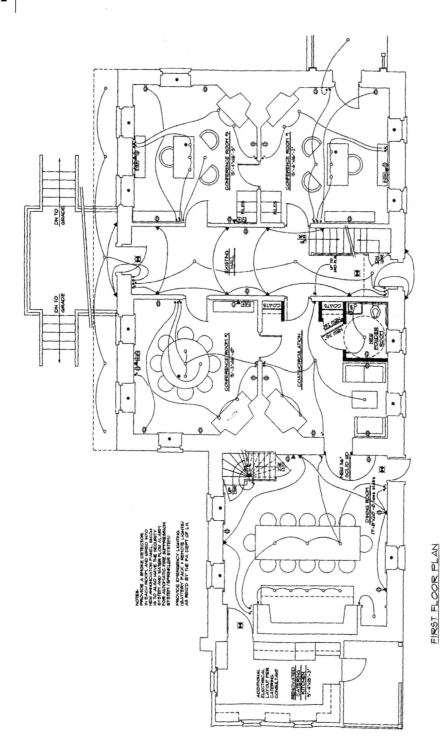

FIRST FLOOR PLAN

(a)

Fig. 6-32 (a, b, c) Original conventional lighting to be replaced by fiber optics. Courtesy of McFadden Architects.

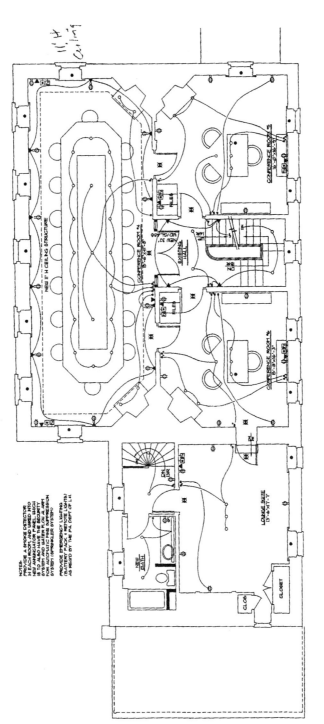

SECOND FLOOR PLAN

Fig. 6-32 (Continued)

(b)

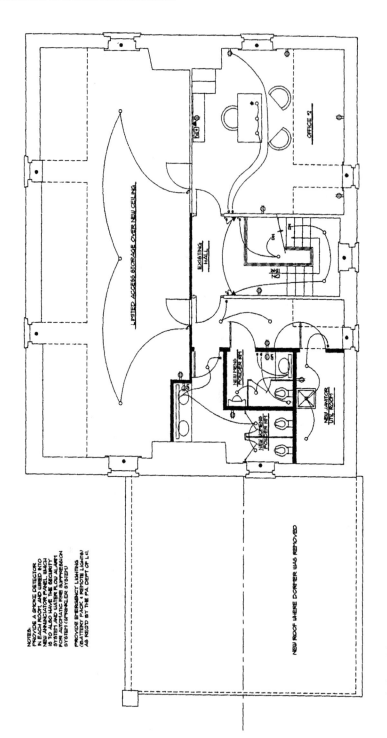

THIRD FLOOR PLAN

(c)

Fig. 6-32 (Continued)

1, 150-watt metal halide projector in middle central basement, west of stairs above

- Southwest quadrant:

  2 candles

  West stair hall: 10 size 7

  SW fireplace: 1 size 24 with adjustable downlight

  Outside: 2 vandal-proof downlights size 36

  1, 150-watt metal halide projector in middle central basement, east of stairs above

- Southeast quadrant:

  2 candles

  East stair hall: 12 size 7

  East fireplace: 1 size 24 with adjustable downlight

  Outside: 3 vandal-proof downlights size 36

Second-Floor Conference Room 4

Light source in mechanical room above ceiling

7 candles

Table: 32 size 24 with adjustable downlights

Third floor: 4 candles

Second-Floor South—Office 6 West

Light source in new cupboard SW corner

3 candles

West fireplace: 1 size 24 with downlight

West stair hall: 7 size 7

Baseboard, conference room 4 door: 1 size 7

Second-Floor South—Office 5 East

Light source in new cupboard SE corner

4 candles

East fireplace: 1 size 24 with adjustable downlight

East stair hall: 7 size 7

Baseboard, conference room 4 door: 1 size 7

Third Floor

Light source in janitor's room

5 candles

West stair hall: 8 size 7

East stair hall: 7 size 7

Figuring out this complicated fiber-optic commission was a great learning experience for the electrical contractor. He went on to the next fiber-optic project confidently and, thoroughly prepared, did an excellent job.

Archeological Sites

An early side-emitting fiber system was installed in Israel in the Beit Govrin Caves,[44] carved in the rock during the Hellenic Period. The light symbolized the water flowing through the channels which filled up the bath at the end. The illuminator is hidden in the bath.

A famous sight in Europe had very primitive lighting that was at the same time inadequate, glaring, and misfocused. Because it was so important, it drew many tourists, but they really could not see the details clearly. This was in dire need of improved illumination.

Libraries

THE HISTORIC LIBRARY BUILDING

Victorian libraries were nineteenth-century temples of learning. Architecturally, many have high atria surrounded by balconies decorated with ornate metalwork. However, they were almost impossible to light, so were usually used only during daylight hours. If expected to last, books, being made of paper and leather, should be illuminated as little as possible. Since conventional lighting components simply could not perform well with the difficult building design and the configuration of the stacks, glass fiber optics was selected. It could provide light in all areas with easy maintenance. Moreover, the cost for the glass came in 10 percent less than bids for traditional equipment. The electrical contractor found the fiber easier to install, too.

LIGHTING THE MAPPA MUNDI

The Mappa Mundi consists of a single sheet of stretched vellum, 1.6×1.3 meters (see Fig. 6-33). Vellum is animal hide scraped thin and is sensitive to moisture and microbiological growth. The work was created probably in Lincoln, England, in about 1290 to "show all of God's creation." It is in the Chained Library at Hereford. The bookcases date from the seventeenth century, but the hundreds of books they contain are from as far back as the eighth century.

Museums

Museums are one of the more difficult venues to light properly because of many outside factors. There is always the matter of finding the money to do the job; conserving valuable objects in the institution's care; presenting visitors with displays that are imaginative, yet readily understandable and visible; and creating lighting, especially in very popular exhibits, with

Fig. 6-33 Lighting the Mappa Mundi. Courtesy of Sir William Whitfield, as shown in Building Services Journal (UK), October, 1996. A box containing glass fiber optics has been added to the lower front of the showcase. Heat is removed directly to the air conditioning plant and the Mappa is bathed in an upwash of soft light. There is also an emergency lighting installation.

maintenance as simple as possible to keep everything working as originally designed.

Several years ago, the Auckland Museum mounted a tribute to those New Zealanders who fought in World War II. It contained all kinds of materials, from textiles to metal, calling for a variety of lighting techniques. In addition to this permanent segment, they also had a temporary show depicting the life of Ghengis Khan. This presented other types of requirements for a flexible and reusable lighting system.

WITH PLASTIC FIBER OPTICS: MUSÉE DE CLUNY, PARIS, FRANCE[45]

Situated in the heart of Paris's Latin Quarter, the Musée de Cluny is a landmark of great historical importance (see Fig. 6-34). It comprises the thermes, or Roman baths, which date from the year 213, and the hôtel, one of only two remaining Gothic residences in the city. Since 1844, it has housed the National Museum of the Middle Ages and one of the world's finest collections of medieval art. The centerpiece of the museum is the celebrated group of 15th century tapestries entitled 'The Lady and the Unicorn'. Displayed in the upper rotunda of the museum, for years, the six tapestries had been illuminated by filtered daylight from the room's high windows. In an effort to allow visitors to view these national treasures in full detail, the French Ministry of Culture ordered a new lighting system. The challenge for the project team was not only to illuminate the

Fig. 6-34 Musée de Cluny, Paris, France—the Unicorn tapestries.

enormous tapestries in a uniform fashion, while protecting them from heat and damaging light rays, but to keep all power sources, transport cables and light fixtures as discreet as possible.

The engineers took advantage of the museum's decision to close off the room's high windows to install light generators at a height of 5 metres in the rotunda's dome. These are equipped with 40 - 50 watt 24° dichroic halogen lamps with a color temperature close to that of natural light. The generators are designed to perform without light leaks or additional ventilation that might detract from the visitor's enjoyment of the collection. The entire unit can be lowered and raised by electric motor for easy maintenance and adjustment. Light is carried from the generators to the 280 end-points of the system by 40 harnesses. Each harness contains 7 cables sheathed in a fireproof material.

To provide museum staff with the greatest degree of flexibility for their lighting needs, the terminations attached to the extremity of each cable are mounted on a miniature ball-and-socket joint that allows them to pivot in all directions. In addition, each light can be individually focused to project a narrower or wider beam. The 280 points of light are positioned in two parallel rows at the periphery of the dome around which the tapestries are hung. The upper row lights the bottom of the tapestries, and the lower row, the top.

PERMANENT EXHIBIT, AUCKLAND MUSEUM, NEW ZEALAND[46]

This description is quoted verbatim from the lighting designer. It is a more eloquent summary of the fiber-optic properties and methods mentioned in previous chapters (see Fig. 6-35).

The Brief:

The exhibition, *Scars on the Heart,* is the first gallery in the museum to be redeveloped at the start of a five-year refurbishment program. The light brief called for a design and installation of the very highest international standards. They were to be achieved in the areas of lighting visual impact and dramatic quality, and also in the area of artifact conservation and museological integrity. Additionally, energy efficiency was a high priority, along with ease of maintenance and practical adjustability of the equipment.

The display material consisted of a wide variety of military and related equipment, in both two- and three-dimensional form. The exhibit areas ranged from conventional cabinets and specialized display cases to theatrical replications of battlefield conditions. It was imperative that the lighting be exceptional in theatrical creativity and perceived drama.

The technique had to deliver tightly focused and highly adjustable pools of light onto targeted artifacts. Very crisp white light was required for

(a)   (b)

Fig. 6-35 "Scars on the Heart" exhibit at the Auckland Museum, New Zealand. (a) Permanent exhibit. (b) Changing exhibit.

accurate color rendering and very defined cutoffs. In addition to visual parameters, conservation was strictly emphasized. The degradation caused by excessive quantities of ultraviolet and infrared rays was to be minimized, while the length of lighting service had to be long. Toward this end, the client concluded that only glass fiber-optics could satisfy all criteria.

The lighting contract was based on a design/supply/installation and commission basis. This required the lighting designer to interpret the generalized lighting brief supplied, and to develop it into a complete proposal. This was to be followed with full installation supervision and commissioning responsibilities. The required light levels specified went between 50 lux and 250 lux centre beam illuminance at various points around the displays, and with nominal beam diameters also specified.

The budget allocated for this project was realistic, considering the complexity. The client was prepared to accommodate the capital costs of top-class technology and equipment, because he recognized the need for this equipment to perform over the long term.

The Solution:

Glass fiber technology was deemed to be the most suitable option, considering the required longevity of the installation. A mixture of metal halide and low voltage halogen fiber-optics projectors was selected. Metal halide lamps, particularly those of larger size, were used to deliver the higher light levels. Low voltage halogen was employed in smaller displays.

Additionally, some supplementary lighting was used. 200 watt halogen uplighters provided diffused light through tent-like canvas drapes for the Sinai-Palestine display, recreating the atmosphere of a Near Eastern marketplace. Larger wall-mounted murals (not antique) inside showcases have been lit with the new T2 miniature fluorescent lamps (7mm diameter), incorporating electronic control gear.

The fiber-optic equipment uses a range of luminaires to distribute the light. The predominant one is a miniature eyeball fitting used both with and without optical quality glass lenses. These fittings are fully focusable and some incorporate color filters. Other display areas employ fiber-optics wands for light distribution, while still others use extended-neck spotlights.

The prevailing design philosophy with the fiber-optic lighting was to minimize the visual intrusion of the equipment itself. The display material was to be the "star of the show," and great pains were taken to hide the lighting equipment from the gaze of the viewer. This task was greatly assisted by the extremely small dimensions of the components. The fiber-optic projectors were discreetly hidden away within cabinets and ceiling cavities. Much detail work was required in order to ensure that these spaces had sufficient cooling airflows, and were readily accessible for routine maintenance. The fiber-optic harnesses incorporated a number of tail sizes from 7mm^2 cross sectional area to 24mm^2. These custom-designed looms were exactly tailored to the requirements of each individual display area.

Non-lensed fiber-optic fittings were used for lighting in close proximity to the displayed object, and where a wide distribution diffused light effect was desired. Conversely, lensed fittings were used where the light beam had to be thrown over some distance and tightly focused, with crisp cutoff light pools.

The lighting design was undertaken using intuitive and qualitative techniques, leaning heavily on theatrical lighting fundamentals. Such well-known effects as grazing, backlighting, shadowing and modelling were used to provide the required enhancement of each display. Following the design of the exhibits, trial mock-ups were made to prove the theory. Considerable fine-tuning was necessary to refine ideas and improve technical and creative effects and illusions. At this stage, light measurements were taken in order to establish compliance with the quantitative area of the design brief.

The prevailing premise on which the lighting design was developed was that ambient lighting levels in the main gallery building would be very low or non-existent. Thus, the display lighting would be allowed to articulate the attributes of the display material fully, without intrusion of generalist light that would undoubtedly reduce the vitality and visual interest of the exhibits.

Great care was taken in the lighting design with the fundamentals of the physics of light. Very detailed attention was paid to ensure the correct angles of light projection, dealing with the issues of glass reflections and minimizing the effects of reflective display material. A particular challenge was to illuminate (from a long distance) the narrow linear information rails. These had to be functionally lit while still not undermining the drama of the displays.

Results:

This project, believed to be the largest application of glass fiber optics yet seen in New Zealand, has clearly proved to be a technical and practical success. The museum curators appreciate the conservation advantages delivered by this technology. This world-leading application of fiber-optics has yielded a result that helps underpin the commercial and museological goals of the client. The realism of the displays, the powerful imagery, and the sometimes macabre depictions of the horrors of war, help to create a memorable experience in the mind of the visitor.

On a practical note, the total installed wattage is only 4.2 kilowatts, and the energy utilization is a meager 10.9 watts/m². Glass fiber-optics equipment included 11 - 150 watt metal halide, and 10 - 50 watt halogen projectors. These operating economies, coupled with the very small number of lamps employed, make this project an extremely practical site to maintain.

In all, the use of advance technology, combined with creative application, has enabled a visual result that simply could not be obtained through any other means. As such, lighting has provided the major impetus to the memorable presentation of the history of New Zealand's military endeavors.

CHANGING EXHIBIT

This same museum presented a wonderful traveling exhibition from the period of Ghengis Khan. In a previous venue, the method of dealing with conservation light level for the textiles and leather was with a single dim bulb over Plexiglas floor cases. There was no graceful physical position the viewer could assume to avoid the glare. Consequently, the bright colors and the beautiful weaving were not seen or appreciated. The interior of a life-size tent filled with native artifacts was barely discernible. In fact, whoever looked into the entrance of this exhibit might have thought it was closed! Those who persevered found an unusual treat in spite of the illumination. It is always interesting to compare the same art exhibited in different places. Sometimes, because of the lighting, the pieces are almost unrecognizable (see Fig. 6-36).

The picture brightened in Auckland. Here the tents, costumes, and jewelry came alive. Three-dimensional objects no longer looked flattened,

(a)   (b)

Fig. 6-36 (a) Single lamp reflecting in case, making Ghengis Kahn display difficult to see exhibit. (b) Color is flat.

and visitors could imagine being in this ancient campsite pulsating with these exciting people (see Fig. 6-37).

A LIGHTING PANEL ON GLASS FIBER OPTICS—PLASTIC VS. GLASS

Some years ago, a lighting panel presented the two divergent views of fiber optics—plastic vs. glass. No definite conclusion was reached, because the applications were so different, and both clients were relatively satisfied with the outcome. Naturally, there were partisans on both sides in the audience, which led to a very lively discussion. Because the first museum[47] was far from a metropolitan center, it could not find a competent lighting designer in the area familiar with fiber optics, so it worked directly with the installer/supplier of a plastic system from another state. The administration had not been aware of the glass version.

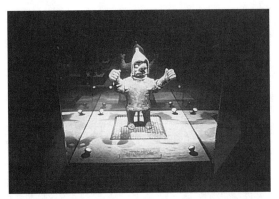

Fig. 6-37 Same collection shown under glass fiber-optic lighting at the Auckland Museum.

In contrast, the director of exhibits in a major museum in a large city, with a much more sophisticated brief requiring extensive highlighting and special effects, felt that use of a lighting consultant was absolutely essential. The curator of the department was very insistent on using glass fiber optics, because of his long experience with scientific instructions equipped with it. A theatrical lighting designer[48] on his first attempt with fiber optics, came up with outstanding ideas employing the technology.

In the first application, only reasonably uniform low light levels at the open displays (5–10 fc), with even less illumination (1–2 fc) outside the display areas, was required. A glass-enclosed multi-tiered open storage system displayed North American Indian, French Paleolithic artifacts and pre-Columbian ceramics. A low-profile lighting (LPL) system was installed inside the display cases behind cast-iron mullions to prevent reflection on the glass front. Fibers were spaced 1 in apart in the LPL channel. The fiber optics, which are small enough to illuminate from behind display supports out of view, provide an even wash of light along the shelf bays that line the exterior perimeter of the glass box.

Metal halide light sources with color temperature-reducing filters were located at basement level in a maintenance space with the rest of the mechanicals, such as air handling and climate control systems. Here lamps could be accessed and changed without going into the collection and having to disturb any of the objects on the shelves.

A total of 30 illuminators are located on the ceiling of the basement, each one below a vertical mullion. From there, the fibers run up into the glass box and into tiny holes in the LPL fixtures, which are mounted on the back of the cabinet mullions in 13-ft runs. A variable aperture (mechanical mesh) dimming system was designed for the illuminators so that the museum curator has control over each display area independently, while maintaining constant color temperature.

Although the many objects on the shelves are lighted by fiber-optics, the work space in the center of the glass box, requiring higher light levels, is not, the architect reverting to a conventional system there.

CONVENTIONAL LIGHTING CAN'T HOLD A CANDLE TO FIBER OPTICS

Problem:

In a large museum, over 100 period rooms filled with very valuable antique furniture and artwork were kept exceedingly dark for conservation purposes. The only illumination was from harsh orange-colored electric candles. Because this glare temporarily blinded visitors as they entered from brighter-lit hallways, people kept knocking into the fragile tables and chairs. Also, to highlight the decorative details, the many docents constantly turned their flashlights (torches) on objects, exposing the pieces to destructive ultraviolet rays and defeating the very purpose of the low light levels.

Solution:

There was no in-house lighting designer and no architectural drawings, the structure having been randomly erected. The museum called in a consultant/supplier, who brought along an engineer, architect, and electrical contractor. Over the course of three months, this team first created working architectural drawings and then devised glass fiber-optic lighting that would answer all the needs of the prototype exhibit selected. Because of its size and the irregular construction, which did not allow clear passage for the light guides, the drawing for the room was divided into four quarters. This method facilitated balancing the number of tails from each light source. Proprietary flickering glass fiber-optic eighteenth-century beeswax candles completed the design. They give off a soft glow similar to real candlelight. All illumination was chosen to be very protective of the wood, textiles, and paintings, yet let the artifacts be seen. Sufficient ambient light from a grid of tiny adjustable downlights in the ceiling provides a guiding path through each setting. In addition to this low-level ambient light, slightly brighter highlights played on the carvings on furniture, the fireplace garniture, the oil-on-wood portraits, and the eighteenth-century hand-painted playing cards. Separate projectors powered the candles in the central metal chandelier and candlesticks dispersed around the room. To eliminate "black holes," the imitation windows were also gently lit.

The two foyer entrances to this room also had to have improved illumination. One contained miniature furniture samples that were suffering under very hot incandescent lights. A collection of china, which could withstand the heat, was displayed in the other foyer, but not adequately lit. The capacity of the projectors was enough to include tails to take care of these spaces, too.

The entire project took four 150-watt metal halide light sources for the sizes 7 and 12 glass tails, and two 50-watt tungsten units for the candles.

A VITRINE IN A MUSEUM[49]

The entrance to this museum's important Oriental galleries had a large show window at one side. It contained an elegant Japanese paper screen behind a low table with a teapot on top of it. Conservation light level was necessary. Unfamiliar with glass fiber-optic display lighting, the curious director wanted to try a small pilot project. A 150-watt metal halide light source was positioned in the dropped ceiling above the display case to power 12 glass tails with adjustable spotlights. To conceal the tails, the ingenious exhibit staff built baffles similar to a picture frame that was painted to match the marble surround. Although this was their first attempt at glass fiber optics, the team of five worked well together, each contributing ideas. Cooperation of the curators and conservators, as well as the inventive exhibit staff, arrived at a conclusion satisfactory to all. It was left to the carpenter to do the focusing, and he did an exceptional job.

Initially, six tails were positioned on either side, providing even light on the background screen and highlights for the table and teapot. Getting bolder, the exhibit team experimented with putting two tails in the ceiling, two in the floor playing up on the table, three on either side for the screen, and two on the side for the ends of the table. This would enable them to eliminate the original yellowish ceiling incandescent light altogether. The only other detail was to put a glass dichroic color filter into the light source to counteract the effect of the ¼-in-thick green-tinted case glass, which somewhat dulled the vibrant colors of the display.

Under the single incandescent light in the case, what had looked like a black table and a monochromatic screen, turned out to be a dark red lacquer table with mother-of-pearl inlay, and a multicolor screen with red, white, and flesh tones, none of which had ever been noticed before. The change was remarkable (see Fig. 6-38). Seeing what this different illumination can do has been an incentive for the

Fig. 6-38 Sample lighting in vitrine at the Nelson-Atkins Museum, Kansas City, MO.

institution to seek funds for upgrading the lighting for the entire museum.

ENTRANCE TO HISTORIC MUSEUM

The 24-ft-wide entrance lobby to a monumental museum needed improved lighting. Within the past few years, at least three unsuccessful versions had been tried to attract more visitors and reduce maintenance in this large space. Along with even illumination requested for the vaulted ceiling, there was also a portable easel announcing the day's events at the entrance to the main staircase. This needed a bright directional beam.

The fiber-optic consultant suggested that the light sources be mounted and concealed on top of the wooden construction just beyond the entrance doors. The size-36 and -48 glass tails would be directed toward the vaulted ceiling; the size 96 would go the distance leading into the main staircase. Equipment included four 150-watt metal halide illuminators with glass color filters to recreate the historic light level. The two outside projectors served two glass harnesses with size-36 and -96 tails. The inner two light sources took care of the two harness with size-48 and -96 glass tails. An additional light guide was aimed at the changing notice board. A sudden change in administration put the project on hold.

COSTUME EXHIBIT AND ASSOCIATED CASES[50]

Light levels for costume exhibits are determined by the age of the textiles. Of course, it is not the intention to allow illumination to fade reproduction fabrics either, but the older garments must certainly be protected to extend their lives as long as possible. For this private museum, in addition to the costumes used in a movie, other artifacts pertaining to the making of that film were displayed in cases on the floor below.

Ideally, the projectors should be housed within the top section of the cases and the adjustable downlighters also fitted into this section. The back of the case should have a louvered panel, and there should be an access hatch for lamp changes when required. However, the physical layout did not permit this, and the light sources had to be put in the bottom of the cases, requiring longer tails which added to the cost. There was the added danger of heat making its way up to the objects, if the case separations were not sound.

The cases required controlled environment. The sealing of the cabinet should be left to the cabinetmakers. The downlighters should be mounted in an artificial void (a double skin) within the case to retain the integrity of the environment during maintenance. A resealable door should be provided for access for changing exhibits to protect the remaining objects from varying temperature/humidity levels during case rearrangement. As usual, the fittings are installed so as not to be seen by the viewer. A preliminary estimate for case lighting was submitted without knowing what objects would be shown. It was later learned that items ranged from three-dimensional metal statues to paper scripts and other ephemera. One of the stumbling blocks was the existence of 250-W floodlights playing on pictures and graphics on the walls above the cases. To counteract this high light level, it would have been necessary to increase the size of the tails serving below to an unacceptable intensity and cost. Eventually, the client was convinced that the illumination in the area should have universally lowered levels, so that both the material above and the cabinets below could be lit with the same light sources, to be easily visible. New quotations were prepared as additional cases and lighting effects were added. The complexity of this task can be seen from the list of display cases to be lit.

Display Cases:

First floor: three 8-ft cases made from 2 × 4 ft units fitted together

2, 7-ft cases

1 raked case 20 ft long × 24 in deep (18 in high in back; 5 in high in front)

2 cases 4 ft w × 6 ft h × 1 ft d

1 case 4 ft d × 12 ft w × 6 ft h - in high light level space

Second floor: two 8-ft cases made from 2 × 4 ft units fitted together.

2, 7-ft cases.

1, 6 ft h × 12 ft w × 18 in d

1, 6 ft h × 9 ft w × 24 in d with translucent shelves

Months went by and still no one decided what items were to be put into the cases. Lighting three-dimensional metal figures is quite different from papers laid flat on the case floor, or textiles propped up on a slant. Lacking any details on the contents, providing an even light with a few spare tails for directional accents, appeared the only answer.

The Costume Room:

The projectors for this segment were to be housed in the ceiling void above the room where they could be reached (see Fig. 6-39). The lighting would all be from the ceiling level with adjustable fittings. Special effects pertaining to the objects were requested:

1. *To provide atmospheric background wall color:* Two 150-W metal halide projectors with four-color dichroic wheel and motor drive were used to produce the colors blue, purple, grey, and deep blue/purple.

2. *For individual sequential lighting of each of 10 figures:* To provide maximum variation and control of this dramatic lighting in the simplest mode, 75-W MR16 tungsten halogen sources with 3000-hour lamp life were chosen. The MR16 lamp is readily available everywhere. The sequential operation will not exhaust these lamps as quickly as the metal halides in the display cases, which will be on continuously throughout the day. Equipment included ten 12-V 75-W tungsten halogen projectors with HF (high-frequency) electronic transformer (for smooth transition of lighting up and down). There was one controller with variable on and off timed to switch each projector as required. The times can be automatically set to suit the exhibit. The device will also contain a detector to avoid operation when there are no visitors.

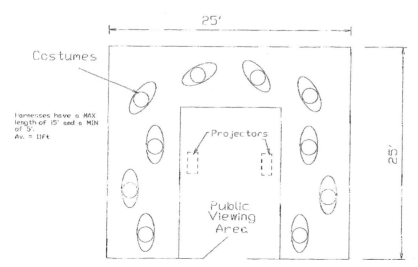

Fig. 6-39 Preliminary sketch for costume display.

Obviously, with this level of sophisticated illumination, mock-ups should definitely be done. However, with only a few weeks before opening (and the cabinets yet to be fabricated and the objects not yet selected for inclusion in them), this did not happen. Indecision was the obstacle to creating striking lighting effects. This certainly was not the fault of the exhibit designer, the lighting people, or the curators. The client was simply too busy to instruct the team. After all, it was his money being spent and his possessions not being shown to their best advantage.

- A museum wanted to eliminate the labor-intensive lamp replacement in the high ceiling of its changing exhibit space. It also wanted to reduce the oppressive electricity bills (see Fig. 6-40).

- The following is an example of a Danish firm[51] that has been supplying glass fiber optics for the past 30 years (see Fig. 6-41).

LIGHTING ARMOR

Because of its sheen, armor used to be difficult to light directly. It had to be surrounded by luminous surfaces. If daylight were not available to reflect off the walls, ceiling uplighting usually had to be provided to fall down on it. The following examples are of two museums, 4000 miles apart, which independently came to the same conclusions to use fiber optics, even if they spell the word armor/armour differently. Note that both plastic and glass versions were tried in the second location.

Royal Armouries Museum, Leeds, England:[52]

This is the largest new museum built in Europe in the twentieth century. The company making the display cases has successfully employed glass fiber optics throughout this massive five-story structure for all cases, freestanding exhibits on the floor, and dramatic center-floor tableaux. The fittings used were surface mounted because they afforded more flexibility than the flush type, which do look neater. However, the designer felt they might have been hidden by mullions or a "picture frame" surround (see Fig. 6-42).

The Detroit Institute of Arts, Detroit, Michigan:[53]

The armor cases were designed in house, and custom fabricated by a local millwork shop. They are constructed principally of clear tempered glass and wood and are movable by means of concealed casters. A variety of schemes were explored, including toplighting, uplighting and sidelighting. After seeing the mock-ups, toplighting was selected. Uplighting produced

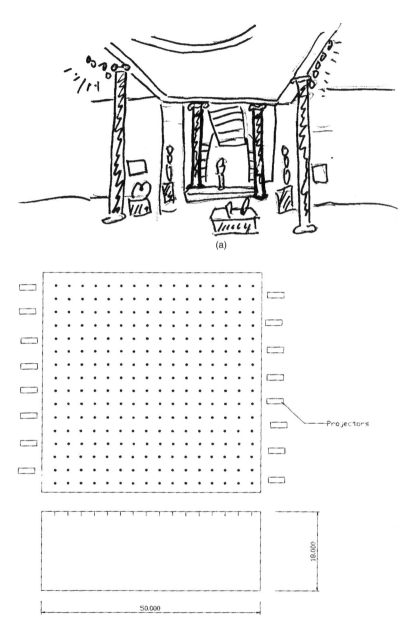

(a)

(b)

Fig. 6-40 (a) Rough sketch of entrance to changing exhibit room. (b) Drawing showing grid lighting on 3-ft (l-m) centers to provide very flexible illumination for all types of objects.

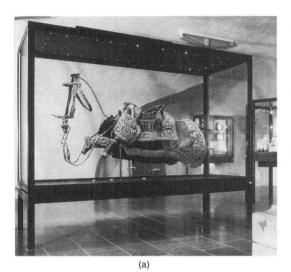

(a)   (b)

Fig. 6-41 (a & b) Glass fiber optics at Rosenborg Castle, Copenhagen, Denmark.

an unnatural effect, while sidelighting from the corners was visually distracting when the armor was viewed from the side (see Fig. 6-43).

For desired color rendition, a light source was selected using glass fiber-optics with a 3000°K metal halide lamp. Initially, the projector was going to be housed in the base of the case. However, two issues led to placing the unit in the 'light attic'. First, the projector required ventilation to dissipate its heat. Placing the unit on top naturally aided the convection. Secondly, by placing the unit above, shorter glass tails could be used, substantially reducing cost.

Lenses were used to focus the light onto the armor. The fiber-optic lighting illuminates the artifact and its workmanship, complementing the abundant daylight which fills the Great Hall. This illumination also renders the collection effectively during evening hours.

For the Arms Case, wishing for further experimentation with fiber-optics, and addressing the problem of multiple objects to be exhibited, it was decided to use a different yet complementary lighting approach. Since the objects would be viewed only from the front, sidelighting could be used along with toplighting. Working closely with the fiber-optics lighting system manufacturer, a concept of a proscenium was developed after exploring various approaches. This enabled effective toplighting combined with sidelighting, utilizing a standard extruded aluminum corner track section welded into an inverted U-shaped configuration. This provided the housing for both the plastic fiber bundles and fixtures.

For this portion of the work, use of reels of plastic fiber, rather than the completely assembled glass harnesses, were chosen in anticipation of

(a)

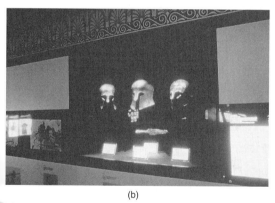

(b)

Fig. 6-42 Royal Armouries Museum in Leeds, England. (a) Rows of cases. (b) Dramatic display of helmets.

unforeseen conditions of installation, even though the case was fully designed in advance. Its limitations, in addition to having to cut and splice the tails on site, were the bending radius capability for concealing within casework, and its ultimate brittleness. Both materials need to be evaluated from long term and initial cost perspectives.

A MR16 tungsten lamp was the light source here, with a significant difference in lower lamp life (about 20% of metal halide). However, maintenance for this exhibit is relatively simple since the illuminator is housed in the base. The fixtures provide excellent flexibility for individual focusing and dimming capabilities.

LIGHTING IVORY[54]

Ivory is one of the most fugitive organic materials. For a special exhibit of medieval carvings, glass fiber optics was selected because it could provide the clearest light, even at conservation level (see Fig. 6-44).

(c)

(d)

Fig. 6-42 (Continued) (c) Life-sized mounted armoured knight. (d) Cases of armour at Leeds.

Fig. 6-44 Special ivory exhibit at Detroit Institute of Art.

Fig. 6-43 Armor at the Detroit Institute of Art.

EDGE-LIGHTING GLASS PORTRAITS

Although they were very inexpensive, the existing fluorescent tubes proved very unsatisfactory for edge-lighting glass portraits, so another method was sought. The sketched plan shows 36 of these to be staggered and back-to-back (see Fig. 6-45). The light sources could be housed on the top of the displays. One light source could supply six portraits, with five glass tails per picture. The assumption is that there will be, or is already, a fitting to hold the fibers tight onto the glass in the correct position. The fiber must be actually touching the edge of the glass. If there is an air gap, the effect will be diminished considerably, which happens whenever light rays have to go through more than one medium. The edges that glow must be occluded (ground, etched, or sandblasted). Equipment included six 150-watt metal halide projectors with six 30-tail S12 glass harnesses (see Fig. 6-46).

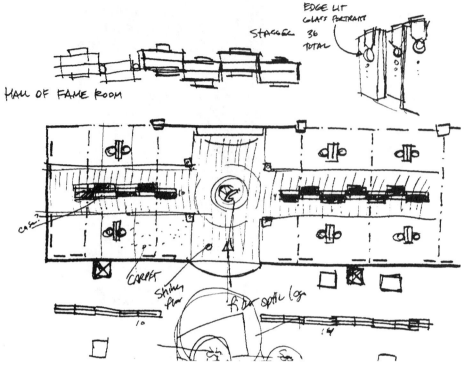

Fig. 6-45 Preliminary sketch for 36 edge-lit portraits. Courtesy of Fricker Studio.

A DOUBLE-SIDED PAINTING

In a large ultramodern hospital, the project was to light a 3½-ft-square double-sided Victorian oil painting in the mini-museum lobby situated in front of a three-sided seating area (see Fig. 6-47). The 42-in-high wooden base supporting the 74-in-high case containing the picture was right in the

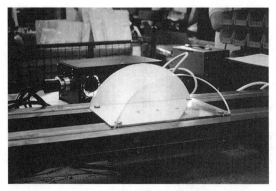

Fig. 6-46 Factory test for edge-lighting for a Durban, South Africa hotel. Courtesy of Flair Lighting, UK.

path of large double doors and presented a hazard as people rushed in and out. It had been put at a 45° angle to avoid collisions, but you would almost think it was positioned to fill the accident ward. The architect rejected conventional lighting outside the case because of the glare. He also did not want to channel out the terrazzo floor for power nor did he want exposed wiring coming down from the ceiling and entering the enclosure.

Also, coming up from the base would not be acceptable because there would be no mullions

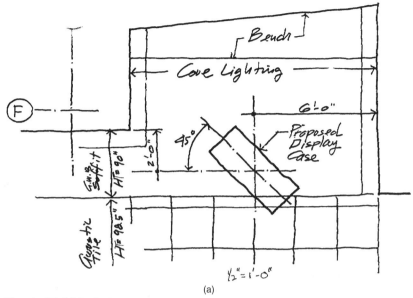

Bench

Cove Lighting

F

45°

6'-0"

Proposed
Display
Case

2'-0"

H = 90"
Gin. Soffit

H = 98.5"
Gypsum Tile

½" = 1'-0"

(a)

Fig. 6-47 (a) Preliminary sketch for double-sided painting.

in the painting's protective Plexiglas. At one point, he was thinking of changing to real glass and then putting a UV (ultraviolet) film on the glass, because sunlight streams into this glass building, flooding the founder's portrait with color-fading rays.

The alcove with the three sides of benches was lit with large hot down-lights and harsh cove lighting of a different color. The surrounding windows and the encircling cove lighting presented considerable competition to the illumination of future picture exhibitions in that space. There was also a lot of reflection from the stainless steel/glass staircase immediately in front of the double painting. The mock-up on-site was done in the presence of an audience of doctors, administrators, architects, and construction people. As usual, there were more opinions than people, but a consensus was arrived at eventually.

Two size-48 glass tails positioned on either side of the painting would eliminate glare from the shiny surface. The light comes from adjustable downlights in the dropped ceiling above, where the light source is located equidistant above the ceiling between the painting and the bench wall. To light future paintings to be displayed on the wall above the back bench, additional tails were arrayed to cover the top, middle, and bottom of the space. They were fitted with circular plate and ball units to ensure com-

(b)

Fig. 6-47 (Continued) (b) Exhibit space behind painting.

plete flexibility when the as-yet-unknown wall art arrives. A few downlights over the bench for ambient light were also provided.

Hint: If frames for paintings are deep or ornate, the light on them will have to be arranged so that the art itself is not hidden in shadow created by the higher surround. Solving one problem (hot spots resulting from shiny surfaces that occur with oil paintings, or photographs covered with reflecting glass) by sidelighting, may create another. That is where light will hit the side of the frame, and not the material below it. Here is where experimentation with various techniques is essential.

Playgrounds[55]

A 20-ft-long concrete Chinese dragon composed of three parts was a playground element. The separate pieces of concrete appear to be undulating through the grass, although they only show just the humps of the tail above grade. Concerned with maintenance and safety for the children, the designer wanted size-12 glass fiber optics for the eyes, nostrils, and open mouth of the 4-ft head. Vandal-proof lenses and a concealed light source and harness kept the object in operation, while being safe for children to touch, even on wet ground. The light source could be installed below grade.

Bridges

LIGHTING A BRIDGE ACROSS THE THAMES RIVER, LONDON, ENGLAND[56]

After trying several different types of illumination, the problem of vandalism of the components lighting the pedestrian walk persisted (see Fig. 6-

48). Finally, glass fiber optics was tried. 150-watt metal halide projectors in weatherproof enclosures were slung under the bridge structure. Glass tails with lens assemblies were mounted 100 mm (4 in) above the deck of the bridge. These were manufactured in marine-grade stainless steel with half-frosted lenses, to allow the observer to actually see the source of the light as well as to produce the visual architectural feature of a fan-shaped beam to illuminate the deck. The glass harness lengths are up to 12 m long. The harnesses also have marine stainless steel ferrules to avoid any possible galvanic action. The light sources are mounted under the bridge, out of sight of vandals. Even if prospective miscreants knew where the projectors were located, they would have to be in a boat in the middle of the river and extend a two-story ladder to reach them.

Since the bridge opens to allow small craft to pass though, this presented further complications to the design of the lighting system. The same manufacturer designed and fabricated the motor controller system for the moving section of the bridge as well as specifying the floodlighting and installing all the lighting, fiber optics, and electrical equipment.

Fig. 6-48 Vandal-proof lighting on a bridge over the Thames at Docklands, London, England.

Hospitals

A hospital wanted special lighting to direct patients to the treatment areas. There are two sections required, one ribbon of light approximately 30 ft long and the other approximately 60 ft long. The arrows would each consist of 10 end-emitting glass tails and would be spaced at approximately 4-ft centers. End-emitting fiber is used to provide a brighter light than side-emitting can provide. A static color filter would help to see the arrows more clearly against a light colored ceiling, which has other luminaires on it. Using the following tail lengths, projectors are to be placed in a central spot above the ceiling. Employing three 75-watt tungsten light sources, there would be one 60-tail size-1 glass harness, and two with 75 tails (see Fig. 6-49). This directional lighting was safe and very low maintenance.

Houses of Worship

Stained glass and the art and architectural features of the interior and exterior of religious institutions are now being lit with long-lasting glass fiber optics. Existing decorative chandeliers can also be retrofit to include unobtrusive downlights for reading the prayer books. Specialist architects and lighting designers should be employed to ensure that the congregation is getting the most for its money. Volunteer designers

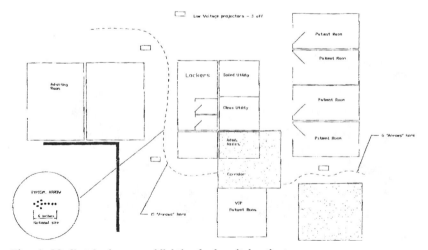

Fig. 6-49 Sketch of proposed lighting for hospital patients.

(a)

would do better to donate money rather than services for this technical type of work.

NANTES CATHEDRAL, FRANCE[57]

An ambitious lighting project for ten of Nantes' principal buildings and monuments was developed, with the cathedral as the centerpiece (see Fig. 6-50). The plan called for key city sites to be illuminated with a blue light, the shade of which would change with the rise and fall of the tide in the Loire basin. The task had proved relatively simple for other edifices, where traditional floodlighting provided a dramatic effect. But the cathedral posed special problems of its own. For centuries, the church's rich architectural detail had been all but invisible to the passing visitor. Most statues were located far too high on the structure to be fully appreciated,

(b)

Fig. 6-50 (a & b) Cathedral at Nantes, France.

and tended to blend in with the color of the façade. How could the dozens of architectural details be highlighted without overdoing the final effect? And how could the city's color system be used on such a huge scale without sending costs soaring higher than the cathedral's spires? Again, the solution was fiber-optics.

Working with the designer to establish the most efficient routes for the tails, the engineering team mapped out the cathedral façade section by section, dividing it into 80 areas that contain over 1,900 points of illumination. Each area is provided with a separate set of light guides, with 9 to 48 tails per harness, depending on the number of statues to be lit. Each light source is equipped with 4 electronically controlled color filters and protected with a custom-designed forced-air cooling system. A metal halide lamp was used with 13,500 lumens, 5900° K, CRI > 80.

The large number of projectors necessary to power the system could not be placed inside the building itself. Instead, they were put fully accessible in weatherproofed cases located on the exterior gangways. The tails' sheathing is galvanized steel. Using an optical train of glass lenses, the engineers tapped into the beam of each fiber at an angle almost parallel to the light flow, avoiding the need to adjust the position of each fixture, simplifying the maintenance of the equipment and reducing the dispersion of light between projectors.

A SMALL RELIGIOUS CENTER[58]

Problem:

In an auditorium of about 33 × 53 ft with a dropped ceiling height of 9 ft, there is a 2-ft space between the dropped ceiling height of 9 ft and the original one. There are currently 400 lineal feet of glaring fluorescent tubing, which makes it difficult to see. At some times, there are only 55 seats on the floor, but the total number could be as many as 70. Since everyone attending the meetings spends much time reading small print, comfortable lighting assists the learning process.

Solution:

Seventy-two lighting points were proposed for the reading/seating area, with 54 having different specifications for the surrounding areas (see Fig. 6-51). Note that this system will not throw any light onto the ceiling, unless the walls/floors are highly reflective. Low-power uplighters (by others) fitted on the walls are recommended to "lift" the ceiling. Only about 10 auxiliary units are needed in all.

The calculations show that each lighting point will provide approximately 740 lux (74 footcandles) onto the seat of the chairs. The lighting

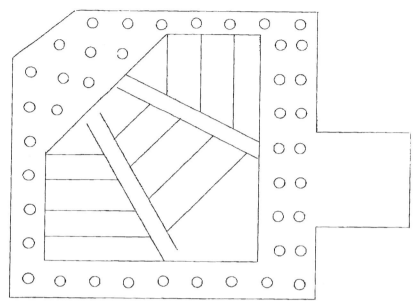

Over the seating/reading area there would be 72 lighting points fed by 18 light sources.

Over the rest of the area there would be the fittings as shown, with different lenses to produce a lower light level.

The ceiling will appear very dark with this system we would recommend the use of some low power uplighters on the walls to "lift" the ceiling

Fig. 6-51 Preliminary sketch of church space.

around the outer areas will be between 100 and 120 lux, plus any contribution from the wall-mounted uplighters.

In addition to glare-proof illumination, maintenance will be reduced to replacing a few lamps. Energy savings will be considerable, with fewer lamps running and at a cool temperature that does not add to the ventilating/air conditioning load.

Equipment for seating/reading area:

18, 150-watt metal halide projectors

18, 4-tail S36 glass harnesses

72 white lens holders and lenses

Equipment for surrounding areas:

9, 150-watt metal halide projectors

9, 6-tail S30 glass harnesses

54 white lens holders and lenses

A VICTORIAN CHURCH

Problem:

Conventional lighting was intended for this church refurbishing, unless access or maintenance demanded fiber optics. The elaborately stenciled interior had handsome original brass chandeliers that gave too little light for the parishioners to see their hymnals. Maintenance was particularly difficult because of the sloped flooring. The architect was loath to break into the original fabric of the ceiling to install winches. There was plenty of space in the attic above to house the illuminators. Because there were seven spheres interspersed with the strapwork ornament on the stems of these combination gas/electric fixtures (see Fig. 6-52), bringing the glass fiber-optic tails down 22 ft from the ceiling unobtrusively was not the best choice.

Solution:

At first, an auxiliary black conduit enclosing the glass fiber-optic tails was considered, but that would be too visible and interfere with the reflectivity of the globes. A flexible pipe finished to match the metal was then suggested and rejected. Finally, the concept of concealing the light sources within the chandeliers was recognized as the most practical solution. Even with the addition of winches to lower them for relamping, the very short tails required made this combination of systems affordable.

The compact 100-watt metal halide illuminator would give additional punch to the high ceilings, yet take up little space hidden within the arms of the combination gas/electric fixture. Each "kit" was composed of two light sources with one 18-tail S18 glass harness for the gas portion, and one 18-tail S4 harness for the candles. Eighteen lenses concentrated the light where needed. Once the "how" was resolved, the lighting designer asked for additional tails for uplighting the ceiling, and additional downlights.

In addition, they wanted to light up the vaulted ceiling, which was also inaccessible for relamping. Here, long-length side-emitting fiber was suggested to supply a gentle glow. The dome had side-emitting fiber tucked behind the cornice, powered by another 100-watt metal halide projector. The difficult maintenance had been corrected, and the

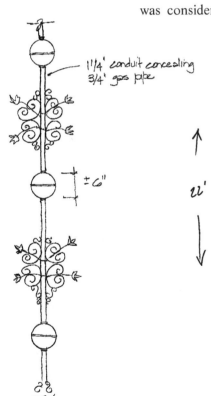

1¼" conduit concealing
3/4" gas pipe

± 6"

22'

Fig. 6-52 Detail of church chandelier.

electricity bill was considerably lessened. Best of all, the churchgoers could see to read and appreciate the beautifully painted interior.

TWO METHODS OF LIGHTING TAPESTRIES

With Glass Fiber Optics: A Nineteenth-Century Church

1. *The narthex tapestries* (20 × 12 ft). Two tapestries are hung facing each other on either side of the space. The distances required to project the light are considerable, however, using 8 × 13° lenses per tapestry, four from the balcony and four from the top of the wood screen, the calculations show an average level of 90 to 110 lux over the area of each tapestry.

   The harnesses can be very short, and the lens holders are a simple variation of a standard type with a saddle bracket to enable adjustment in two planes. Equipment was four 150-watt metal halide projectors with 4-tail size-36 glass tails. Lens holders with 13° lenses were used (see Fig. 6-53).

2. *Church library tapestry* (9 ft 2 in × 8 ft 1 in). There is no problem lighting this tapestry other than the location of the light source and the harness/lenses. The library section shows a castellated ceiling detail. The scale shows that a light source/harness/lens combination could be housed inside one of these sections. Equipment was one-150 watt metal halide illuminator with 4-tail size 36 harness plus 13° lenses.

Schools and Universities

- An early twentieth-century college wanted to update the main building. There were existing pendant incandescent fixtures in the main corridor where important paintings were hung. A more unified color in the area could be presented if the lighting for the paintings and the hallway were from the same source. Using glass fiber optics to retrofit the existing hall chandeliers could accomplish this and reduce maintenance and energy costs. Using a 26° lens with ten size-12 glass tails would give an average light level of 70 lux at floor level (140 lux at 3 ft above the floor).

   Three 150-watt metal halide light sources could provide lighting on the 12 paintings and the hallway. If it proved to be too expensive to break into the ceiling to locate the projectors in the attic space

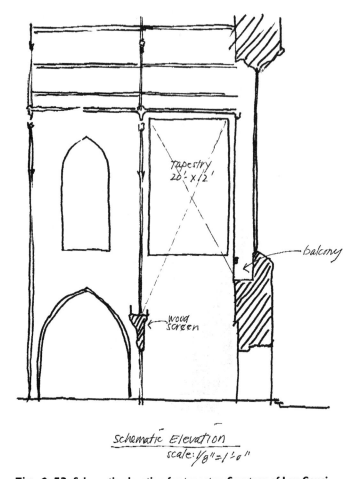

Fig. 6-53 Schematic elevation for tapestry. Courtesy of Lou Gauci.

above, the projectors could be disguised with a GRP (glass reinforced plaster) molding to simulate stonework. This would enable them to be surface mounted but unobtrusive and vandal proof. In the high ceiling, 1-in downlighters take care of the ambient hall light, while 26 adjustable eyeball fittings play on the artwork. The client was also interested in installing glass fiber-optic baseboard emergency lighting.

- Schoolrooms and laboratories need specific task lighting for reading and working. Long-lasting glass fiber optics would be very useful for these purposes.

Water Features

This segment includes pools, fountains, waterfalls, and aquariums for institutional, commercial, and residential use.

Fountains

SEA HORSE FOUNTAIN, KANSAS CITY, MISSOURI[59]

Problem:

This massive sculpture (see Fig. 6-54) was brought from Italy at the turn of the century by the visionary developer, J. C. Nichols, who created Country Club Plaza, the United States' first shopping center in Kansas City, Missouri. Age and deterioration necessitated new lighting within the varied parameters set by the city and the environmental conditions. The design of the 100-ft-diameter fountain matched the original, but the materials were different, exchanging marble for sandstone with a limestone surround.

Fig. 6-54 The Sea Horse fountain, Country Club Plaza, Kansas City, MO.

The fountain, surrounded by grass, is within a traffic circle on a major street. In addition to satisfying local electrical codes and safety standards regarding placement of fixtures near water, the city did not allow any lighting equipment to be installed in the grassy areas, thus eliminating use of pole-mounted fixtures. Burial units also had to be avoided because of the potential glare distracting drivers. Sources had to be low-brightness, well-concealed, and require low maintenance.

Solution:

The lighting designer devised a system incorporating low-voltage incandescent units and fiber optics. The low-voltage sources, which are a specific type required by the city in public spaces, have been placed in the fountain foundation to highlight the beginning, middle, and end of water arcs, bubble jets, the central sculpture base, and the sea horse statues. Plastic fiber-optic cables illuminated with amber-filtered metal halide sources housed in concealed illuminators, highlight sculpture details and the 316-in outer perimeter of the fountain.

The projectors are concealed in a preexisting main vault on the south side, and in three added custom-designed smaller satellite vaults on the north, east, and west sides. The main vault houses five light sources to light the sculptures, and two for the wall. The three smaller flange-type vaults are watertight and can withstand heavy truck weight. They contain two 150-watt or one 400-watt illuminator.

Because the light sources need ventilation to dissipate the heat produced by them, 6-in-diameter conduits have been installed to connect the main vault to the satellites. Cooling air, 250 CFM, is blown from the main vault through the conduits and boosted from vault to vault by minifans at each vault. The underground air tubes also help to act as air-cooling tubes. Corings allow water and fiber-optic cables into the sea horses; the lower bowl (six cables), the upper bowl (three cables), and one cable to the dolphin's mouth held by the cherub at the top. Two bundles of fiber optics are run around the outside perimeter of the fountain to graze the irregular set stones of the surround, so if one lamp in an illuminator burns out, the second strand, connected to the second illuminator in each small vault remains intact and produces half light.

The two 50-strand fiber cables (two per illuminator) exit the vaults through 2-in copper conduit; enter the inside of the pool, are run up the wall, back through the wall above water line, and trace the perimeter wall under the perimeter lip to the next vault.

An interesting detail concerns the mounting of the fiber-optic cables underneath the stone ledge around the perimeter. Since the unevenness of the stones creates a bright spot in the cable wherever there is a gap between the cable and the stone surface, a 1½-in-wide sheet metal lip has been mounted beneath the stone ledge and in front of the cable to conceal it, so that only the soft grazing effect is visible. The metal strip has been painted to look like the stones.

Aquariums

There is a big business in making aquariums for doctors' offices, airports, restaurants, etc., as well as for large institutional displays. According to one ichthyologist, light emissions directly from fiber must be in excess of

15,000 lux for exotic fish. Lighting must penetrate water to provide intensities of 15,000 lux for the first 4 to 8 inches, 12,000 lux down to 12 to 15
inches, and 10,000 lux down to 24 inches. Other details are:

Water specific gravity = 1.021 to 1.024

Average temperature = 76 to 80°F

Bulbs must emit light with color temperature of +5000 K with CRI =
92+. The fish expect bluish light. For example, a 150-gallon tank (7×20 ft $\times$
24 in) would require 50,000 lumen output (standard halide) over the entire
surface area. All materials must be made of inert, nontoxic materials, which
are totally noncorrosive. All light guides must be able to bend 90°.

For a normal 5-ft tank, a minimum of two conventional metal halide
pendant fixtures would be used above the container, with lamp height 1 to
2 in from the top of the water surface. Employing glass fiber optics, the
inert tails can be placed right in the water, dispensing with intensive maintenance and the danger of the electric lights falling into the water.

A LARGE AQUARIUM, TERMINAL 3, HEATHROW AIRPORT, LONDON[60]

The tropical fish are quite happy and thriving in the tank lit with glass fiber
optics, and they provide a great attraction for travelers. The color wheel is
linked to a timer that alters the color of the light depending on the time of
day. This essentially simulates the color of the light the fish would experience in their natural habitat.

For some reason, quantities of low-iron glass (clear, as opposed to green-
ish tint) are not available in the United States. It is the material of choice for
expansive panes in large-scale aquatic displays, because it transmits the light
better than acrylic and, thus, is more energy efficient. It is also more resistant
to being scratched by sharks and other huge inhabitants of the tanks.

Waterfalls

WATERFALL AND CHANNEL[61]

A water channel emerging from a waterfall in a city zoo had to be lit. Considerations included safety for curious children and the possibility of vandalism. In winter there would be snow on the ground, which might seep
into pits containing the light sources. Having had prior experience with
turbulent waters under waterfalls, the designer evolved an ingenious plan
(see Fig. 6-55). Equipment included:

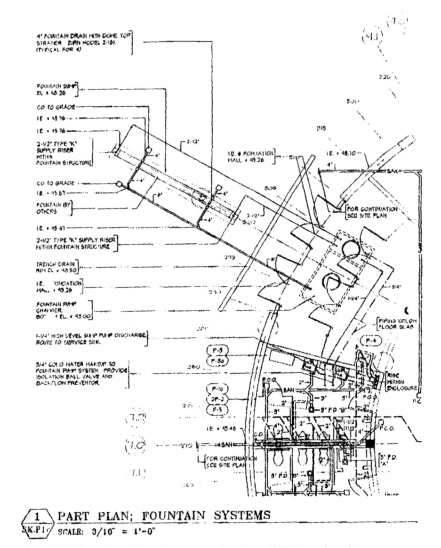

Fig. 6-55 Part plan of fountain systems. Courtesy of Wilkinson Associates.

3, 150-watt metal halide projectors 120 volt for external/damp conditions

1, 8-tail S48 glass harness, diameter of each tail = 8.0 mm

1, 10-tail S36 glass harness, diameter of each tail = 6.6 mm

1, 10-tail S 24 glass harness, diameter of each tail = 5.56 mm + 5 × S12 @ 3-m diameter of each tail = 4.03 mm

All threaded tail ferrules in marine-grade stainless steel

18 stainless steel lens holders with frosted lens to diffuse light

The 2-in conduits leading from each of the projectors will be large enough for each of the three harnesses. They should be as short as possible for ease of pull. The ends in the waterfall itself are marine-grade stainless steel with glass lenses. They will resist a reasonable amount of vandalism. The frosted lenses will not need focusing; however, the waterproof membrane needs to be protected.

There are a variety of accessories that are used to protect the integrity of waterproof membranes. For the lens holders specified, it would be necessary to know how each fiber penetrates the base of the waterfall. Puddle flanges with stainless steel couplers will accept the waterproof connectors, which allow for lens holders to be removed without allowing water to penetrate the membrane. These are more expensive but will prevent vandals from causing any serious damage. Before pouring concrete, all necessary preliminary work has to be done so that the final installation will be as simple as possible (i.e., placing the projectors in the pit, drawing the tails through the conduit, sealing the bottom of the trough; and providing the ventilation).

Please see Appendix E for method of determining the size of conduit to encase the fiber optics.

Pools

RESIDENTIAL INDOOR POOL[62]

The owner of an indoor pool $100 \times 60 \times 16$ ft high, with a 5-ft Jacuzzi™ jet at one end, requested "spectacular" lighting. The design professional did not indicate where the light sources could be located, so the assumption was below the floor at the end of the room for the main pool lighting, and the Jacuzzi™ projector at the other end, again below the floor. If the projectors could be located closer to the pool, below the floor, the tails would be shorter and the cost, less. Continuous and static color changes and "sparkle" within the water were added.

The client wanted decorative light over part or all of the pool area. When water is still, the surface reflects the ceiling lighting for a dazzling effect, particularly at night. These light sources can be located at the edge of the pool in the ceiling void for easy maintenance. Color and sparkle wheels can also be fitted if desired.

Equipment for main pool lighting:

2, 150-W metal halide light sources

2, 5-tail S48 glass harnesses with 316 stainless steel ferrules

10 pool lighting accessories

Equipment for Jacuzzi™:

1, 150-W metal halide light source

1, 8-tail S24 harness with 316 stainless steel ferrules

18 stainless steel lens holders c/w lenses

Equipment for 20 × 20 ft starlight ceiling over water:

1, 150-W metal halide light source with motor drive and sparkle wheel

1, 400-tail S1C harness with fittings

A FREE-STANDING POOL HOUSE

Although a similar application to the one above, by using the new 100-watt metal halide light source, the size of the tails could be reduced.

- Lighting inside the pool:

    4, 100-watt projectors with 4-color wheel (nonsynchronized).

    4, 4-tail S36 glass harnesses

    16 pool lights

- Lighting inside the hot tub:

    1, 100-watt projector as above

    1, 6-tail S24 glass harness

    6 pool lights

- Ambient lighting over pool and hot tub:

    8, 100-watt projectors—white light

    8, 10-tail S24 harnesses

    80 lenses

- Ambient lighting over seating area:

    3, 100-watt projectors—white light

    3, 10-tail S24 harnesses with adjustable lenses

SECTION 3. RESIDENTIAL

As with all construction, people doing residential fiber optics must be ready to react quickly to unexpected changes. Within four weeks, the character of one house interior changed abruptly from avant garde to early-nineteenth-century style, with an entirely different color scheme and feeling. Light levels and colors of light then had to agree with the new surroundings. With the addition of neutral density filters, dichroic glass color filters, and different lenses, this metamorphosis was accomplished.

AN APARTMENT[63]

Situated in a landmark early-twentieth-century building, this 15-room duplex flat has an interior more luxurious than the Doges Palace in Venice, from which it was copied. It is used exclusively for lavish entertaining. To enhance the valuable art collections and furnishings, the client wanted very discreet lighting that had excellent color rendition, yet would conserve the fugitive materials of textiles, paper, leather, lacquer, ivory, and wood.

Each time another treasure was brought in, additional glass fiber-optic lighting was devised for it. The details of the formerly dark vaulted coffered ceiling in the entrance hall can now be seen. One room contains two monumental inlaid seventeenth-century cabinets of museum quality, which are beautifully highlighted. The dressing rooms are lit to allow the garments' true colors to be seen. The grand staircase, lined with paintings, now has adequate illumination without glare. The main salon, hung with Old Masters and with rich cut-velvet upholstery on the furniture, has a light level suited to the Renaissance ambiance, yet everything can be easily viewed.

A guest bathroom suite has antiquities displayed amid ornamental painting, marble, and gold plumbing fittings. In fact, the sight of all this luxury is so startling, most people forget why they entered the room! The glass fiber optics was plastered into place and painted out, to be as inconspicuous as possible.

The dining room has a variety of light levels for various occasions. The food on the plate is quite visible, but the guests are not made uncomfortable by the overhead lighting. The fiber-optic task lighting in the library makes searching for a book, or reading one, a pleasure.

A 27-ROOM ART DECO HOUSE[64]

An electrical contractor who worked regularly for a private client wished to do something unusual in this 70-year-old house (see Fig. 6-56). Pre-

Fig. 6-56 Sketch of living room with items to be highlighted.

liminary steps included having the consultant/supplier photograph and accurately measure rooms and family paintings (including the depths of the frames) in the study, drawing room, library, and the vaulted hallway. During a mock-up, adding an extra glass tail to highlight parts of a Victorian scene of a couple picnicking alongside a lake with a steep bluff on the opposite shore, the owner suddenly noticed rocks under the water which he had never seen in the painting before. He was also amazed to see that the hill in the background became almost three-dimensional when the light guides were moved onto it in a certain way.

Both the rooms and the pieces of art are in very large scale. Multiple tails in sizes 36 and 48 glass are required to cover the areas and counteract all the daylight streaming in from the many windows. Although first requesting lighting for only two large paintings, the owner soon became interested in doing more. This included retrofitting the crystal chandeliers in the library and dining room, lighting two 3-shelf shell-shaped recessed cabinets, the large live tree in the living room, and the expansive black-and-white marble entrance. He was delighted that it was possible to dim the crystal chandelier in the dining room while keeping the paintings lit fully. In fact, he treated his discovery of glass fiber optics as a new toy and sought more and more ways to use it.

The main hall has a ceiling painted as sky. There are five vaulted sections that will be painted with murals. All is to be illuminated from the 3½-in ornamental cornice moldings. At last the owner saw the true colors of the sample murals. He had thought they were mostly brown under the old lighting, when they were really greens and blues.

Investigations were made for space on the second floor above the rooms to be lit. Closets and hallways provided locations for the light sources. A butler's pantry adjoining one of the principal rooms, and the top shelves of tall bookcases on either side of the drawing room, also offered convenient places for the projectors. The light sources for the two shell cabinets can be put in the bottom of each.

The small study had dark fabric walls and one small window, making the room quite dim. The work in this area entailed lighting the five paintings (two size 24 each on the larger ones, and one tail each on the two small ones), plus retrofitting the two wall sconces with size 4s. Also, lighting was added to the gun case in the vestibule entering this room. That light source will be in one corner in the floor above.

In this room, there were two existing table lamps with an unflattering yellow colored light, which should be replaced at least with compact fluorescents. The contrast between the clear white light from metal halide and that of the incandescents was very marked, and affected the color perceived in the paintings. The dingy lampshades needed to be changed too.

A MEDIA ROOM[65]

For a newly built residence, the client wanted a media room where he could entertain clients and friends watching sports events on film or television projected onto a wall-size motorized screen (see Fig. 6-57). For the two-level space, he wanted dimmable ambient light, which was not too bright. In addition, he wanted actual star constellations in the dark ceiling, which would be visible during the projection. The installer coordinated the existing dimming system with the light sources. Illuminators were concealed in the loft above the media room, allowing the shortest possible tails. Installation took three days.

This was only a secondary home and used just a few months a year. The interior designer preferred tungsten light and, since usage would be brief, it was decided to use 250-watt tungsten halogen light sources, even with the shorter lamp life. They were specially wired for dual voltage so that when dimming occurs, the fan motor continues to dissipate heat from

(a)

Fig. 6-57 Progress shots of installation of ambient and decorative light in a media room. Matt Cunniff, interior designer. (a) Searching for space above the ceiling.

the lamp. Controls for the ambient downlighting and the constellation were separate for complete flexibility.

- Ceiling downlighting:

    2, 250-watt tungsten halogen projectors

    1 harness of 17 size-12 glass tails

    1 harness of 16 size-12 glass tails

    33 adjustable miniature downlights arranged in a grid pattern

- Constellation:

    1, 250-watt tungsten halogen projector

    1 harness of 200 size-1 glass tails, average length 3.5 m

    200 bullet lenses

On his own, the electrician foreman took a celestial atlas and selected five star constellations that could be fashioned with the 200 tails available. Normally, the designer would have done a diagram; but in this case, the installer was allowed to express himself. He did a wonderful job.

Prior to the introduction of the fiber optics, another electrical contractor had put in large-diameter downlights in the ceiling. They were permanently turned off when the tiny fiber-optic miniature fittings were installed, because sufficient light levels were obtained from them alone.

ENTRANCE HALL

This new, large ultramodern residence contains an entry with a domed skylight. The staircase lighting will be done by glass fiber-optic fittings placed at the 10-ft height above the balcony, in between the luminous glass panels around the edge of the dome. The illumination for the walls of the dome can also be performed from the same area, but, of course, facing upward. The 24 glass fibers are behind the luminous glass panels, with

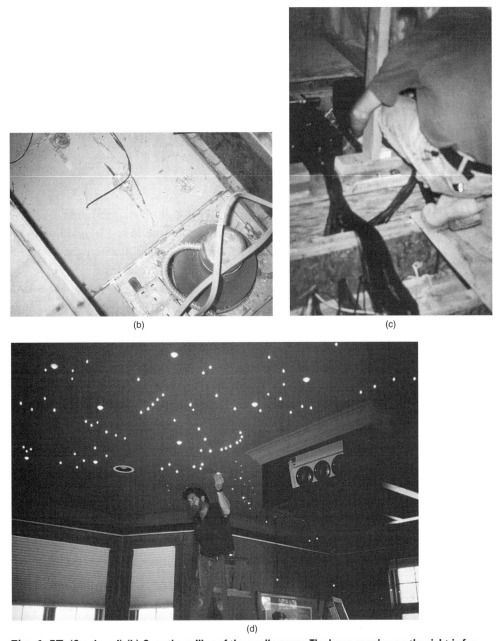

Fig. 6-57 (Continued) (b) Over the ceiling of the media room: The large opening on the right is for the original conventional downlights installed before glass fiber optics were considered. The small holes to the left are for the tails making the constellations. The large lights were subsequently turned off permanently. (c) Pulling the tails through the ceiling. (d) The larger dots of light are for dimmable ambient light. The star effect works independent from the room illumination.

two fibers per panel. The drop from the downlighters to the floor is over 21 ft, and to the top of the stairs is 10 ft. Size-48 tails were figured. The projectors will be housed in the ceiling voids. The exit angle of the fiber is 68°. Therefore, in uplighting the walls toward the dome, because of this beam spread, lenses are not required.

Although requested to, it was not possible to quote on lighting paintings under the stair until location, size, color, and material of this artwork is determined. These details should be decided before construction closes in, to avoid additional costs.

PIER LEADING TO A GAZEBO ON A LAKE[66]

In front of a newly built house on a lake, the client wanted to illuminate the sides of the walkway leading to a gazebo on the water. In addition to the decorative treatment outside, additional up-and-down lighting within the structure was needed for entertaining in the evenings.

The gazebo lighting could be provided by one light source and a 36-m (118.20-ft)-long length of side-emitting plastic fiber fed from BOTH ends. The installer tried 7- and 12.7-mm tails in both clear and diffused versions, and found that the 7 mm diffused was more visible over the water. An additional 150-watt projector with size-12 glass tails was added to light the interior. The pier required two light sources because, if the fiber can only be fed from one end, the light level will fall off toward the end of the run.

- For the exterior of the gazebo:

    1, 150-watt metal halide projector

    26 m of 7-mm plastic side-emitting fiber c/w special insulating coupler

- Pier outlining:

    2 new type 150-watt metal halide projectors

    26 m of 7-mm plastic side-emitting diffused c/w special insulating coupler

    30 m of 7-mm plastic side-emitting diffused c/w special insulating coupler

By the time the owner made a decision to proceed, the new 100-watt metal halide lamp and the improved glass side-emitting fiber became available commercially, so it was back to the drawing board.

A DINING ROOM[67]

This hostess does a great deal of entertaining, with many different table configurations. Having seen it abroad, her interior designers were anxious to start using glass fiber-optic architectural lighting. Two 250-watt tungsten halogen projectors with 8-tail size-24 glass harnesses power a grid of adjustable downlights for ambient illumination. For a "conversation piece," 75 points of light in a decorative design formed from small glass tails are provided in the ceiling. They are served by a 75-watt 12-volt illuminator (see Fig. 6-58).

MASTER BATHROOM

A Japanese-style bath, plus double sinks, and enclosed shower and toilet areas are to be lit by two 100-watt metal halide light sources with 11 miniaturized adjustable downlights. One harness was a 6-tail glass size 24. The other was 5-tail size 24. With two projectors, part of the lighting can be turned off, if not needed (see Fig. 6-59).

KITCHENS

This room should be illuminated to a relatively high level with good color rendition. The lighting should also be positioned so that there is no shadowing on work surfaces, stove, and sink areas. Matte finishes would be preferable. Careful focusing should cut down light bouncing off of shiny finishes.

Undercounter lighting, plus downlights in the center aisle and over the eating and work counters, should be included. Fully adjustable recessed eyeball fittings powder coated to match the ceiling will allow maximum flexibility. If projectors cannot be located in the middle of the room's ceiling, perhaps they can put into one of the upper shelves of a centrally located cabinet. In an average-size kitchen, two 100-watt metal halide illuminators could be used with 6-tail size-24 glass tails. If there is an eat-in table with seating, additional points of light should be provided.

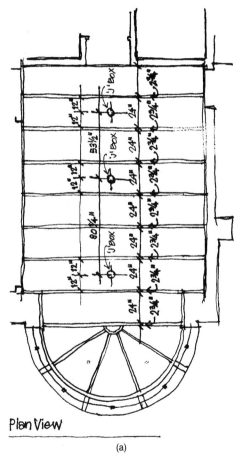

Plan View

(a)

Fig. 6-58 Dining Room. Courtesy of Eberlein Design. (a) Location of beams in ceiling which have to be fished through.

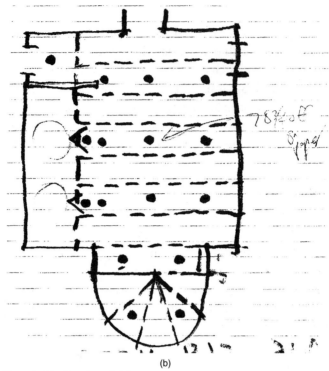

(b)

Fig. 6-58 (Continued) (b) Indication of where ambient light tails are to be located. 75 decorative smaller tails are interspersed and controlled separately.

RECESSED BRICK STEPLIGHTS

A builder of a large house forgot to install the recessed brick steplights before pouring the concrete. How was lighting to be provided in two locations? There were no bullnoses, so lights couldn't be put under each step. However, small vandal-proof lenses lit with glass fiber optics could be located through the wall on both sides of each step. Since this was an area that could have snow cover, the lights were place ABOVE the tread, aimed obliquely toward the center. Only very small light guides were necessary.

BEDROOM

An interior designer requested side-emitting glass fiber optics to encircle a queen-size bed mounted on a platform. A harness of 3 × S8 strands, 9.6 meters long, fed at one end from a 150-watt metal halide with a 3000 K

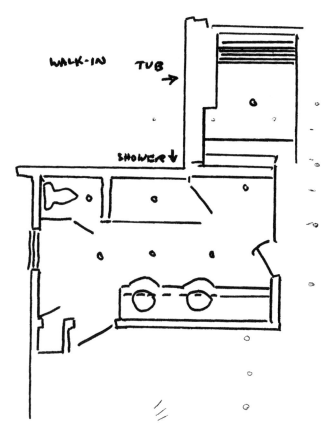

Fig. 6-59 Master bathroom showing existing conventional lights. Courtesy of Eberlein Design.

lamp makes a gentle glow that is not hot. It also will not fade the custom bed covers.

SECTION 4. DAYLIGHTING WITH FIBER-OPTIC SYSTEMS

This subject, which has intrigued scientists the world over, is being well covered elsewhere. However, mention of it here, however briefly, should be made. Progress on this topic is being made almost daily. International lighting conferences are filled with speakers reporting the latest research. It seems the desire for daylighting (using the sun as a free source of light) and conducting the gathered sun's rays through light pipe or fiber optics indoors has become the search for today's Holy Grail. Great strides have already been made in Japan. According to one report,[68] a Japanese system[69] powers itself with solar cells and tracks the sun using a sensor and software. A honeycomb of Fresnel lenses (105 mm diameter) focuses the sun's light onto the ends of glass optical fibers. In 1996, they stated that a six-tail quartz fiber, 130-foot cable per lens, emits 1182 lumens under 98,000 lux of direct sunlight, which is comparable to the light output of a 75-watt incandescent lamp. It is used where initial cost is less of an issue than operating costs, or where special decorative effects are needed.

An English product[70] also provides energy-free daylight for commercial buildings. This system entrains sunlight thorough a clear acrylic dome mounted above roof level. The light is magnified through a mirrored, reflective pipe to the room below. A translucent ceiling fixture then diffuses the natural light evenly around the room (see Fig. 6-60). It can feed sunlight into basements 7 m (21 ft) below roof level and is available in two dome sizes—330 and 530 mm for illuminating rooms of approximately 21 and 42 m² respectively.

Costs of daylighting in 1997 could range from $7000 to $300,000. Therefore, the possibility of eventual payback through energy saving has to be carefully considered. There are also concerns about the enormous amount of heat generated by collecting sunlight, so choice of materials that can withstand these temperatures is important. Even if using glass light guides, there MUST be some form of forced cooling at the collection end of this system, and some very good quality infrared filters between the collector device and the common end and each tail, plus whatever directional device is used at the other end of the harness. Dr. Lorne Whitehead reports that the most cost-effective daylighting systems have active (moving) components.

SKI LODGE IN THE CANADIAN ROCKIES

As an example, in a ski lodge in the Canadian Rockies, the owner wanted to capture sunlight and conduct it into the basement recreation room. This might involve use of a three-tail, 5-meter-long size-360 glass harness. Only tails of this large size could bring down sufficient light to be significant, taking into account the

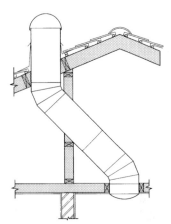

Fig. 6-60 Drawing of "SunPipe."

physical light loss per meter. A parabolic reflector of appropriate material to withstand heat and of proper shape to direct all light rays efficiently into the glass harness is needed.

SECTION 5. GARDENS AND LANDSCAPING

Illumination in these areas is needed for personal convenience and safety outdoors. However, fragile plant material, which cannot stand the heat normally produced by artificial light, must also be protected. The best method available today of lighting these features is with COOL miniaturized glass fiber optics (see Fig. 6-61). The owner benefits from the longevity of the glass, so that the grounds do not have to be dug up unnecessarily after the initial installation. In addition, excellent color rendition is obtained at whatever light level and distance is desired.

Possible problems in landscape lighting include children or intentional vandalism, motor vehicles, lawnmowers, animals, chemicals, and extreme environmental conditions. Because the light sources can be hidden along with the tails, vandalism is essentially defeated. It is advisable to encase the light guides in some type of conduit if run underground. This is to avoid accidental damage. This extra protection is not needed for fiber optics in underwater features.

For a very cost-effective installation, the most fragile plant materials, which have to be highlighted in a controlled manner, should be done with glass fiber optics, while large areas of general floodlighting can be of a conventional material. In the absence of other lighting in the area, 1 to 2 footcandles are sufficient for exterior garden illumination. Of course, if there are streetlights or brightly lit adjacent buildings, a little higher light level is needed.

Permanent provision for outdoor seasonal lighting and entertaining (for food service and

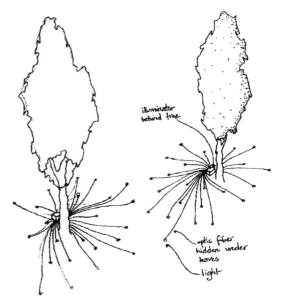

Fig. 6-61 Sketch for garden lighting. Courtesy of L'Observatoire International.

music/sound) should be included at the same time as the illumination. This again will eliminate multiple excavations. Underground electric, water, gas, and telephone/communication lines must be clearly marked and given easy access. All of these utility companies must be notified BEFORE excavating, to avoid accidental disruption of service.

Please spare the trees by not nailing lighting and/or wiring onto their trunks. Instead, use a freestanding pole, or mount the equipment on another building, being careful to keep glare out of the viewer's eyes. Note that in regions that get snow cover, since there is no heat emerging from fiber-optic lighting placed on the grade, the snow will not be melted, as with conventional fixtures. In those cases, fittings should be installed above ground.

- *A tropical garden.* On one project whose grand opening was to be telecast nationwide, all lighting equipment had been meticulously concealed behind plantings in a 4-acre tropical garden. Many preliminary photographs and drawings were made to include every detail. Trees were dramatically highlighted, and flowering bushes were lit to show their vibrant colors. Paths were evenly lit by overlapping the patterns of light. However, Mother Nature chose to bring an unheard-of string of three subzero days that blackened all the foliage and caused it to fall off, just in time for the telecast. The upstanding conduits and lighting fittings, instead of the landscape, were all that was visible to the crowds celebrating this event. "The best laid plans. . . ."

- **Historic gardens.** Surrounding period houses, these gardens are enhanced by glass fiber optics because the components are so unobtrusive. Proprietary flickering glass fiber-optic candles provide a safe and authentic ambience without having to replace burned-out bulbs constantly. By the same token, contemporary structures and their surrounds can have very sophisticated outdoor lighting, matching the architectural design.

- **A mountain landscape.** An application where fiber optics would not be cost-effective would be to provide security lighting around the 600-ft (200-m) perimeter of a large tract of land 100 ft away from a big house. This would entail much trenching and many very long tails mounted on poles to clear possible heavy snow cover.

SECTION 6. DECORATIVE

Since there is considerable material available on this application, only a few suggestions for using fiber optics are given here. No doubt every artistic and ingenious user will develop many more applications.

EUROPEAN BANK FOR RECONSTRUCTION AND DEVELOPMENT, LONDON, ENGLAND[71]

In the staff restaurant of this organization, the architect wanted to create a symmetrical pattern of "dots" of light, 8 mm in diameter, colored blue on two centers of 150 and 300 mm. The effect was achieved by designing a cylindrical lens that accepted a size-1.5 fiber and once in position, appeared to be 8 mm in diameter. The viewing angle is approximately 90°, which provides a varied effect depending on the viewer's position within the area. The blue color was achieved by using a borosilicate-based dichroic filter within each projector. There are a total of 2200 "dots" around the restaurant, fed from 10 light sources housed within the ceiling void. Imagine the maintenance cost of constantly replacing 2200 little conventional bulbs in a busy restaurant.

A PROMOTIONAL MODEL

For a promotional display, a 21-ft model of a group of three-dimensional high-rise buildings needed all the little windows illuminated. Approximately 300 to 400 size-1 glass tails with a maximum length of about 7 m (21 ft) to a minimum length of about 4 m (12 ft [= average length 5.5 m]), would light all the windows in the rectangular structures on each side. The fiber-optic lighting will eliminate the problem of many burned-out lamps in these windows. Equipment per side was one 150-watt metal halide source with a 300-tail harness.

THE GIRAFFE

Huge outdoor three-dimensional displays such as this and the Wayland Flame (following) would be difficult to do without end-emitting fibers. A 20-ft openwork metal model of a giraffe stands on a traffic island, as the symbol of the adjacent store. Since it is outside in all kinds of weather, vandal-proof and long-lasting lighting that would not be affected by heat, cold, or wet, was sought. The head, horns, and ears are outlined using side-emitting plastic fiber that carries on down to the 14 ft 6 in level. Below this point, the fiber is sleeved in black to make it invisible. The rest of the animal is lit with broken (so it sparkles) side-emitting glass fiber with a light source at both ends. There is a 4-color change option for holidays. Components included five 100-watt metal halide illuminators with 4-color wheel. There were two 44-tail broken glass side-emitting harnesses with two common ends, and 25 meters of 7-mm diffuse plastic side-emitting fiber with insulating coupler.

THE WAYLAND FLAME[72]

This eternal flame was applied to a five-story front/side façade wall of the Learning Center building.

The frame of the flame is made of welded steel with braced vertical risers, backed by anodized bronze. Stained glass panes in a variety of sizes and patterns were created and joined to form "snail trails" for fiber-optic tubing to follow, concealed between the glass and luminescent white panels affixed to the frame.

During the day, natural light radiates through the stained glass, reflecting off the white luminescent panels and back through the glass. The fiber-optics are programmed to illuminate at night, where the white panels serve as a diffuser to allow the same evenly distributed light patterns as during the day.

Equipment: 7 - 400 watt HID illuminators with 640' of side-emitting tubing. The HID light sources, combined with bundled and twisted fiber-optic strands densely packed and extruded through the tubing, produce a brilliance comparable to the effect achieved by natural light during the day.

It is to be noted that most stained glass creations are not lit at night, negating the effect they exhibit during the day.

This use of fiber optics offered a solution to the problem.

A DECORATIVE CEILING

Normally, whoever designs the lighting confers with equipment suppliers during the design process to determine the types and amount of equipment that will do the job properly. This was not the case here, and it was obvious that the otherwise competent professional was not completely familiar with the three-part components of a fiber-optic system and had confused plastic with glass sizes. Not only the quantity of light sources, but whether they had to be synchronized or not; the size, quantity, and length of tails; size and type of fittings; and the actual design of the points of light, along with the wiring diagram, were either vaguely specified or not mentioned altogether. Those bidding the job, although not having been given complete drawings, knew from experience that only five projectors would be sufficient, instead of the 10 specified. The maximum number of fibers, 160,000 for a metal halide light source, would determine the quantity of projectors, assuming the distances were manageable. Moreover, size-4 glass tails would be adequate for this simple decorative purpose rather than the size 12 specified.

Consequently, the manufacturer, his representative, and the bidders were "in the dark" about the lighting requirements. The only thing to do was to present individual prices "cafeteria style" for the client to chose his preference from an unknown quantity of 150-watt metal halide projectors with color and flicker wheels:

1. Single motor (color and flicker work together for each projector)

2. Twin motors (color and flicker work separately on each projector)

3. Synchronized projectors (all do the same thing at the same time)

A DECORATIVE CEILING IN A COMMERCIAL VENUE[73]

A 1900-square-foot starlight ceiling was requested. In this new skylighted building, there was no interstitial space to house the projectors, so they had to be placed on the roof in GRP (glass reinforced plaster) enclosures for external use. Five 150-watt metal halide light sources for 40-tail size-8 glass tails were ordered with ability for dimming, color change, and twinkle.

Close cooperation among the engineer, lighting designer, roofers, ceiling people, electrical contractor, the general contractor, and the fiber-optic supplier is needed to ensure proper installation. The roofing contractor will know the suitable sealant to use in external penetrations.

Hint: For restaurants or other locations with large plate glass picture windows, an interesting touch would be to use masses of the small glass fibers like fabric. Bundles of up to 350 such tails of miniature sparkling lights can be powered from a single light source. They can be had in lengths up to 20 m (60 ft). It is perfectly safe to touch and can be hung as curtains, otherwise draped, or even be immersed in water.

To see the outside view during daytime, the tails can be easily held aside with a 3-in-wide tape. Color effects may be added. In open, glazed entrance areas, a contrast ratio greater than 3 to 1 between source and background allows fiber optics to work best.

FIBER OPTICS WOVEN INTO CARPETING OR DRAPERIES

The curtains separating hospital beds could have safe glass fibers introduced into them, advising patients of fire alarm drills or when to go to therapy. Fine fiber can be introduced into heavy-duty carpeting or window covering for overall design or directional guidance. Concealed pressure-pads in the rugs could activate otherwise invisible fiber-optic patterns, and a series of related pictures could evolve sequentially as each pressure-pad is depressed.

FIREWORKS

Whenever funds were contributed to a museum celebrating its 100th anniversary, fiber-optic fireworks (see Fig. 6-62) were set off from the roof of the architectural model of the building placed in the main lobby. To create these fireworks, three 50-watt tungsten light sources were used. There were different speed motors in each projector and independent fiber harnesses for each, so that they would change color randomly and separately. The upward thrust of the light guides was achieved by encasing the glass side-emitting fibers in a clear enclosure strong enough to keep them from falling back on themselves.

It is fitting that this book ends with a fiber-optic version of fireworks, one of the oldest lighting effects, which was devised by the ancient Chinese. It celebrates the ongoing progress leading to even more wonderful developments in the future.

Epilogue: In the Future

The August, 1996, *Lighting Equipment News* (UK) contained a roundup of coming attractions in lamps, light guides, and projectors. It finishes with a summary of the current state of fiber optics.

Fig. 6-62 Glass fiber-optic fireworks.

... More often than not, only fiber-optics can resolve a particular lighting problem. But all advantages can be lost through poor [design and] installation.

Another watchword for fiber optics is honesty between designer and client. Despite wonderful mathematical attenuation calculations, the best solution is to replicate the required effect by experimentation [mock-ups] and then to make sure that this can be adhered to [maintenance]. If not, the effect will be lost.

Fiber-optics and light pipe are not a panacea for every illumination problem, but a useful resolve in the designer's armoury. Those who grasp this fact could be first to benefit.

This book reflects just the first chapter in the odyssey of this revolutionary technology.

General Lighting Terms[1]

ambient light general lighting in an area. It can come from artificial or natural sources.

American National Standards Institute (ANSI) consensus organization that coordinates voluntary standards for the physical, electrical, and performance characteristics of lamps, ballasts, luminaires, and other lighting and electrical equipment.

American Society for Testing and Materials (ASTM).

ballast auxiliary piece of equipment designed to start and properly control the flow of power to gas discharge light sources such as fluorescent and high intensity discharge (HID) lamps. This is also called *control gear* or transformer.

High frequency electronic ballasts run the lamp at frequencies between 20 and 40 kHz and:

- Consume up to 30% less circuit power than a wire wound ballast for a given light output.

---

[1]Definitions gathered from General Electric and Philips catalogs; *Good Practice Guides* 160 and 199 from the Department of the Environment (UK), and *Energy Efficient Lighting in Industrial Buildings* from the Commission of the European Communities Directorate General for Energy DG XVII.

- Are lighter in weight than their wire wound equivalents.

- Are silent in operation.

- Lamps start at the first attempt without annoying flashing.

- Lamps last longer.

- The quality of light is improved with the elimination of flicker and stroboscopic effects.

- There is automatic switch off at the end of life, eliminating any lamp flashing.

- The lamp can often be operated at less than its nominal voltage.

- Lamps are overvoltage protected.

Note: Protection against harmonic effects caused by electronic ballasts must be taken.

candela (CD)   international unit (SI) of luminous intensity. Sometimes the older term *candlepower* is used to describe the relative intensity of a source.

candlepower   luminous intensity expressed in candelas.

Cartesian coordinates   mathematical system named for René Descartes, seventeenth-century philosopher/scientist, representing relative position of points in a plane or space. A point in space may be specified by the triple of numbers *x, y,* and *z* representing the distance from three planes determined by three intersecting straight lines not all in the same plane.

coefficient of elasticity   ratio of the internal stress to the strain giving rise to it. In this usage, it is affected by temperature changes.

coefficient of utilization (CU)   percent of initial lamp lumens that reaches the work plane as determined by surface reflectances, room shape (RCR), and fixture efficiency.

color rendering index (CRI)   measurement of the color shift an object undergoes when illuminated by the light source, as compared to a reference source at the same color temperature. Color rendering is measured on an index from 0 to 100, with natural daylight and incandescent lighting both equal to 100. Objects and people viewed under lamps with a high color rendering index generally appear more true to life. Light from lamps with good (70–80 CRI) and excellent (80+ CRI) color rendering properties is said to be "high-quality light," because objects and people look more appealing and the light level itself is perceived to be higher.

The CRI is critical in settings where it is important that people appear natural, in retail applications where merchandise must look inviting, and in restaurants where food must look appetizing. In office and factory uses, CRI can increase visual clarity and create a more pleasing and productive work environment. Obviously, in art or museum situations, it is particularly significant.

color temperature (chromaticity)   scientific measurement of the balance of wavelengths making up any "white" light. The unit of measurement is Kelvin, abbreviated *K*. A high color temperature means a cooler, bluer light source. Incandescents are 2800 K (warm); halogens are 3000 K; some fluorescents are 3500 K (neutral white, flattering to skin tones); and metal halides are 4000 K (clear white). Metal halides are also available in 3000 K; noon sunlight is 5000 K; an overcast sky is 7000 K.

cost of light   determined primarily by the cost of the electricity used to power the lamp. In the United States, 80 to 88% of the cost of light is money spent on electricity. Labor (8%) and cost of the lamp (4%) make up the balance of 100%. While the purchase price of energy-efficient systems may be higher than conventional ones, the rapid payback more than makes up for the initial outlay.

daylighting

1. Bringing the sun's rays into a building via glass fiber optics or light pipe
2. Augmenting natural daylight with artificial light, usually by automatically switching the latter on when a certain low level of sunlight is reached

decibel   (dB) = $\frac{1}{10}$ of a bel (named for Alexander Graham Bell), a measurement of intensity of sound.

dichroic lamp   type of light source in which heat, normally produced by light, is directed backward, away from the path of the light, where it can be dissipated by a fan or natural ventilation.

directional light   lighting aimed at an area or object to accomplish a task or to highlight.

discharge lamp   one whose illumination is produced by an electrical discharge through a gas, a metal vapor, or a mixture of gases and vapors.

DMX512 protocol   DMX is an acronym for *digital multiplex.* It was first developed in 1986 by a committee of the USITT (U.S. Institute of Theatre Technology) as a means to control dimmers from lighting consoles via a standard interface.

efficacy   lumens per watt (lpW). The ratio of luminous flux emitted by a lamp to the power consumed by the lamp. This is a critical consideration when evaluating a light source because lighting represents 30 to 50% of the total operating cost of a typical installation and can affect related costs such as air conditioning. A lighting system that uses energy efficiently is also beneficial to the environment. When the power consumed by control gear is taken into account, this term is sometimes known as *lamp circuit efficacy.*

electromagnetic spectrum   continuum of electric and magnetic radiation that can be characterized by wavelength or frequency. Visible light encompasses a small part of the electromagnetic spectrum in the region from about 380 nanometers (violet) to 770 nanometers (red) by wavelength.

footcandle   American System (AS) unit used to measure how much total light is reaching a surface, such as a wall or table. One lumen falling on 1 square foot of surface produces illumination of 1 footcandle.

fluorescent lamp   one in which electric discharge of ultraviolet energy excites a fluorescing coating (phosphor) and transforms some of that energy into visible light. This requires a transformer/ballast.

gobo   plate or slide made of brass, stainless steel, chrome-coated glass or borosilicate into which an image is cut so that all parts are physically connected to keep the image from "falling apart." Light is then passed through it to project that image on a surface. Gobos can be permanent or temporary. Similar to a stencil for painting.

halogen lamp   short for tungsten halogen lamp. These are high-pressure incandescent lamps containing halogen gases, such as iodine or bromine, which allow the filaments to be operated at higher temperatures and higher efficacies. A high-temperature chemical reaction involving tungsten and the halogen gas recycles evaporated particles of tungsten back onto the filament surface.

high-intensity discharge lamps (HID)   general term for mercury, metal halide, and high-pressure sodium lamps. HID lamps contain compact arc tubes that enclose various gases and metal salts operating at relatively high pressures and temperatures. These lamps require a transformer for the operating voltage.

illuminance   density of light (lumens/area) incident on a surface. The amount of light arriving on a surface is illuminance. It is measured in lumens per square meter, usually referred to as *lux*. An American rule of thumb is to divide the number of lux by 10 to reach footcandles.

incandescent lamp   one that provides light when a filament is heated to incandescence by an electric current. It is the oldest form of electric lighting technology. It does not require a transformer.

infrared radiation   electromagnetic energy radiated in the wavelength range of about 770 to 1106 nanometers. Energy in this range cannot be seen by the human eye, but can be sensed as heat by the skin.

kelvin (K)   a unit of measurement of color temperature.

kilowatt (kW)   watts $\times$ 1000 = kilowatts.

kilowatt hour (kWh)   measure of electrical usage from which electricity billing is determined. For example, a 100-W bulb operated for 1000 hours would consume 100 kWh (100 W $\times$ 1000 hours = 100 kWh). At a billing rate of $0.10/kWh, this source would cost $10.00 (100 kWh $\times$ $0.10/kWh) to operate.

LAN   local area network.

light   radiant energy capable of producing a visual sensation in a human observer.

lumen   basic unit of measurement for light. This is the quantity of light energy per unit time arriving, leaving, or going through a surface. The unit of luminous flux is the lumen (lm). A dinner candle shines at about 12 lumens. If a uniform point source of 1 candela is at the center of a sphere of 1-foot radius, which has an opening of 1-square-foot area at its surface, the quantity of light that passes through is called a *lumen*. The sphere has a total surface area of 12.57 square feet. Since, by definition, a lumen flows to each square foot of surface area, a uniform point of 1 candela produces 12.57 lumens.

lumens per watt (lpW)   measure of the efficacy of a light source in terms of the light produced for the power consumed.

luminaire   conventionally, a light fixture with one or more lamps and housing. It controls the distribution of light from a lamp and includes all the components. In fiber-optic technology, it is the point of light from an end-emitting tail, with a controlling lens, if necessary.

luminance or brightness luminance is a measurable quantity, whereas brightness is a subjective sensation.
1. The human eye does not see the light arriving, but the light reflected from an object, which is called its *brightness* or *luminance.*
2. It is usually expressed in candles per square inch or lamberts or foot lamberts.
3. Luminance of a surface is equal to luminance × reflectance. In metric, it is measured in candelas per square meter, abbreviated to cd/m². Before the modern term *candela,* the luminous intensity, or strength of light in a given direction, had the older term *candle-power.*

lux SI (International System) unit of illumination, which is 1 lumen uniformly distributed over an area of 1 square meter.

maintained illuminance average illuminance over the reference surface at the time maintenance has to be carried out by replacing lamps and/or cleaning the equipment and room surfaces.

maintenance cycle point in time when maintenance needs to take place. This could be lamp and luminaire cleaning, room surface cleaning and/or lamp replacement.

metal halide lamp high-intensity discharge light source in which the light is produced by the radiation from mercury, together with halides of metals such as sodium and scandium.

micron One millionth of a meter.

nanometer One billionth of a meter.

photometry a system developed to measure light, taking into account the psychophysical aspects of the human eye/brain system. It takes accurate measurements of the distribution of light within the scene.

task (or local) lighting lighting designed to illuminate a task area.

total harmonic distortion (THD) measure of the distortion of the sine wave on alternating current (ac) systems caused by higher-order waves superimposed on the fundamental (usually 60-Hz) frequency of the system. Expressed in percent, THD may refer to individual electrical loads (such as a ballast) or a total electrical circuit or system in a building. The ANSI recommendation is for THD to be no greater than 32 percent, although some electric utilities may require lower THDs on some systems. Excessive THDs on electrical systems can cause efficiency losses as well as overheating and deterioration of system components.

ultraviolet (UV) radiation   radiant energy in the range of about 100 to 380 nanometers (nm). For practical applications, the UV band is broken down further as follows:

Ozone-producing	180–220 nm
Bactericidal (germicidal)	220–300 nm
Erythemal (skin reddening)	280–320 nm
"Black" light	320–400 nm

The International Commission on Illumination (CIE) defines the UV band as UV-A (315–400 nm); UV-B (280–315 nm); and UV-C (100–280 nm).

watts   amount of power in. Lumen = amount of power out.

wavelength   scientific term for the color of the light traveling in the fiber.

To Sum Up—Lumens, Candlepower, and Footcandles

In lighting, the basic measure for the amount of light produced by a light source is called a *lumen*. As with any unit of measure, one must start with a standard. The starting point for lumens is historically a candle. If it is of specific composition and size, it emits 1 candlepower. If this candle is placed in a sphere with a 1-foot radius, 1 lumen by definition will fall on 1 square foot of the sphere's surface. Since, from geometry, the total surface area of a 1-foot-radius sphere is 12.57 square feet, there are 12.57 lumens given off by that candle. One lumen falling on 1 square foot of a surface produces illumination of 1 footcandle.

Definitions Used for Glass Fiber-Optic Lighting

active diameter   diameter of the glass in a trail or light guide excluding the ferrule thickness (sometimes called the optical diameter).

attenuation   term used to describe the losses in the fiber, i.e., loss per m is usually written in dB/km. For most quality lighting applications, the glass would be below 150 dB/km, measured at 450 nm.

bundle   trade unit of quantity. One bundle consists of 400, 50-μm diameter fibers. (One bundle is known as *size 1,* two bundles as *size 2,* and so forth).

cladding   outer sheath of glass (usually a minimum thickness of 1.5 μm) that surrounds the core glass.

common end   termination of a harness where two or more tails meet in parallel to engage with the projector.

core   center of a fiber, usually about 48 μm in diameter.

crimp ferrule   type of tail termination that clamps the fiber and sheathing.

harness   fiber-optic loom, consisting of two or more tails.

interstice   space between each fiber, about 20 percent of the total optical area.

light guide   term to describe one tail, usually with a ferrule at both ends or a ferrule at one end and a common-end ferrule at the other.

machined ferrule   termination of a light guide or tail specially machined to suit the application. This is usually threaded to accept a fitting.

mechanical dimmer   device within the projector to obstruct the light falling on the common end. It is particularly useful when low levels are required without loss of color temperature.

projector   lamp housing into which the common end of the harness is plugged (sometimes referred to as the *light source* or *illuminator*).

randomization   process that distributes a percentage of the fibers in each tail (50%, 25%, 12.5%, etc.) so that the fibers are evenly distributed over the common end. Randomization ensures that each tail emits the same amount of light.

sheathing   protective material that covers the glass in a tail or light guide, such as PVC, silicon, marine-grade stainless steel, or Megalon.

size   trade unit giving the number of strands (fibers) of glass in a tail or light guide. (This can vary between harness makers; therefore, it is advisable to specify the number of fibers you estimate you will require.) The following formula for active diameter to size conversion should cover most requirements:

For a 6.0-mm-diameter tail:
$$\frac{(\text{Active Diameter}^2)}{1.21} = \text{size}$$

$$\frac{(6.0 \text{ mm})^2}{1.21} = \text{size}$$

Thus, if size 1 has 400 fibers, then size 32 will have 12,800 fibers (assuming a 50-μm diameter fiber).

tail   two or more light guides meeting at the common end.

tail-end fittings   light fittings (luminaires) into which the tails are fitted, usually described in the same way as conventional luminaires, i.e., downlighter, wallwasher, etc.

tail ferrule   termination of a light guide or tail. The metal ferrule can be the crimp type or machine threaded, depending on application.

Terms Familiar to the Glass Communication Fiber-Optic Industry[1]

[1]Courtesy of *Lennie Lightwave's Guide to Fiber Optic Installations*, published by The Fiber Optic Association, Boston, MA, Fotec, Inc. and The Fiber Optic Test Equipment Company.

This article shows the similarities and differences between this use and architectural lighting applications:

- Fiber optics sends signals down hair-thin strands of glass or plastic fiber. The light is "guided" down the center of the fiber, called the *core*. The core is surrounded by an optical material called the *cladding* that traps the light in the core. The core and cladding are usually made of ultrapure glass, although some fibers are plastic. The fiber is coated with a plastic covering called the *buffer coating* that protects it from moisture and other damage. More protection is provided by a cable that has an outer covering called a *jacket*.

- Multimode and single-mode fiber are the two types in common use. Multimode has a larger core (almost always 62.5 μm—a micrometer is one-millionth of a meter) and is used with light-emitting diode (LED) sources at wavelengths of 850 and 1300 nm—a nanometer is one-billionth of a meter—for local area networks (LANs). *Wavelength* is the scientific term for the color of the light traveling in the fiber.

- Except for plastic fiber, which uses a bright LED light, all fiber-optic systems use light in the "infrared" region that is invisible to the human eye.

- Single-mode fiber has a much smaller core, only about 9 μm, and is used for telephony and CATV with laser sources at 1300 and 1550 nm. Plastic optical fiber (POF) is large-core (about 1-mm) fiber that can be used for short, low-speed networks. Glass fiber has more strength and greater tolerance to abuse than copper power wire.

- Cable affords the fiber the protection it needs to survive in all the places it is installed. Cables include strength members to pull with, various ways to protect the fibers from the elements, and sometimes even armoring to discourage rodents from chewing through it. Cables installed inside buildings must meet fire codes by using special jacketing materials. Cables may have from one to hundreds of fibers inside them.

- Connectors are used to mate two fibers, or fibers to equipment, where they are expected to be disconnected occasionally for testing or rerouting. *Note:* They are not used with glass fiber-optic architectural lighting.

- Splices are permanent connections between two fibers made by welding them in an electric arc (fusion splicing) or aligning them in a fixture and gluing them together (mechanical splicing). *Note:* This procedure is not used for glass fiber-optic architectural lighting.

- Loss is the amount of light that is lost in a mated pair of connectors, a splice, or in a long length of fiber. It is expressed in decibels (dB) where −10 dB means a reduction in power by 10 times; −20 dB means another 10 times, or 100 times overall; −30 dB means another 10 times, or 1000 times overall, and so on.

- Most connectors have a loss of about 0.5 dB. A splice has about 0.2-dB loss. Fiber losses are a function of wavelength. Losses decrease rapidly at longer wavelengths. Multimode fiber losses are a function of length and wavelength. Figure about 3 dB per km (5 dB per mile) at 850 nm and 1 dB per km (1.6 dB per mile) at 1300 nm. Single-mode fiber losses are about 0.4 dB per km at 1300 nm and 0.3 dB per km at 1550 nm. POF has very high loss, about 0.2 dB per m!

- Optical power is measured in dBm, or decibels referenced to 1 milliwatt of power. While loss is a relative reading (one power relative to another), optical power is an absolute measurement, referenced to the following standards:

- Standards: Most of what we call standards are *voluntary,* created by an industry group to insure product compatability. The only common *mandatory* standard in the United States is the NEC (National Electrical Code) #770. The NEC specifies fire prevention standards for communication fiber-optic cables. Other criteria are merely *guidelines.*

- Standards for optical power measurements are set by NIST (The United States National Institute of Standards and Technology). ANSI (the American National Standards Institute) has chartered The Fiber-Optic Association and the National Electrical Contractors' Association (NECA) to develop installation standards for communication fiber optics, including workmanship.

- Safety: Optical sources used in fiber optics generally are of much lower power levels than lasers. Also, they are not focused into a small spot like lasers. The main risk is from small scraps of bare fibers and the various chemical cleaners and adhesives employed.

- Cleanliness is next to impossible, but very important! Tolerance to dirt is near zero. Airborne particles are about the size of the core of a single-mode (SM) fiber and usually silica based. They may scratch connectors if not removed. Dirt is the biggest cause of scratches on polished connectors and high-loss measurements.

Approximate Light Levels for Glass Fiber Using Metal Halide

APPROXIMATE LIGHT LEVELS OF GLASS FIBER OPTICS WITH METAL HALIDE SOURCE

| TAIL SIZE | NOMINAL TAIL DIAMETER IN MM (APPROX.) | NUMBER OF FIBERS PER TAIL | LUX LEVELS (FOR APPROXIMATE FOOTCANDLES, DIVIDE BY 10) | | | | MAXIMUM NUMBER OF TAILS PER METAL HALIDE LIGHT SOURCE[3] | BEND RADIUS IN MM |
			WITH NO LENS 68–70°	LENS 36°	LENS 26°	LENS 13°		
0.75	1.0	435	8 lux	11	43	62 lux	435	5
1.5	1.5	600	15	22	80	150	270	8
3	2.0	1,200	33	45	171	250	135	15
8	3.0	3,200	57	79	301	438	52	20
14	4.0	4,800	99	135	515	751	33	25
18	4.5	7,200	150	200	700	1,000	22	30
24	6.0	9,600	198	270	1,031	1,503	17	50
36	7.2	14,400	297	406	1,546	2,254	12	60
48	8.0	19,200	437	579	2,277	3,318	8/10	80
72	9.5	28,800	594	812	3,092	4,508	5	95
96	10.0	38,400	890 lux	1,158	4,554	6,636 lux	4	100

NOTES: Larger sizes are available. The above table is only intended to give the user a guide to what light levels to expect from different size tails and beam angles. Actual values may vary due to different optical systems within projectors.

To determine the approximate number of tails per light source:

For 150/250-W tungsten halogen lamp: 300 ÷ tail size = number of tails per source

For 150-W metal halide lamp: 400 ÷ tail size = number of tails per source

Lux values are for one tail *3.0 m* long made from a minimum of 150 dB/Km glass with a throw distance of *1.0 m*, using a single-ended 150-W HQI 4000 K lamp. For throw of *2 m*, divide by 2 × 2; for *3 m* throw, by 3 × 3, etc. Readings are taken at the center of the beam. More efficient lamps will yield better lux values. Less light may be derived from a maximum-loaded projector.

68–70° is the beam angle of the light emitted from the glass fiber without a lens.

Collimating lenses come in sizes from 10 to 80°. They can intensify the light from a tail.

The maximum number of each size *glass* tails per harness is based on a 25-mm-diameter area of glass in the 30-mm common end. Approximate maximum number of fibers using a combination of glass tail sizes powered by one metal halide source = 160,000.

To increase light level with same size tail, add stronger collimating lens (which will decrease footprint of light) or use multiple tails on same area.

To achieve *even* light, use randomized fibers and overlap the footprint of light from a series of tails arrayed horizontally or vertically.

Megolon™ = halogen-free, self-extinguishing cable sheathing that fulfills fire protection standards.

Specify whether end ferrules are to be smooth or threaded to accept fittings.

Specify silicone booting at tail end for extra flexibility in tight spaces.

Rule of thumb for bend radii = 10 times diameter of light guide.

SOURCE NOTE: Figures for randomized glass courtesy of Schott Fiber Optics. (Figures revised by Scott Glass.)

Representative Types of Miniature Lenses for Glass Fiber

Courtesy of Flair Lighting Ltd., UK.

For:	Type:
Note: Give tail size and degree of lens	
Soft edge beam	Convex frosted
Small surface; very wide beam for background	Concave clear
Soft-edge wide beam, back lighting	Concave frosted
Low light level—confined space	Convex clear
Soft-edge beam—low-level light	Convex frosted
Wall/floor mounted—low-level light	Convex clear
Reduced bezel lens holder—front area insufficient for standard top hat fitting	Convex clear
Downlight—no architectural detail	Convex clear
Downlight—source invisible, wide beam	Convex frosted
Downlight—source seen, architectural detail	Convex clear
Downlight—source seen, architectural detail, soft-edge shallow lens mount	Convex frosted

Downlight—source seen, architectural detail, very wide beam, backlighting	Convex clear
Downlight—flush with ceiling	
MR16 glass reflector replacement	Convex clear or frosted; eyeball required
MR11 glass reflector replacement	Convex clear; eyeball required
MR11 replacement—soft-edge beam	Convex frosted
Extra-deep recessed lens for walkway	Convex clear/ ½ frosted

Also: decorative sparkle lights; eyeball downlights; swimming pool lights; framing projectors (recessed on track or surface mounted); plus custom combinations and adjustments as required.

Fittings arew provided fixed or adjustable, painted, plated or with outdoor/corrosive finishes.

Bend Tolerances for Glass Tails Without Silicone Booting

SIZE	ACTIVE DIAM. APPROX.	NO. FIBERS	MIN. BEND RADII PER HARNESS	MAX. TAILS PER MH PROJECTOR	OUTER Ø (MM) INCLUDING FERRULE
0.75	1.0 mm	435	5 mm R	435	2.20 ± 0.1
1.5	1.5 mm	600	8 mm R	270	2.70 ± 0.1
3	2.0 mm	1,200	15 mm R	135	3.85 ± 0.15
8	3.00 mm	2,800	20 mm R	52	4.85 ± 0.15
14	4.0 mm	4,800	25 mm R	30	6.35 ± 0.15
18	5.0 mm	7,200	30 mm R	22	
24	6.0 mm	9,600	50 mm R	16	8.70 ± 0.3
36	7.2 mm	14,400	60 mm R	12	10.10 ± 0.3
48	7.57 mm	19,200	35 mm R	8/10*	
96	10.00 mm	38,400	40 mm R	4	
And so forth					

*10 size 48 tails may be used on one harness but there may be slight light falloff on the outer tails.

Do not bend tails past 90°. This might break individual strands, lessening the light level.

Common-end diameter to a metal halide light source = 30 mm.

Figures for randomized glass courtesty of Schott Fiber Optics.

Reference Groups

The Lighting Center, Rensselaer Polytechnic, Troy, New York

USITT (United States Institute for Theatre Technology), New York

CIBSE (Chartered Institute of Building Services Engineers), United Kingdom

Universe Stage Lighting, New York

Professional Lighting and Sound Association (PLASA), United Kingdom

SAFA (Finnish Architectural Association), Helsinki, Finland

Production Arts Lighting Inc., New York

Plastic manufacturers: Mitsubishi, Japan (FibreStars); Rohm & Haas, Philadelphia; Ultratec, Burnaby, Canada

Glass fiber manufacturers: Schott Glaswerke, Germany; Mitsubishi, Japan

Philips Lighting, The Netherlands and France

General Electric Company, Nela Park, Ohio

Roblan Fibre-Optics, Denmark

Flair Lighting, United Kingdom

TIR Systems Ltd., Canada

Click Systems, United Kingdom

Rosco, United States

3M Company, United States

Illuminating Engineering Society of North America, New York

Illuminating Engineering Society, Toronto, Canada

Electronic Industries Association (EIA)

Lightscape Technologies, California

Association of Energy Engineers, United States

Society of Automotive Engineers, United States

Topaz Ltd, Israel

The Victoria and Albert Museum, London, England

The Wallace Collection, London, England

Derksen Light Technology, California, United States

SuperVision, Orlando, Florida

BLV Licht und Vakuumtecknik, Germany

Osram, Europe

CIE (Commission Internationale de L'Écairage), the world authority on the science, technology and standardization of lights, lighting, and vision

Library of the New York School of Interior Design, New York

Determine the Volume of the Fiber Bundle for Size of Conduit

Courtesy of Flair Lighting Ltd., UK.

Example, using $8 \times$ size-48 tails:

$$8 \times S48 = 8 \times 6.5 \times 6.5 \times 3.142 = 1062 \text{ mm}^2.$$

To accommodate the fibers comfortably, add 30% to the figure, which becomes 1381 mm^2.

To determine the diameter of pipe (conduit) to contain tails, simply divide by 3.142 and take the square root, then double the answer:

$1381 \div 3.142 = 439.53$; square root of 440

$$= 20.96 \times 2 = 42 \text{ mm} = 1.65 \text{ in.}$$

Therefore, a 2-in-diameter pipe will be adequate.

Example of Calculations to Determine Light Level at Floor

Courtesy of Flair Lighting Ltd., UK.

Below are the lighting calculations to achieve 17–18 footcandles at the floor from 30 ft (9.30 m):

150-watt metal halide source = 11,500 lumens

Mounting height: 9.30 m (30.49 ft)

Array diameter: 2.86 m (9.37 ft) from faxed drawing

Fiber size: 96; no. of tails per harness = 4 @ maximum 5 m long

Lens detail: 17° beam, plano convex 17.3 mm ϕ

Floor area = 3.142 × [tan 8.5° × 9.30]2

Illumination = lumen output × system efficiency × [floor area] × transmission loss

$$= 11,500 \times \frac{0.624}{20} \times \frac{1}{3.142 \times [\tan 8.5° \times 9.30]2} \times \text{transmission loss}$$

= 60 × lux × transmission loss

$$\text{Transmission loss} = \frac{150}{10} \times \frac{5}{1000} = 0.075$$

Antilog of 0.075 = 1.188 The reciprocal of 1.188 = 0.84 = 84% transmission

Light level on the floor from 1 tail therefore = 60 × .084 = 50.4 lux

There is a 3.7 overlap, therefore the average light level = 50.4 × 3.7 = 186.48 lux

Nominally = 17 to 18 footcandles

A Good First Estimation of Illuminance vs. Application

Courtesy of Schott Fibre Optics (UK) Ltd. 1997.

ILLUMINANCE (LUX)	APPLICATIONS
<0.2	(Moonlight)
1–10	Emergency escape lighting for public buildings
20	Gangways in warehouses, car parks, railway platforms
50	Conservation objects, site ladders/platforms/stairs
100	Warehouses, store rooms, lifts, cloakrooms, theatres, cinemas, external spotlighting
300	Larger working space areas in industry/commerce/retail
500	Task lighting, desk top, inspection, all localized work areas
1000	Precision assembly/inspection, small object tasks
1000–5000	Retail spotlighting, studios
40,000–100,000	(direct sunlight)

Special project requirements may cause variations from these recommended values.

Examples of the Great Range of Fiber-Optics Components Available

1. Any size glass tail, from #1 to #360, can be made as required. There are also increasing numbers of plastic tails now available. Their variety is limited by their capability to survive the heat and ultraviolet rays of the lamp source.

   If the application is emergency baseboard lighting, lengths up to 15 m of glass in any direction out of the projector can be provided. However, if color rendition is important, the maximum glass tail length recommended is 8–10 m (24–30 ft) in any direction out of the light source. Therefore, with light guides going to the right and left out of the projector, a maximum area of 48–60 ft can be covered.

   Refer to the individual plastic manufacturers for their specifications, which differ slightly.

   Only use highest quality end- and side-emitting fibers. Side-emitting tails are for decorative use only as a replacement for neon.

   Glass harnesses are delivered fully assembled, ready for insertion into the light source, while plastic has to be cut and put together on the job.

2. Choose a manufacturer with the capacity to make whatever type light source is needed. Stock types include:

   6000-hour 150-W metal halide (3000 or 4000 K)

   From 300- to 3000-hour 75- to 250-W tungsten halogen

All projectors can be made dust- or waterproof, or for corrosive areas.

GRP enclosures are available for outdoor mounting.

Select projectors that work silently and in any position.

3. Fittings shown in a catalog are only the beginning. Select a supplier who can adjust stock units or can custom make lenses and holders to suit a particular application.

4. Dimming, color, and motion can be simply achieved by the additional of motors onto the basic projector.

For multiple automated operations, an input can be provided for DMX512 protocol, or any other sophisticated control necessary.

Installation of Glass Fiber-Optics Architectural Lighting

Consider this just another lighting project.

Investigate existing electric service for condition and ability to accept new loads.

Establish full communication and coordination with design professionals and all adjacent trades.

When received, check equipment immediately for damage during shipment.

Make freight claim at once for missing or damaged parts, so as not to delay the job.

Count and mark all components at once.

Acquaint all members of the team of the fiber optics at the beginning of construction.

Study the building to find the shortest paths from light source to where light is to emerge.

Wiring for power and controls can be done at the same time as bringing the light guides through the structure to where needed.

Store in a clean and safe place until ready for use.

Do a mock up with a piece of ceiling/wall/floor material through which the tails must be put. Practice making the holes and threading the tails through them.

Locate light sources in an always accessible and convenient spot.

Allow enough air space to:

a) Dissipate the heat

b) Relamp

Fish the glass tails through interstitial spaces just like copper wire.

DO NOT bend past 90°

DO NOT twist tails—hold light guide and turn fitting on to the threaded ferrule

Focus the lights carefully and secure them from unwanted movement.

As soon as practicable, light up a portion of the work to show the team what it looks like.

Prepare a scheduled relamping program and show personnel how to do it.

Notes

Chapter One

1. Details from the CIBSE *Newsletter,* August 1997.
2. From an article by Hugh King in *Building Services & Environmental Engineer* magazine (UK), September 1997.
3. By the 3M Specified Construction Products Department, St. Paul, Minnesota.
4. Product of DuPont Chemicals, USA.
5. To Mitsubishi Rayon, Japan.
6. TIR Systems Ltd., Vancouver, BC, Canada.
7. Such as products of the 3M Company—*Scotchlamp*™ and *Silverlux*™.
8. TIR.
9. Developed by Fusion Lighting Systems, Maryland.
10. Reported in *Architectural Lighting,* July/August 1994. Designers Francesca Bettridge and Stephen Bernstein, New York.
11. Reported in *Architectural Lighting,* TIR equipment.
12. Design by Helen Diemer with TIR equipment, as reported in *Lighting Dimensions.*

13. By TIR.

14. Helmut Jahn, Chicago.

15. Design by Lorne Whitehead with TIR equipment.

16. Design by Roland Zeev Friedman of Topaz Ltd., Haifa, Israel.

17. Adapted from an article by Bernard Crocker and Dr. Lorne A. White-
    head in *Lighting Magazine,* Canada, April 1997.

18. Ongoing series in *Electrical Contractor,* by Paul Rosenberg,
    1996–1997.

19. Philips Lighting, The Netherlands.

20. BLV, Germany, and Ushio, Japan.

21. Such as Rosco, maker of theatrical color filters.

22. Conservation Lighting International (CLI), Philadelphia, PA.

23. DMX512 from Strand or Apollo.

24. Flair Lighting, England.

25. *Electrical Contractor.*

26. Courtesy of Rohm & Haas, Philadelphia, PA.

27. FibreStars, California; Ultratec, Burnaby, Canada; Rohm & Haas,
    Philadelphia, PA.

28. Ultratec Fibre-Optics, Burnaby, Canada.

29. Rohm & Haas, Philadelphia, PA.

30. FibreStars, Fremont, California.

31. Drawings courtesy of SuperVision.

32. Courtesy of Fiberstars.

33. Rohm & Haas, Philadelphia, PA.

Chapter Three

1. With DMX512 protocol, such as products of Strand or Apollo.

2. The Wallace Collection, London. Reported in the *Good Practice Guide*
   no. 160. The Department of the Environment, UK.

3. Reported by Wanda Jankowski in *Architectural Lighting,* January, 1994.

4. Lightscape Technologies, San Jose, California.

5. This description is adapted from Lightscape Visualization System (LVS)™ literature from Lightscape Technologies. Other tools include Autodesk 3D Studio; Wavefront Composer (on a Silicon Graphics workstation); Cineon/Vistavision high-resolution file format (100 MB per frame); Chyron Liberty 64. Another article on the subject was written by Barrett Fox in *Cadence,* June 1996. Additional programs include PaintShop Pro image editing and conversion and QuickTime VR and AVI formats, as mentioned in the article "Lightscape NT" by David Duberman in *3D Design* (May 1996). Further data from "Vegas gets an old look for a new movie (CASINO)" by Diana Philips Mahoney in *Computer Graphics World,* January 1996.

Chapter Four

1. From *Lighting Futures,* the newsletter of the Lighting Research Center of Rensselaer Polytechnic Institute in Troy, New York.

Chapter Five

1. Quoted from *Recommended Practice for DMX512.* Adam Bennette, PLASA, 1994.

2. Philip Johnson, Alan Ritchie, architects; Ann Kale, lighting designer; Flair Lighting equipment, through CLI, Philadelphia, PA.

Chapter Six

1. Lloyd Jary, architect; lighting design by CLI.

2. Lewis Sternberg, lighting designer.

3. Details courtesy of Philips Lighting, The Netherlands.

4. Design by CLI.

5. Design by CLI.

6. Furnished and installed by Flair Lighting, England.

7. Design by Flair Lighting.

8. Designed and installed by Flair Lighting.

9. Design by Flair Lighting.

10. Product of Schott Fibre-Optics, Germany.

11. Jones, January 8, 1998.

12. Design by Flair Lighting.

13. Design by William Allen and Paul Ruffles, England.

14. Design by Julian Harrap, England.

15. Information courtesy of Paul Tear, Curator of the Wallace Collection, London, England.

16. Cases furnished by Helmut Guenschel, Baltimore, MD.

17. Paul Morgan Lighting Design; FibreStars equipment.

18. Quoted from Philips Lighting, The Netherlands.

19. Design by Dr. Reuven Azoury, Jerusalem, Israel, with Flair equipment.

20. Supplied and installed by Flair Lighting.

21. Installed by Flair Lighting.

22. Quoted from Philips Lighting, The Netherlands.

23. Design by Dr. Reuven Azoury, Jerusalem, Israel, with Flair equipment.

24. Quoted from Philips Lighting, The Netherlands. Campo de Las Naciones Convention Center, Madrid, Spain. Designer: Ricardo Bofill, Taller De Arquitectura. Completed April 1993.

25. Furnished and installed by Flair Lighting Ltd.

26. Design by Flair Lighting.

27. Details courtesy of Philips Lighting, The Netherlands.

28. Details from Philips Lighting, The Netherlands.

29. Design by Flair Lighting.

30. Of Fisher Marantz Renfrew Stone, New York.

31. Ian Grant, architect; Rosie Winston, interior designer; Flair Lighting equipment.

32. TIR installation in the Callahan Tunnel, Boston, MA.

33. Data courtesy of Anthony Elderhorst, clockmaster, PA.

34. From *InFocus,* Fall 1995. Published by Production Arts Lighting, New York.

35. Reported in *Lighting Equipment News* (UK). August 1996.

36. The quotation is from *Lighting Historic Buildings,* by Derek Philips. New York: McGraw-Hill; UK: Butterworth, 1997.

37. Furnished and installed by Flair Lighting, England.

38. Designed by Peter Lawson-Smith, England.

39. Robert Neiley, restoration architect; lighting design by CLI.

40. Commissioned for CLI; executed by William T. Whiting, Philadelphia; lighting designed by LeMar Terry.

41. Jack Murray, Exhibit Director at the University Museum, Philadelphia.

42. Design by Conservation Lighting International (CLI), Philadelphia.

43. Design by CLI.

44. Design by Roland Zeev Friedman, Topaz Ltd., Israel, with Flair equipment.

45. Details courtesy of Philips Lighting, The Netherlands.

46. Design by Mark Kirkham, Modus Lighting, using Click Equipment. Quotation courtesy of Click Systems, England.

47. Logan Museum of Anthropology, Beloit College, Wisconsin. Account adapted from an article by Christina Trautwein in *Architectural Lighting,* October, 1995. Installation by Lightly Expressed Ltd., Virginia.

48. Design by Paul Mathiesen; Dan Rahimi, Director of Exhibits, Royal Ontario Museum, Toronto, Canada.

49. The Nelson-Atkins Museum, Kansas City, MO.

50. Details courtesy of Dextra Frankel, exhibit designer, CA.

51. The Green Cabinet in Rosenborg Castle, Copenhagen, designed and fitted by Roblon Fiber Optic, Denmark.

52. Details courtesy of Click Systems, England.

53. Quoted from the account of Lou Gauci, Director of Exhibits, Detroit Institute of Art, MI.

54. Design by Lou Gauci, Detroit Institute of Art.

55. Design by Grenald, Waldron Associates, Narberth, PA.

56. Designed and installed by Flair Lighting.

57. Quoted from Philips Lighting, The Netherlands.

58. Design by Flair Lighting.

59. Designer, Tim Trobel, Kansas. Quoted from an article by Wanda Jankowski in *Architectural Lighting.* April/May, 1994.

60. Designed and installed by Flair Lighting.

61. Design by Flair Lighting.

62. Design by Flair Lighting.

63. Design by LeMar Terry, New York.

64. Design by CLI.

65. Design by Flair Lighting.

66. Design by CLI.

67. Interior Design, Eberline, Philadelphia; lighting designed by CLI with Flair equipment.

68. Reported in *Lighting Futures,* Lighting Research Center, Rensselaer Polytechnic, Troy, New York.

69. *Himawari,* from Mitsubishi.

70. The SunPipe, Monodraught Ltd. UK.

71. Installed by Flair Lighting.

72. At Wayland Baptist University, Plainview, Texas. Designer, Berg Studios, with equipment by FibreStars.

73. Design by Fisher Marantz Renfrew Stone, New York.

Bibliography

General

Recommended Practice for Strand DMX512, A Guide for Users and Installers. Adam Bennette (A.B. Micro). London, 1994.

Fibre-Optic Lighting and Sensing Technology. Paul Timson and Barry Gregson (Eurotec). London, 1993.

The Stage Lighting Handbook, 4th ed. Francis Reid (A&C Black, Ltd.). London, 1993.

CIBSE, UK, various publications.

A Guide to Good Urban Lighting. CIBSE and ILE (Institution of Lighting Engineers). Jed Griffiths. August, 1995.

Lighting Historic Buildings. Derek Phillips, New York: McGraw-Hill; UK: Butterworth. 1997.

Fibre-Optics Without Tears. Del Bennett (Flair Lighting). London, 1995.

Lighting Designers' Handbook for Fibre Optic Systems. Schott Fibre Optics (UK) Ltd. 1997.

Mechanical/Electrical Systems for Historic Buildings. G. N. Kay: New York: McGraw-Hill. 1992.

ICOMOS Guidelines on Education (mechanical/electrical segment). Paris, 1993. (International Council on Monuments and Sites—a group of 90 nations).

ASTM Standards for Preservation and Rehabilitation (mechanical/electrical segment). G. N. Kay: Philadelphia: American Society for Testing and Materials. 1996.

Magazines

United States

Consulting/Specifying Engineer.

Electrical Contractor, magazine of the National Electrical Contractors' Association.

Lighting Design + Application, magazine of the Illuminating Engineering Society of North America.

The Construction Specifier, magazine of the Construction Specifications Institute.

Architectural Lighting.

Architectural Record—Lighting.

Lighting Dimensions International.

CEE (Contractors' Electrical Equipment).

Exhibit Builder.

VM&SD—Visual Merchandising and Store Design.

Energy Users' News.

Lighting Futures. Troy, New York: Renssalear Polytechnic.

Foreign

Lighting Equipment News, UK.

Lighting Magazine, Canada.

Professional Lighting, Canada.

Energy in Buildings and Industry, UK.

Building Services Journal, UK.

Architectural Journal, UK.

Cabltalk, magazine of the Electrical Contractors' Association of Scotland.

Light and Lighting, magazine of the CIBSE Lighting Division, UK.

The Lighting Journal, official journal of The Institution of Lighting Engineers, UK.

Building Services & Environmental Engineer magazine, UK.

HAC Building Services Engineering, UK.

Other publications

Good Practice Guides—various, The Department of the Environment, UK.
Energy Efficient Lighting in Industrial Buildings, Commission of the European Communities Directorate General for Energy, Belgium.

Catalogs

General Electric 9200 lamp catalog
Philips Catalogue SAG-100
Flair Lighting Ltd., UK
TIR Systems, Canada
Strand
SuperVision
FibreStars
Lumenlyte
Derksen Graphic
Rosco, USA
Ultratec, Burnaby, Canada
Rohm & Haas
Ushio, USA
BLV, Germany
Osram
Venture Lighting

Material from conferences

International Architectural Conference. Kaoshiung, Taiwan. March, 1995.
World Congress on Art Deco. Brighton, England. July, 1995.
International Lighting Exposition. Toronto, Canada. September, 1995.
CIBSE Lighting Conference. Bath, England. April, 1996.
American Association of Museums. Minneapolis, MN. May, 1996.
Finnish Architectural Association. Helsinki, Finland; St. Petersburg, Russia. September, 1996.

Association of Energy Engineers. Milwaukee, WI. September, 1996.

The American Institute for Conservation of Historic & Artistic Works. St. Paul, MN; Cleveland, OH; and Pleasant Hills, KY. 1995–1996.

Midwest Regional Conservation Guild. Kansas City, MO. April, 1997.

World Congress on Art Deco. Los Angeles, CA. May, 1997.

The American Association for State and Local History. Denver, CO. October, 1997.

International Lighting Exposition. Toronto, Canada. October, 1997.

South Bank University, London, England. March 1998.

CIBSE/ASHRAE, London, England. 1998.

Construction History Society, London, England. 1998.

Electrical Contractors' Association of Scotland, Midlothian, Scotland. 1998.

ASTM International Symposium on Historic Preservation, Atlanta, GA. April 1998.

Workshop #35, LIGHTFAIR, Las Vegas, NV. May 1998.

AIC National Conference, Arlington, VA. June 1998.

Pennsylvania Historical & Museum Commission, Harrisburg, PA. June 1998.

American Institute of Architects, Historic Resources Committee, Nantucket, MA. August 1998.

Lighting Dimensions International, Phoenix, AZ. November 1998.

Index